Bibliographies for Biblical Research

New Testament Series

in Twenty-One Volumes

General Editor

Watson E. Mills

Bibliographies for Biblical Research

New Testament Series

in Twenty-One Volumes

Volume I

The Gospel of Matthew

Compiled by

Watson E. Mills

MBP

MELLEN BIBLICAL PRESS

Lewiston/Queenston/Lampeter

Library of Congress Cataloging-in-Publication Data

The Gospel of Matthew / compiled by Watson E. Mills.
    p.   cm. -- (Bibliographies for biblical research.   New
Testament series)
    Includes index.
    ISBN 0-7734-2347-8
    1. Bible, N. T. Matthew--Criticism, interpretation, etc. -
-Bibliography. I. Mills, Watson E. II. Series.
Z7772.M1G674 1993
[BS2575.5]
016.2262'06--dc20   93-30864
                                                                          CIP

This is volume I in the continuing series
Bibliographies for Biblical Research
New Testament Series
Volume I ISBN 0-7734-2347-8
Series ISBN 0-7734-9345-X

A CIP catalog record for this book is available from the British Library.

The Edwin Mellen Press   The Edwin Mellen Press
        Box 450   Box 67
Lewiston, New York   Queenston, Ontario
     USA 14092   CANADA L0S 1L0

The Edwin Mellen Press, Ltd.
Lampeter, Dyfed, Wales
UNITED KINGDOM   SA48 7DY

Printed in the United States of America

Dedication

To Brenda, Sherry
world-class sisters-in-law
with much affection

Contents

Contents

Introduction to the Series

This volume is the first of a series of bibliographies on the books of the Hebrew and Christian Bibles as well as the deutero-canonicals. This ambitious series calls for some 35-40 volumes over the next 4-6 years complied by practicing scholars from various traditions.

Each author (compiler) of these volumes is working within the general framework adopted for the series, i.e., citations are to works published within the twentieth century that make important contributions to the understanding of the text and backgrounds of the various books.

Obviously the former criterion is more easily quantifiable than the latter, and it is precisely at this point that an individual compiler makes her/his specific contribution. We are not intending to be comprehensive in the sense of definitive, but where resources are available, as many listings as possible have been included.

The arrangement for the entries, in most volumes in the series, consists of three divisions: scriptural citations; subject citations; commentaries. In some cases the first two categories may duplicate each other to some degree. Multiple citations by scriptural citation are also included where relevant.

Those who utilize these volumes are invited to assist the compilers by noting textual errors as well as obvious omissions that ought to be taken into account in subsequent printings. Perfection is nowhere more elusive than in the citation of bibliographic materials. We would welcome your assistance at this point.

We hope that these bibliographies will contribute to the discussions and research going on in the field among faculty as well as students. They should serve a significant role as reference works in both research and public libraries.

I wish to thank the staff and editors of the Edwin Mellen Press, and especially Professor Herbert Richardson, for the gracious support of this series.

Watson E. Mills, Series Editor
Mercer University
Macon GA 31211
July 1993

Preface

This Bibliography on the Gospel of Matthew provides an index to the journal articles, essays in collected works, books and monographs, dissertations, commentaries, and various encyclopedia and dictionary articles published in the twentieth century through 1992 (a few titles for the early months of 1993 are included when these were available for verification). Technical works of scholarship, from many differing traditions constitute the bulk of the citations though I have included some selected works that intend to reinterpret this research to a wider audience.

Two extant bibliographies on the Gospel of Matthew proved most helpful in the preparation of this text: Günter Wagner, *An Exegetical Bibliography of the New Testament: Matthew and Mark* (Mercer University Press, 1983) and the exhaustive three-volume work by Paul-Émile Langevin, *Bibliographie biblique* (Les Presses de l'Université Laval, 1972, 1978, 1985). The first covers a far more representative sampling of traditions and confessions (especially from Europe) but contains listings only by scriptural citation; the second is heavily slanted toward Catholic publications but particularly the third volume begins to move toward a more balanced perspective. Langevin's work is very heavy in citations to French literature, but is meticulously indexed by scriptural citation as well as subject and contains detailed indexes.

Building the database necessary for a work of this magnitude was a tedious and time-consuming task. I acknowledge the administration of Mercer University for granting me a sabbatical leave during the 1991-1992 academic year. Also, I acknowledge with gratitude the Education Commission of the Southern Baptist Convention which provided funds for travel to overseas libraries.

I want to express my gratitude to the staff librarians at the following institutions: Baptist Theological Seminary (Rüschlikon, Switzerland); Oxford University (Oxford, UK); Emory University (Atlanta, GA); Duke University (Durham, NC); University of Zürich (Zürich, Switzerland); Southern Baptist Theological Seminary (Louisville, KY).

I wish to thank especially, Valerie Edmonds, Coordinator of Reference, Mercer University Library and Paul Debusman, Reference Librarian at the Southern Baptist Theological Seminary Library for their considerable help in verifying citations in this work. Finally, I gratefully acknowledge the invaluable assistance given me in technical aspects of this work by my long-time associate Ms. Irene Palmer.

Watson E. Mills
Mercer University
Macon GA 31211
July 1993

Abbreviations

ABR	Australian Biblical Review (Melbourne)
AmER	American Ecclesiastical Review (Washington, DC)
AnBib	Analecta Biblica (Rome)
Ang	Angelicum (Rome)
ANQ	Andover Newton Quarterly (Newton Centre, MA)
AnnT	Annales Theologici (Rome)
Ant	Antonianum (Rome)
ARefG	Archiv für Reformationsgeschichte (Gütersloh)
AsSeign	Assemblées du Seigneur (Paris)
ASTI	Annual of the Swedish Theological Institute (Leiden)
ATB	Ashland Theological Bulletin (Ashland, OH)
ATJ	Asbury Theological Journal (Wilmore, KY)
ATLA	American Theological Library Association: Proceedings (Menuchen, NJ)
ATR	Anglican Theological Review (Evanston, IL)
AugR	Augustinianum (Rome)
AUSS	Andrews University Seminary Studies (Berrien Springs, MI)
BA	Biblical Archaeologist (Ann Arbor, MI)
BAR	Biblical Archaeology Review (Washington, DC)
BB	Bible Bhashyam: An Indian Biblical Quarterly (Vadavathoor)
BET	Berträge zur evangelischen Theologie (Munich)
BETL	Bibliotheca ephemeridum theologicarum lovaniensium (Louvain)

Bib	Biblica (Rome)
BibL	Bibel und Leben (Düsseldorf)
BibN	Biblische Notizen: Beiträge zur exegetischen Diskussion (Munich)
BibO	Bibbia e Oriente (Brescia)
BibR	Biblia Revuo (Ravenna, Italy)
BibTo	Bible Today (Collegeville, MN)
BibView	Biblical Viewpoint (Greenville, SC)
Bij	Bijdragen: Tijdschrift voor Filosofie en Theologie (Nijmegen)
BJRL	Bulletin of the John Rylands University Library (Manchester, UK)
BK	Bibel und Kirche (Stuttgart)
BL	Bibel und Liturgie (Vienna)
BLE	Bulletin de Littérature Ecclésiastique (Paris)
BLT	Brethren Life and Thought (Oak Brook, IL)
BQ	Baptist Quarterly (Oxford, UK)
BR	Biblical Research (Chicago)
BRev	Bible Review (Washington)
BSac	Bibliotheca Sacra (Dallas, TX)
BT	Bible Translator (Aberdeen, UK)
BTB	Biblical Theology Bulletin (St. Bonaventure, NY)
BTF	Bangalore Theological Forum (Bangalore)
BTZ	Berliner Theologische Zeitschrift (Berlin)
Burgense	Burgense: Collectanea Scientifica (Burgos)
BVC	Bible et Vie Chretienne (Paris)
BZ	Biblische Zeitschrift (Paderborn)
BZAW	Beihefte zur Zeitschrift für die alttestamentliche Wissenschaft (Berlin)
BZNW	Beihefte zur Zeitschrift für die neutestamentliche Wissenschaft (Berlin)
CahJos	Cahiers de Joséphologie (Copenhagen)
CalTJ	Calvary Theological Journal (Grand Rapids, MI)
CanaCR	Canadian Catholic Review (Saskatoon)
Cath	Catholica: Vierteljahresschrift für ökumenische Theologie (Münst)

CBG	Collationes Brugenses et Gandavenses (Gent)
CBQ	Catholic Biblical Quarterly (Washington, DC)
CBTJ	Calvary Baptist Theological Journal (Lansdale, PA)
CC	Christian Century (Chicago)
CE	Cahiers Évangiles (Paris)
Ch	Churchman (London)
ChH	Church History (Berne, IN)
ChJR	Christian Jewish Relations (London)
Chr	Christus (Paris)
CICR	Communico: International Catholic Review (Spokane, WA)
CJ	Concordia Journal St. Louis, MO)
ClerR	Clergy Review (London)
CM	Clergy Monthly (Ranchi)
Coll	Colloquium: The Australian and New Zealand Theological Review (Vols 1-2 New Zealand Theological Review) (Auckland, Sydney)
CollT	Collectanea Theologica (Warsaw)
Conci	Concilium (New York)
CQ	Covenant Quarterly (Chicago)
CrNSt	Cristianesimo nella Storia (Bologna)
CrozQ	Crozer Quarterly (Chester, PA)
Crux	Crux (Vancouver)
CS	Chicago Studies (Chicago)
CSR	Christian Scholar's Review (Grand Rapids, MI)
CT	Christianity Today (Des Moines, IA)
CThM	Currents in Theology and Mission (Chicago)
CTM	Concordia Theological Monthly (St. Louis, MO)
CTQ	Concordia Theological Quarterly (Fort Wayne, IN)
CuBi	Cultura Biblica (Madrid)
CumSem	Cumberland Seminarian (Memphis, TN)
CVia	Communio Viatorum (Prague)
DBM	Deltío Biblikôn Meletôn (Athens)
Dia	Dialog (Minneapolis, MN)
Diakonia	Diakonia (Vienna)
Did	Didascalia (Otterburne, Canada)

Div	Divinitas (Laterano, Italy)
DivT	Divus Thomas (Piacenza)
DR	Downside Review (Bath, UK)
DTD	Disciples Theological Digest (St. Louis, MO)
DTT	Dansk Teologisk Tidsskrift (Copenhagen)
DunR	Dunwoodie Review (Yonkers, NY)
EAJT	East Asia Journal of Theology (Singapore)
EB	Estudios Bíblicos (Madrid)
EE	Estudios Eclesiásticos (Madrid)
ÉgT	Église et théologie (Ottawa, Canada)
E-I	Eretz-Israel (Jerusalem)
Emmanuel	Emmanuel (New York)
EMQ	Evangelical Mission Quarterly (Wheaton, IL)
Enc	Encounter (Indianapolis, IN)
EQ	Evangelical Quarterly (Exeter, UK)
Era	Eranos: Acta philologica Suecana (Uppsala)
ERT	Evangelical Review of Theology (Exeter)
EstT	Estudios Teológicos (Guatemala City)
ET	Expository Times (Edinburgh, UK)
ETL	Ephemerides Theologicae Lovanienses (Louvain)
ÉTR	Études Théologiques et Religieuses (Montpellier)
ÉtudF	Études Franciscaines (Barcelona)
EV	Esprit et Vie (Langres)
EvErz	Der evangelische Erzieher (Frankurt/M)
EvJ	Evangelical Journal (Myerstown, NJ)
EvT	Evangelische Theologie (Stuttgart)
FilN	Filologia Neotestamentaria (Córdoba)
FM	Faith and Mission (Wake Forest, NC)
Forum	Forum (Sonoma, CA)
Found	Foundations (Arlington, MA)
FV	Foi et Vie (Paris)
GeistL	Geist und Leben (Würzburg)
GOTR	Greek Orthodox Theological Review (Brookline, MA)
GR	Gordon Review (Boston)

Greg	Gregorianum (Rome)
GTJ	Grace Theological Journal (Winona Lake, IN)
GTT	Gereformeered Theologisch Tijdschrift (Kampen, Neth)
HBT	Horizons in Biblical Theology: An International Dialogue (Pittsburg, PA)
HeyJ	Heythrop Journal (London)
Hokhma	Hokhma (Bordeaux)
Horizons	Horizons: The Journal of the College Theology Society (Villanova, PA)
HPR	Homiletic and Pastoral Review (New York)
HTR	Harvard Theological Review (Cambridge, MA)
HTS	Hervormde Teologiese Studies (Pretoria)
HUCA	Hebrew Union College Annual (New York)
IBMR	International Bulletin of Missionary Research (New Havem CT)
IBS	Irish Biblical Studies (Belfast)
IEJ	Israel Exploration Journal (Jerusalem)
IJT	Indian Journal of Theology (Calcutta)
IKaZ	Internationale Katholische Zeitschrift "Communio" (Frankfurt/M)
IKZ	Internationale Kirchliche Zeitschrift (Bern)
IliffR	Iliff Review (Denver, CO)
Immanuel	Immanuel: A Bulletin of Religious Thought and Research in Israel (Jerusalem)
Int	Interpretation (Richmond, VA)
IRM	International Review of Mission (Geneva)
ITQ	Irish Theological Quarterly Kildare, Ireland)
ITS	Indian Theological Studies (Bangalore)
JAAR	Journal of the American Academy of Religion (Atlanta, GA)
JASA	Journal of the American Scientific Affiliation (Durham, NH)
JBL	Journal of Biblical Literature (Atlanta, GA)
JBQ	Jerusalem Biblical Quarterly (Jerusalem)

JBR	Journal of Bible and Religion (Philadelphia, PA)
Je	Jeevadhara (Kerala, India)
JEH	Journal of Ecclesiastical History (Cambridge, UK)
JES	Journal of Ecumenical Studies (Philadelphia, PA)
JETS	Journal of the Evangelical Theological Society (Jackson, MS)
JGES	Journal of the Grace Evangelical Society (Roanoke, TX)
JJS	Journal of Jewish Studies (Oxford UK)
JLR	Journal of Law and Religion (St. Paul, MN)
JNES	Journal of Near Eastern Studies (Chicago)
JPC	Journal of Pastoral Care (Decatur, GA)
JPT	Journal of Psychology and Theology (La Mirada, CA)
JQR	Jewish Quarterly Review (Philadelphia, PA)
JR	Journal of Religion (Chicago)
JRH	Journal of Religious History (Sydney)
JRT	Journal of Religious Thought (Washington, DC)
JSNT	Journal for the Study of the New Testament (Sheffield, UK)
JSS	Journal of Semitic Studies (Oxford, UK)
JTS	Journal of Theological Studies (Oxford, UK)
JTSA	Journal of Theology for Southern Africa (Cape Town)
Jud	Judaica (Zürich)
K	Kairos (Salzburg)
KD	Kerygma and Dogma (Göttingen)
KIsr	Kirche und Israel: Theologische Zeitschrift (Neukirchen)
LB	Linguistica Biblica (Bonn)
Lead	Leadership: A Practical Journal for Church Leaders (Carol Stream, IL)
LexTQ	Lexington Theological Quarterly Lexington, KY)
List	Listening: Journal of Religion and Culture (Romeoville, IL)
LouvS	Louvain Studies (Louvain)
LQ	Lutheran Quarterly (Milwaukee, WI)
LQHR	London Quarterly and Holbon Review (London)
LTJ	Lutheran Theological Journal (Adelaide)

LTQ	Lutheran Theological Quarterly
LV	Lumen Vitae (Brussells)
LVie	Lumière et Vie Lyon)
Marianum	Marianum: Ephemerides Mariologiae (Rome)
MarSt	Marian Studies (Dayton, OH)
May	Mayéutica (Marcilla)
McMJT	McMaster Journal of Theology (Hamilton, Ontario)
MD	Maison-Dieu (Paris)
MeliT	Melita Theologia (Rabat, Malta)
MelJT	Melanesian Journal of Theology (New Guinea)
Miss	Missiology: An International Review (Scottsdale, PA)
MSR	Mélanges de Science Religieuse (Lille Cedex)
MTZ	Münchener theologische Zeitschrift (München)
NBlack	New Blackfriars (London)
NedTT	Nederlands theologisch tijdschrift (Gravenhage, Neth)
Neo	Neotestamentica: Journal of the New Testament Society of South Africa (Pretoria)
NovT	Novum Testamentum (Leiden, Neth)
NovVet	Nova et Vetera (Fribourg)
NRT	Nouvelle revue théologique (Tournai)
NTheoR	New Theology Review (Collegeville, MN)
NTS	New Testament Studies (Cambridge, UK)
NTT	Norsk teologisk tidsskrift (Oslo)
OCP	Orientalia christiana periodica (Rome)
Orient	Orientierung (Zürich)
Pacifica	Pacifica: Australian Theological Studies (Brunswick, East, Victoria, Australia)
PalCl	Palestra del Clero (Rovigo)
PatByzR	Patristic and Byzantine Review (Kingston, NY)
PerT	Perspectiva Teológica (Belo Horizonte, Brazil)
PJ	Perkins Journal (Dallas, TX)
Pneuma	Penuma: The Journal of the Society for Pentecostal Studies (Gaithersburg, MD)

P&P	Priest & People (London)
PPsy	Pastoral Psychology (New York)
Pro	Proyeccíon (Granada)
PRS	Perspectives in Religious Studies (Lewiston, NY)
PSB	Princeton Seminary Bulletin (Princeton, NJ)
QR	Quarterly Review: A Journal of Theological Resources for Ministry (Nashville, TN)
RAfT	Revue Africaine de Théologie (Alger)
RB	Revue biblique (Paris)
RBib	Rivista Biblica (Bologna)
RBR	Ricerche Bibliche e Religiose (Milan)
RCB	Revista de Cultura Bíblica (San Paulo)
RCT	Revista Catalana de Teología (Barcelona)
REA	Revue des Études Augustiniennes (Paris)
RechSR	Recherches de science religieuse (Paris)
REd	Religious Education (New Haven, CT)
Reformatio	Reformatio: (Evangelische Zeitschrift für Kultur, Politik, Kirche (Zürich)
RevAug	Revista Augstiniana (Madrid)
RevB	Revista Biblica (Buenos Aires)
RevExp	Review and Expositor (Louisville, KY)
RevQ	Revue de Qumran (Paris)
RevSR	Revue des sciences religieuses (Strasbourg Cedex)
RHPR	Revue d'historie et de philosophie religieuses (Strasbourg Cedex)
RJ	Reformed Journal (Grand Rapids, MI)
RL	Religion in Life (Nashville, TN)
RoczTK	Roczniki Teologiczno-Kanoniczne (Lublin)
RQ	Restoration Quarterly (Abilene, TX)
RR	Reformed Review (Holland, MI)
RSPT	Revue des sciences philosophiques et théologiques (Paris)
RSR	Religious Studies Review (Valapariso, IN)
RT	Revue Thomiste (Paris)
RTAM	Recherches de Théologie Ancienne et Médiévale (Louvain)

RTL	Revue théologique de Louvain (Louvain)
RTP	Revue de Théologie et de Philosophie (Geneva)
RTR	Reformed Theological Review (Hawthorne, Australia)
RW	Reformed World (Geneva)
SacD	Sacra Doctrina (Bologna)
Sale	Salesianum (Rome)
Salm	Salmanticensis (Salamanca)
SBFLA	Studii Biblici Franciscani Liber Annuus (Jerusalem)
SBib	Sémiotique et Bible (Lyon)
SBLSP	Society of Biblical Literature Seminar Papers (Atlanta, GA)
SBT	Studia Biblica et Theologica (Pasadena, CA)
ScanJT	Scandinavian Journal of Theology (Oslo)
ScE	Science et Esprit (Montreal)
Schrift	Schrift (Landstichting, Neth)
Scr	Scripture (Scripture Bulletin after 1968; London)
ScrB	Scripture Bulletin (London)
ScripT	Scripta theologia (Pamplona, Spain)
ScrSA	Scriptura: Journal of Bible and Theology in South Africa (Stellenbosch, South Africa)
SE	Sciences Ecclésiastiques: Revue philosophique et théologique (Montreal)
SEÅ	Svensk Exegetisk Årsbok (Lund)
SEAJT	South East Asia Journal of Theology (Manila)
Semeia	Semeia (Atlanta, GA)
SJOT	Scandinavian Journal of the Old Testament (Copenhagen)
SJT	Scottish Journal of Theology (Edinburgh, UK)
SLJT	Saint Luke's Journal of Theology (Sewanee, TN)
SM	Studia Missionalia (Rome)
SNTU-A	Studien zum Neuen Testament und seiner Umwelt (series A; Linz)
SouJT	Southwestern Journal of Theology (Fort Worth, TX)
SR	Studies in Religion/Sciences religieuses (Waterloo, Ontario)
SThV	Studia theologica Varsaviensia (Warsaw)
STK	Svensk teologisk kvartalskrift (Lund)

StL	Studia Liturgica (Nieuwendam)
StPa	Studia Patavina: Revista di scienze religiose (Padova)
Stud	Studium (Madrid)
SuC	La Suola Cattolica (Milan)
SVTQ	St. Vladimir's Theological Quarterly (Crestwood, NY)

Tarbiz	Tarbiz (Jerusalem)
TBe	Theologische Beiträge (Wuppertal)
TD	Theology Digest (Duluth, MN)
Teologia	Teologia (Brescia)
TerreS	Terre sainte (Jerusalem)
TexteK	Texte und Kontexte: Exegetische Zeitschrift (Berlin)
TF	Theologische Forschung (Hamburg)
TGl	Theologie und Glaube (Paderborn)
Themelios	Themelios (Leicester, UK)
Theology	Theology (London)
Thomist	Thomist (Washington, DC)
TijT	Tijdschrift voor Theologie (Nijmegen)
TischWo	Am Tische des Wortes (Stuttgart)
TJT	Toronto Journal of Theology (Toronto)
TLife	Theology and Life (Hong Kong)
TLZ	Theologische Literaturzeitung (Leipzig)
TR	Theologische Rundschau (Tübingen)
TriJ	Trinity Journal (Deerfield, IL)
TS	Theological Studies (Washington, DC)
TT	Theology Today (Princeton, NJ)
TTQ	Tübinger Theologische Quartalschrift (Stuttgart)
TTZ	Trierer Theologische Zeitschrift (Trier)
TU	Texte und Untersuchungen zur Geschichte der altertumswissenschaftliche Reihe (Berlin)
TV	Theologische Versuche (Berlin)
TXav	Theologica Xaveriana (Bogotá)
TynB	Tyndale Bulletin (London)
TZ	Theologische Zeitschrift (Basel)

| Unitas | Unitas: International Quarterly Review (Garrison, NY) |
| UnSa | Una Sancta (Freising) |

USQR	Union Seminary Quarterly Review (New York)
VD	Verbum Domini (Rome)
Way	Way (London)
WesTJ	Wesleyan Theological Journal (Marion, IN)
Worship	Worship (Collegeville, MN)
WS	Word and Spirit: A Monastic Review (Still River, MA)
WTJ	Westminster Theology Journal (Philadelphia)
ZAW	Zeitschrift für die alttestamentliche Wissenschaft (Berlin)
ZDPV	Zeitschrift des Deutschen Palästina-Vereins (Wiesbaden)
ZDT	Zeitschrift für dialektische Theologie (Kampen, Neth)
ZEE	Zeitschrift für Evangelische Ethik (Gütersloh)
ZKT	Zeitschrift für Katholische Theologie (Innsbruck)
ZNW	Zeitschrift für die neutestamentliche Wissenschaft (Berlin)
ZRGG	Zeitschrift für Religions- und Geistesgeschichte (Erlangen)
ZTK	Zeitschrift für Theologie und Kirche (Tübingen)

PART ONE

Citations by Chapter and Verse

1:1-13:52

    0001   T. Fornberg, *Matteusevangeliet 1:1-13:52*. Uppsala: EFS-förlaget, 1989.

1-11

    0002   G. Danieli, "Storicita di Matteo 1-11: Stato Present della la Discussione," *CahJos* 19 (1971): 53-61.

1-5

    0003   John Goldingay, "The Old Testament and Christian Faith: Part 1. Jesus and the Old Testament in Matthew 1-5," *Themelios* 8/1 (1982): 4-10.

1:1-2:23

    0004   N. Casalini, *Il evangelo di Matteo come racconto teologico. Analisi delle sequenze narrative*. Jerusalem: Franciscan Press, 1990.

1:1-4:16

    0005   John M. Gibbs, "Mk. 1,1-15, Mt. 1,1-4,16, Lk. 1,1-4,30, Jn. 1,1-51. The Gospel Prologues and their Function," in F. Cross, ed., *Studia Evangelica IV*: Papers Presented to the Third International Congress on New Testament Studies, Christ Church, Oxford, 1965 (Part I—The New Testament Scriptures). Berlin: Akademie-Verlag, 1968. Pp. 154-88.

1-2

    0006   E. Lohmeyer, "Die Kindheitsgeschichten des Matth.," in *Gottesknecht und Davidssohn*. 2nd ed. Göttingen: Vandenhoeck & Ruprecht, 1953. Pp. 40-46.

    0007   S. Muñoz Iglesias, "Los Evangelios de la infancia y las infancias de los héroes," in *Géneros literanos en los Evangelios*. Madrid: Científica Medinaceli, 1958. Pp. 83-113.

    0008   P. J. Thompson, "The Infancy Gospels of St. Matthew and St. Luke Compared," in Kurt Aland, et al., eds., *Studia Evangelica*: Papers Presented to the International Congress on the Four Gospels, Christ Church, Oxford, 1957. Berlin: Akademie-Verlag, 1959. Pp. 217-22.

    0009   Myles M. Bourke, "The Literary Genius of Matthew 1-2," *CBQ* 22 (1960): 160-75.

0010   E. Galbiati, "Evangeli," *BibO* 4 (1962): 20-29.

0011   G. Strecker, "Die Reflexionszitate in Mt. 1-2," in *Der Weg
            der Gerechtigkeit: Untersuchung zur Theologie des
            Matthäus*. Göttingen: Vandenhoeck & Ruprecht, 1962. Pp.
            51-63.

0012   C. H. Cave, "St. Matthew's Infancy Narrative," *NTS* 9
            (1962-1963): 382-90.

0013   Edgar Krentz, "The Extent of Matthew's Prologue," *JBL*
            83 (1964): 409-14.

0014   Krister Stendahl, "Quis et unde? An Analysis of Mt. 1-2,"
            in Walther Eltester, ed. *Judentum, Urchristentum, Kirche*
            (festschrift for Joachim Jeremias). Berlin: Töpelmann, 1964.
            Pp. 94-105.

0015   G. Danieli, "Vangeli dell'infanzia," in *Il Messaggio della
            salvezza*. 5 vols. Torino: Leumann, 1966-1970. 4:150-203.

0016   R. Pesch, "Der Gottessohn im matthaischen
            Evangelienprolog (Mt. 1-2): Beobachtungen zu den
            Zitationsformeln der Reflexionszitate," *Bib* 48 (1967):
            416-19.

0017   K. H. Schelkle, "Die Kindheitsgeschichte Jesu," in *Bibel
            und Zeitgemässer Glaube*. Band II: Neues Testament.
            Klosterneuberg: Kunstverlag, 1967. 2:11-36.

0018   E. Rasco, "Matthew 1-2: Structure, Meaning, Reality," in
            F. Cross, ed., *Studia Evangelica IV*: Papers Presented to the
            Third International Congress on New Testament Studies,
            Christ Church, Oxford, 1965. (Part I—The New Testament
            Scriptures). Berlin: Akademie-Verlag, 1968. Pp. 214-30.

0019   C. Duquoc, "Les enfances du Christ," in *Christologie*. 2
            vols. Paris: Cerf, 1968-1972. 1:23-41.

0020   G. G. Gamba, "Annotazioni in margine alla struttura
            letteraria ed al significato dottrinale di Mateo I-II," in
            *Jalones de la Historia de la Salvación en el Antiguo y
            Nuevo Testamento*. 2 vols. Madrid: Científica Medinaceli,
            1969. 2:59-99.

0021   U. E. Lattanzi, "Il vangelo dell'infanzia è verità o mito?" in *De primordiis cultus marian. IV. De cultu B. V. Mariae respectu habito ad mythologiam et libros apocryphos.* Rome: Mariana Internationalis, 1970. 4:31-46.

0022   E. Peretto, *Ricerche su Mt. 1-2.* Rome: Marianum, 1970.

0023   D. Ashbeck, "The Literary Genre of Matthew 1-2," *BibTo* 57 (1971): 572-78.

0024   B. De Solages, "Réflexions sur les évangiles de l'enfance," *BLE* 72 (1971): 37-42.

0025   S. Muñoz Iglesias, "Midrás y Evangelios de la Infancia," *EB* 47 (1972): 331-59.

0026   K. Schubert, "Die Kindheitsgeschichten Jesu im Lichte der Religionsgeschichte des Judentums," *BL* 45 (1972): 224-40.

0027   J. O. Tuni, "La Tipología Israel-Jesús en Mt. 1-2," *EE* 47 (1972): 361-76.

0028   A. Vögtle, "Die matthäische Kindheitsgeschichte," in *L'Évangile selon Matthieu.* Gembloux: Duculot, 1972. Pp. 153-83.

0029   E. Galbiati, "Genere letterario e storia in Matteo 1-2," *BibO* 15 (1973): 3-16.

0030   A. V. Cernuda, "La dialéctica *gennô-tiktô* en Mt. 1-2," *Bib* 55 (1974): 408-17.

0031   Dan O. Via, "Narrative World and Ethical Response: The Marvelous and Righteousness in Matthew 1-2," *Semeia* 12 (1978): 123-49.

0032   M. R. Mulholland, Jr., "The Infancy Narratives in Matthew and Luke: Of History, Theology, and Literature," *BAR* 7/2 (1981): 46-59.

0033   Raymond E. Brown, "Gospel Infancy Narrative Research from 1976 to 1986: Part I (Matthew)," *CBQ* 48 (1986): 468-83.

0034   G. Segalla, "Matteo 1-2: dalla narrazione teologica della tradizione alla teologia kerygmatica della redazione," *Teologia* 11 (1986): 197-225.

0035   J. Cosslett Quin, "The Infancy Narratives with Special Reference to Matthew 1 and 2," *IBS* 9 (1987): 63-69.

0036   G. D'Urso, "Betlemme: incontri di sguardi tra Gesù e Maria," *SacD* 34 (1989): 557-84.

0037   B. T. Benedict, "The Genres of Matthew 1-2: Light from 1 Timothy 1:4," *RB* 97 (1990): 31-53.

0038   N. Casalini, *Libro dell'origine di Gesù Cristo. Analisi letteraria e teologica di Matt.* Jerusalem: Franciscan Press, 1990.

0039   C. Thomas, "The Nativity Scene," *BibTo* 28 (1990): 26-33.

<u>1:1-25</u>

0040   F. Hofmans, "Maria altijd maagd," *CBG* 8/4 (1962): 475-94; 9/1 (1963): 53-78.

0041   E. Pascual, "La Genealogia de Jesus segun S. Mateo," *EB* 23/2 (1964): 109-49.

0042   O. Da Spinetoli, "Les généalogies de Jésus et leur signification," *AsSeign* N.S. 9 (1974): 6-19.

0043   J. Schaberg, "The Foremothers and the Mother of Jesus," *Conci* 206 (1989): 112-19.

<u>1:1-18</u>

0044   Barclay M. Newman, "Matthew 1:1-18: Some Comments and a Suggested Restructuring," *BT* 2/2 (1976): 209-12.

<u>1:1-17</u>

0045   G. Saldarini, "La genealogia di Gesù," in L. Moraldi and S. Lyonnet, eds., *I Vangelini (Introduzione alla Bibbia).* Torino: Marietti, 1960. Pp. 411-25.

0046   Jacques Dupont, "La genealogia di Gesu secondo Matteo 1,1-17," *BibO* 4/1 (1962): 3-6.

0047   H. Milton, "The Structure of the Prologue to St. Matthew's Gospel," *JBL* 81 (1962): 175-81.

0048   K. H. Schelkle, "Die Frauen im Stammbaum Jesu," *BK* 18/4 (1963): 113-15.

0049   J. E. Bruns, "Matthew's Genealogy of Jesus," *BibTo* 1/15 (1964): 980-85.

0050   M. J. Moreton, "The Genealogy of Jesus," in F. Cross, ed., *Studia Evangelica II*: Papers Presented to the Second International Congress on New Testament Studies, Christ Church, Oxford, 1961. (Part I—The New Testament Scriptures). Berlin: Akademie-Verlag, 1964. Pp. 219-24.

0051   L. Ramlot, "Les genealogies bibliques. Un genre litteraire oriental," *BVC* 60 (1964): 53-70.

0052   H. Schöllig, "Die Zählung der Generationen im matthäischen Stammbaum," *ZNW* 59 (1968): 261-68.

0053   M. D. Johnson, "The Genealogy of Jesus in Matthew," in *The Purpose of the Biblical Genealogies with Special Reference to the Setting of the Genealogies of Jesus.* Cambridge: University Press, 1969. Pp. 139-228.

0054   E. L. Abel, "The Genealogies of Jesus ὁ Χριστός," *NTS* 20 (1974): 203-10.

0055   D. E. Nineham, "The Genealogy in St. Matthew's Gospel and its Significance for the Study of the Gospels" *BJRL* 58 (1976): 421-44.

0056   Herman C. Waetjen, "The Genealogy as the Key to the Gospel According to Matthew," *JBL* 95/2 (1976): 205-30.

0057   J. Lach, "Historycznosc genealogii Chrystusa w Mt. 1,1-17," *SThV* 15 (1977): 19-35.

0058   F. Schnider and W. Stenger, "Die Frauen im Stammbaum Jesu nach Matthaus. Strukturale Beobachtungen zu Mt. 1, 1-17" *BZ* 23 (1979): 187-96.

0059   W. Hammer, "L'intention de la génélogie de Matthieu," *ÉTR* 55 (1980): 305-306.

0060   André Feuillet, "Observations sur les deux généalogies de Jésus-Christ de saint Matthieu (1,1-17) et de saint Luc (3,23-38)," *EV* 98 (1988): 605-608.

0061   R. P. Nettelhorst, "The Genealogy of Jesus," *JETS* 31 (1988): 169-72.

0062   Thomas H. Graves, "Matthew 1:1-17," *RevExp* 86 (1989): 595-600.

0063   K. F. Plum, "Genealogy as Theology," *SJOT* 3 (1989): 166-92.

0064   H. Hempelmann, " 'Das dürre Blatt im Heiligen Buch.' Mt. 1,1-17 und der Kampf wider die Erniedrigung Gottes," *TBe* 21 (1990): 6-23.

<u>1:1</u>

0065   Sebastian Bartina, "Jesus, el Cristo, ben David ben Abraham (Mt. 1,1): Los appelidos de la Biblia y su traduccion al castellano," *EB* 18/4 (1959): 375-93.

0066   Otto Eissfeldt, "Toledot," in *Studien zum Neuen Testament und zur Patristik* (festschrift for Erich Klostermann). Berlin: Akademie-Verlag, 1961. Pp. 1-8.

0067   W. Barnes Tatum, " 'The Origin of Jesus Messiah' (Matt. 1:1, 18a): Matthew's Use of the Infancy Traditions" *JBL* 96 (1977): 523-35.

<u>1:1a</u>

0068   J.-L. Leuba, "Note exégétique sur Matthieu I,1a," *RHPR* 22 (1942): 56-61.

<u>1:2-16</u>

0069   A. Vögtle, "Die Genealogie Mt. 1,2-16 und die matthaische Kindheitsgeschichte (I. Teil)," *BZ* 8/1 (1964): 45-58.

0070   A. Vögtle, "Die Genealogie Mt. 1,2-16 und die matthaische Kindheitsgeschichte," in V. Vajta, ed., *Das Evangelium und die Bestimmung des Menschen*. Göttingen: Vandenhoeck & Ruprecht, 1972. Pp. 57-102.

0071 C. T. Davis, "The Fulfillment of Creation: A Study of Matthew's Genealogy," *JAAR* 41 (1973): 520-35.

1:3

0072 J. P. Heil, "The Narrative Roles of the Women in Matthew's Genealogy," *Bib* 72 (1991): 538-45.

1:5

0073 Yair Zakovitch, "Rahab als Mutter des Boaz in der Jesus-Genealogie (Matth. 1,5)," *NovT* 17/1 (1975): 1-5.

0074 A. T. Hanson, "Rahab the Harlot in Early Christian Tradition" *JSNT* (1978): 53-60.

0075 Jerome D. Quinn, "Is Ῥαχάβ in Mt. 1,5 Rahab of Jericho?" *Bib* 62/2 (1981): 225-28.

0076 Raymond E. Brown, "Rachab in Mt. 1,5 Probably Is Rahab of Jericho," *Bib* 63/1 (1982): 79-80.

0077 J. P. Heil, "The Narrative Roles of the Women in Matthew's Genealogy," *Bib* 72 (1991): 538-45.

1:6

0078 J. P. Heil, "The Narrative Roles of the Women in Matthew's Genealogy," *Bib* 72 (1991): 538-45.

1:16

0079 B. M. Metzger, "On the Citation of Variant Readings of Matt. 1,16," *JBL* 77 (1958): 361-63 (see also, Throckmorton, B. H., Jr., "A Reply to Professor Metzger," *JBL* 78 (1959): 162-63).

0080 H. A. Blair, "Matthew 1,16 and the Matthaean Genealogy," in F. Cross, ed., *Studia Evangelica II*: Papers Presented to the Second International Congress on New Testament Studies, Christ Church, Oxford, 1961. (Part I—The New Testament Scriptures). Berlin: Akademie-Verlag, 1964. Pp. 149-54.

0081 B. M. Metzger, "The Text of Matthew 1,16," in D. E. Aune, ed., *Studies in New Testament and Early Christian Literature* (festschrift Allen Wikgren). Leiden: Brill, 1972. Pp. 16-24.

0082   J. P. Heil, "The Narrative Roles of the Women in Matthew's Genealogy," *Bib* 72 (1991): 538-45.

1:18-2:25
0083   I. Broer, "Die Bedeutung der 'Jungfrauengeburt' im Matthausevangelium," *BibL* 12 (1971): 248-60.

0084   A. Knockaert and C. van der Plancke, "Catéchèses de l'annonciation," *LV* 34 (1979): 79-121.

0085   M. Herranz Marco, "Substrato arameo en el relato de la Anunciación a José," *EB* 38 (1979-1980): 35-55, 237-68.

1:18-2:23
0086   Dominic Crossan, "Structure and Theology of Mt. 1.18-2.23," *CahJos* 16/1 (1968): 119-35.

0087   C. T. Davis, "Tradition and Redaction in Matthew 1:18-2:23," *JBL* 90/4 (1971): 404-21.

0088   M. J. Down, "The Matthaean Birth Narratives: Matthew 1:18-2:23," *ET* 90 (1978): 51-52.

0089   E. A. Ahirika, "The Theology of Matthew in the Light of the Nativity Story," *BB* 16 (1990): 5-19.

1:18-2:19
0090   J. M. Germano, "Nova et vetera in pericopam de sancto Joseph," *VD* 46 (1968): 351-60.

1:18-25
0091   R. H. Fuller, "The Virgin Birth: Historical Fact or Kerygmatic Truth?" *BR* 1 (1957): 1-8.

0092   F. Dumermuth, "Bemerkung zu Jesu Menschwerdung," *TZ* 20 (1964): 52-53.

0093   M. Krämer, "Die globale Analyse des Stiles in Mt. 1,18-25," *Bib* 45/2 (1964): 4-22.

0094   M. Krämer, "Zwei Probleme aus Mt. 1:18-25: Vers 20 und 25" *Sale* 26 (1964): 303-33.

0095   Otto A. Piper, "The Virgin Birth: The Meaning of the Gospel Accounts," *Int* 18 (1964): 131-48.

0096 A. Pelletier, "L'Annonce à Joseph," *RechSR* 54/1 (1966): 67-68.

0097 W. Trilling, "Jesus, der Messias und Davidssohn (Mt. 1,18-25)," in *Christusverkündigung in den synoptischen Evangelien.* Munich: Kösel, 1969. Pp. 13-39.

0098 E. Rasco, "El anuncio a Jose (Mt. 1,18-25)," *CahJos* 19/1 (1971): 84-103.

0099 Joseph A. Fitzmyer, "The Virginal Conception of Jesus in the New Testament," *TS* 34 (1973): 541-75.

0100 K. Grayston, "Matthieu 1:18-25: Essai d'interprétation," *RTP* 23 (1973): 221-32.

0101 P. T. Stramare, "Giuseppe 'uomo giusto' in Mt. 1,18-25," *RBib* 21 (1973): 287-300.

0102 F. Schnider and W. Stenger, " 'Mit der Abstammung Jesu Christi verhielt es sich so: . . .' Struckturale Beobachtungen zu Mt. 1,18-25," *BZ* 25 (1981): 255-64.

0103 Raymond E. Brown, "The Annunciation to Joseph (Matthew 1:18-25)," *Worship* 61/6 (1987): 482-92.

0104 Fred L. Horton, "Parenthetical Pregnancy: The Conception and Birth of Jesus in Matthew 1:18-25," *SBLSP* 26 (1987): 175-89.

0105 D. J. Harrington, "New and Old in New Testament Interpretation: The Many Faces of Matthew 1:18-25," *NTheoR* 2 (1989): 39-49.

0106 T. Kronholm, "Den Kommande Hiskia," *SEÅ* 54 (1989): 109-17.

0107 P. T. Stramare, "L'Annunciazione a Giuseppe in Mt. 1:18-25: Analisi letteraria e significato teologico [pt 1]," *BibO* 31 (1989): 3-14.

0108 P. T. Stramare, "L'Annunciazione a Giuseppe in Mt. 1:18-25: Analisi letteraria e significato teologico [pt 2]," *BibO* 31 (1989): 199-217.

0109   R. N. Longenecker, "Whose Child Is This?" *CT* 34 (1990): 25-28.

0110   F. Olivera, "Interpretación derásica de Mt. 1,18-25," *May* 17 (1991): 281-304.

0111   Sheila Klassen-Wiebe, "Matthew 1:18-25," *Int* 46 (1992): 392-95.

1:18-24
0112   A. Bouton, "C'est toi qui lui donneras le nom de Jésus," *AsSeign* N.S. 8 (1972): 17-25.

1:18-21
0113   F.-J. Steinmetz, "Der Zweifel des Josef, der Heilige Geist und das neue Leben. Meditationsanregungen zu Mt. 1,18-21.24," *GeistL* 47 (1974): 465-68.

0114   Laurence Cantwell, "The Parentage of Jesus: Mt. 1:18-21," *NovT* 24/4 (1982): 304-15.

1:18a
0115   W. Barnes Tatum, " 'The Origin of Jesus Messiah' (Matt. 1:1, 18a): Matthew's Use of the Infancy Traditions" *JBL* 96 (1977): 523-35.

1:18b
0116   James Lagrand, "How was the Virgin Mary 'Like a Man': A Note on Mt. 1:18b and Related Syriac Christian Texts," *NovT* 22 (1980): 97-107.

1:19
0117   Ceslaus Spicq, " 'Joseph, son mari, etant juste. . .' (Mt. 1, 19)," *RB* 70 (1964): 206-14.

0118   David Hill, "A Note on Matthew 1:19," *ET* 76/4 (1965): 133-34.

0119   A. Tosato, "Joseph, Being a Just Man (Matt. 1:19)," *CBQ* 41 (1979): 547-51.

0120   Antonio Vincent-Cernuda, "El domicilio de José y la fama de María," *EB* 46 (1988): 5-25.

1:20-24
> **0121** S. Bartina, "Los sueños o éxtasis de San José (Mt. 1,20-24; 2,13-14, 19-20," *CahJos* 39 (1991): 43-53.

1:20-23
> **0122** J. C. Fenton, "Matthew and the Divinity of Jesus: Three Questions concerning Matthew 1:20-23," in E. A. Livingstone, ed., *Studia Biblica 1978 II*. Papers Presented to the Fifth International Congress on Biblical Studies, Oxford, 1978. Sheffield: JSOT Press, 1980. Pp. 79-82.

1:20
> **0123** F. Sottocornola, "Tradition and the Doubt of St. Joseph concerning Mary's Virginity," *Marianum* 19/1 (1957): 127-41.

> **0124** Pierre Grelot, "La naissance d'Isaac et celle de Jésus," *NRT* 104 (1972): 462-87, 561-85.

1:21-59
> **0125** F. Neirynck, "Apò tóte ērxato and the Structure of Matthew," *ETL* 64/1 (1988): 21-59.

1:21
> **0126** J. M. Germano, "Privilegium nominis messianici a S. Joseph imponendi (Is. 7,14; Mt. 1,21, 23, 25)," *VD* 47/3 (1969): 151-62.

> **0127** A. R. C. McLellian, "Choosing a Name for the Baby," *ET* 93 (1981): 80-82.

1:22
> **0128** James W. Scott, "Matthew's Intention to Write History," *WTJ* 47/1 (1985): 68-82.

1:23-25
> **0129** Andreas Schmidt, "Der mögliche Text von P. Oxy. III 405, Z 39-45," *NTS* 37 (1991): 160.

1:23
> **0130** H. E. W. Turner, "Expository Problems: The Virgin Birth," *ET* 68 (1956): 12-17.

0131   Robert G. Bratcher, "A Study of Isaiah 7:15. Its Meaning
            and Use in the Masoretic Text, the Septuagint and the
            Gospel of Matthew," *BT* 9/3 (1958): 98-125.

0132   M. McNamara, "The Emmanuel Prophecy and Its
            Context-III," *Scr* 15 (1963): 80-88.

0133   J. P. Brennan, "Virgin and Child in Isaiah 7:14," *BibTo*
            1/15 (1964): 968-74.

0134   J. M. Germano, "Privilegium nominis messianici a S.
            Joseph imponendi (Is. 7,14; Mt. 1,21, 23, 25)," *VD* 47/3
            (1969): 151-62.

0135   C. H. Dodd, "New Testament Translation Problems I," *BT*
            27/3 (1976): 301-11.

0136   John T. Willis, "The Meaning of Isaiah 7:14 and Its
            Application in Matthew 1:23," *RQ* 21/1 (1978): 1-18.

0137   J. M. James, "The God Who Is with Us," *ET* 91 (1979):
            78-79.

0138   Frederick Anderson, "The Virgin Birth," *RevExp* 1 (1904):
            28-43.

0139   Georges Arnera, "Du rocher d'Esaie aux douze montagnes
            d'Hermas," *ÉTR* 59/2 (1984): 215-20.

0140   J. Edward Barrett, "Can Scholars Take the Virgin Birth
            Seriously?" *BRev* 4 (1988): 10-15, 29.

0141   W. C. Kaiser, "The Promise of Isaiah 7:14 and the
            Single-Meaning Hermeneutic," *EvJ* 6/2 (1988): 55-70.

1:24

0142   F.-J. Steinmetz, "Der Zweifel des Josef, der Heilige Geist
            und das neue Leben. Meditationsanregungen zu Mt.
            1,18-21.24," *GeistL* 47 (1974): 465-68.

1:25

0143   J. M. Germano, "Privilegium nominis messianici a S.
            Joseph imponendi (Is. 7,14; Mt.1, 21, 23, 25)," *VD* 47/3
            (1969): 151-62.

0144   J. M. Germano, "Et non cognoscebat eam donec . . . 'nquisitio super sensu spirituali seu mystico Mt. 1 25," *Marianum* 35 (1973): 184-240.

2-3

0145   M. S. Enslin, "The Christian Stories of the Nativity," *JBL* 59 (1940): 314-38.

0146   A. R. C. Leaney, "The Birth Narratives in St. Luke and St. Matthew," *NTS* 8 (1962): 158-66.

0147   Armand Beauduini, "The Infancy Narratives: A Confession of Faith," *LV* 39/2 (1984): 167-77.

2:1-23

0148   R. Couffignal, "Le conte merveilleux des mages et du cruel Hérode," *RT* 89 (1989): 97-117.

2:1-12

0149   H. J. Richards, "The Three Kings (Mt. II 1-12)," *Scr* 8 (1956): 23-28.2:1-12

0150   E. Galbiati, "Esegesi degli Evangeli festivi. L'Adorazione dei Magi (Matt. 2,1-12). (Festa dell'Epifania)," *BibO* 4/1 (1962): 20-29.

0151   M. W. Schoenberg, "Why Epiphany?" *HPR* 64/3 (1963): 222-30.

0152   F. Kerstiens, "Unterwegs im Glauben: Homilie zum Feste Epiphanie," *BibL* 6 (1965): 303-306.

0153   J. N. M. Wifngaards, "The Episode of the Magi and Christian Kerygma," *IJT* 61/1 (1967): 30-41.

0154   E. Bettencourt, "Os Magos, Herodes e Jesus," *RCB* 5/10 (1968): 30-42.

0155   P. Gaechter, "Die Magierperikope (Mt. 2,1-12)," *ZKT* 90/3 (1968): 257-95.

0156   L. Zani, "Influsso del genere letterario midrashico su Mt. 2,1-12," *StPa* 19/2 (1972): 257-320.

0157   W. A. Schulze, "Nachtrag zu meinem Aufsatz: Zur Geschichte der Auslegung von Matth. 2:1-12," *TZ* 31 (1975): 150-60.

0158   Raymond E. Brown, "The Meaning of the Magi: The Significance of the Star," *Worship* 49 (1975): 574-82.

0159   W. A. Schulze, "Zur Geschichte der Auslegung von Matth. 2,1-12," *TZ* 31/3 (1975): 150-60.

0160   David C. Steinmetz, "Gedanken zum Dreikönigstag: Reflexionen über die Huldigung der Magier in Mt. 2," *GeistL* 50 (1977): 401-408.

0161   G. Schmahl, "Magier aus dem Osten und die Heiligen Drei Könige," *TTZ* 87 (1978): 295-303.

0162   F. Salvoni, "La visita dei Magi e la fuga in Egitto," *RBR* 14 (1979): 171-201.

0163   Robert W. Bertram, "An Epiphany Crossing: Programming Matthew 2:1-12 for Readers Today," *CThM* 7/6 (1980): 328-36.

0164   Antonio Charbel, "Mateo 2:1-12: los Magos en el ambiente del Reino Nabateo," *RevB* 46/1 (1984): 147-58.

0165   Elmer Matthias, "The Epiphany of Our Lord," *CJ* 10 (1984): 231.

0166   William E. Phipps, "The Magi and Halley's Comet," *TT* 43/1 (1986): 88-92.

0167   O. J. McTernan, *A Call to Witness: Reflections on the Gospel of St. Matthew*. Collegeville: Liturgical Press, 1989.

0168   Donald Senior, "Matthew 2:1-12," *Int* 46 (1992): 395-98.

2:1-7

0169   Antonio Charbel, "Mt. 2,1.7: Os Reis Magos eram Nabateus?" *RCB* 8/1 (1971): 96-103.

0170   Antonio Charbel, "Mt. 2,1.7: I Magi erano Nabatei?" *RBib* 20 (1972): 571-83.

2:2

0171   N. Turner, "The New-Born King: Mt. 2:2," *ET* 68 (1957): 122.

0172   R. A. Rosenberg, "The a Star of the Messiah 'Reconsidered'," *Bib* 53 (1972): 105-109.

0173   M. Küchler, "Wir haben seinen Stern gesehen . . . ," *BK* 44 (1989): 179-86.

2:5-6

0174   Victor J. Eldridge, "Typology: The Key to Understanding Matthew's Formula Quotations?" *Coll* 15 (1982): 43-51.

2:5

0175   Jean Doignon, "Erat in Iesu Christo homo totus (Hilaire de Poitiers, *In Mattaeum 2,5*: Pour une saine interprétation de la formule," *REA* 28 (1982): 201-207.

2:6

0176   Homer Heater, Jr., "Matthew 2:6 and Its Old Testament Sources," *JETS* 26/4 (1983): 395-97.

0177   A. J. Petrotta, "A Closer Look at Matt. 2:6 and Its Old Testament Sources," *JETS* 28/1 (1985): 47-52.

0178   A. J. Petrotta, "An Even Closer Look at Matt 2:6 and Its Old Testament Sources," *JETS* 33 (1990): 311-15.

2:7

0179   Alasdair B. Gordon, "The Fate of Judas according to Acts 1:18," *EQ* 43/2 (1971): 97-100.

2:9

0180   Anon. "What Was the Star of Bethlehem?" *CT* 9 (1964): 277-80.

2:11

0181   Gonzague Ryckmans, "De l'or, de l'encens et de la myrrhe," *RB* 58 (1951): 372-76.

0182   G. W. van Beek, "Frankincense and Myrrh," *BA* 23 (1960): 70-95.

0183   S. Barting, "Casa o caserio? Los magos en Belen," *EB* 25
                (1966): 355-57.

0184   D. H. C. Read, "Three Gaudy Kings," *ET* 91 (1979):
                84-86.

2:13-23
0185   A. Paul, "La fuite en Égypte et le retour en Galilée,"
                AsSeign N.S. 11 (1971): 19-28.

0186   A. R. C. McLellian, "Into Egypt," *ET* 95 (1983): 84-86.

0187   Thomas H. Graves, "A Story Ignored: An Exegesis of
                Matthew 2:13-23," *FM* 5/1 (1987): 66-76.

2:13-18
0188   David Daube, "The Earliest Structure of the Gospels," *NTS*
                5 (1958-1959): 184ff.

2:13-15
0189   N. Walker, "The Alleged Matthaean Errata," *NTS* 9
                (1962-1963): 391-94.

0190   L. Swidler, *Biblical Affirmations of Women*. Fortress, 1979.

0191   B. Bagatti, "La fuga in Egitto: prova per la S. Famiglia,"
                SacD 24 (1979): 131-41.

2:13
0192   K. Rahner, "Nimm das Kind und seine Mutter," *GeistL*
                30/1 (1957): 14-22.

0193   S. Bartina, "Los sueños o éxtasis de San José (Mt. 1,20-24;
                2,13-14, 19-20)," *CahJos* 39 (1991): 43-53.

2:15
0194   Sebastian Bartina, "Y desde Egipto lo he proclamado hijo
                mio (Mt. 2,15)," *EB* 29/1 (1970): 157-60.

0195   T. L. Howard, "The Use of Hosea 11:1 in Matthew 2:15.
                An Alternative Solution," *BSac* 143 (1986): 314-28.

2:16-23
0196   David L. Bartlett, "Jeremiah 31:15-20," *Int* 32/1 (1978): 73-78.

2:16-18
    0197   R. T. France, "Herod and the Children of Bethelem," *NovT* 21/2 (1979): 98-120.

2:16
    0198   R. T. France, "The 'Massacre of the Innocents': Fact or Fiction?" in E. A. Livingstone, ed., *Studia Biblica 1978 II*. Papers Presented to the Fifth International Congress on Biblical Studies, Oxford, 1978. Sheffield: JSOT Press, 1980. Pp. 83-94.

2:17-18
    0199   M. Quesnel, "Les citations de Jérémie dans l'évangile selon saint Matthieu," *EB* 47 (1989): 513-27.

2:17
    0200   M. J. J. Menken, "The References of Jeremiah in the Gospel According to Matthew (Mt. 2,17; 16,14; 27,9)," *ETL* 60/1 (1984): 5-24.

    0201   James W. Scott, "Matthew's Intention to Write History," *WTJ* 47/1 (1985): 68-82.

2:13-14
    0202   S. Bartina, "Los sueños o éxtasis de San José (Mt. 1,20-24; 2,13-14, 19-20," *CahJos* 39 (1991): 43-53.

2:18-25
    0203   F. L. Filas, "Karl Rahner, Saint Joseph's Doubt," *TD* 6 (1958): 169-73.

2:18
    0204   David L. Bartlett, "Jeremiah 31:15-20," *Int* 32/1 (1978): 73-78.

2:19-20
    0205   S. Bartina, "Los sueños o éxtasis de San José (Mt. 1,20-24; 2,13-14, 19-20," *CahJos* 39 (1991): 43-53.

2:20
    0206   Michal Wojciechowski, "Herod and Antipater? A Supplementary Clue to Dating the Birth of Jesus," *BibN* 44 (1988): 61-62.

2:21

0207   R. R. Lewis, "*Epiblēma rakous agnaphou* (Mt. 2,21)," *ET*
                45 (1933-1934): 185.

2:23

0208   W. Caspari, "Nazwraioc Mt. 2,23 nach alttestamentlichen
                Voraussetzungen," *ZNW* 21 (1922): 122-27.

0209   J. A. Bain, "Did Joseph Belong to Bethlehem or to
                Nazareth?" *ET* 47 (1935-1937): 93.

0210   E. Zolli, "Nazarenus Vocabitur," *ZNW* 49 (1958): 135-36.

0211   J. G. Rembry, "Quoniam Nazaraeus vocabitur (Mt. 2,23),"
                SBFLA 12 (1961-1962): 46-65.

0212   J. A. Sanders, "*Nazōraios* in Matt. 2,23," *JBL* 84 (1965):
                169-72.

0213   Ernst Zuckschwerdt, "Ναζωραῖος in Matth. 2,23," *TZ*
                31/2 (1975): 65-77.

0214   W. Barnes Tatum, "Matthew 2:23: Wordplay and
                Misleading Translations," *BT* 27/1 (1976): 135-38.

0215   H. P. Rüger, "Nazareth/Nazara Nazarenos/Nazaraios,"
                ZNW 72/3 (1981): 257-63.

0216   R. Pritz, "He Shall Be Called a Nazarene," *JeruP* 4
                (1991): 3-4.

2:28-30
0217   Hans Dieter Betz, "The Logion of the Easy Yoke and of
                Rest (Matt. 2:28-30)," *JBL* 86/1 (1967): 10-24.

3:1-4:25
0218   N. Casalini, *Il vangelo di Matteo come racconto teologico.*
                Analisi delle sequenze narrative. Jerusalem: Franciscan
                Press, 1990.

3-4
0219   A. Kretzer, "Die Proklamation der Herrschaft der Himmel
                an die Sohne des Reiches," in *Der Herrschaft der Himmel*
                und die Söhne des Reiches: Eine redaktionsgeschichte

Untersuchung zum Base' eiabegriff und Basileiaverständnis im Matthäusevangelium. Stuttgart: KBW, 1971. Pp. 65-92.

3:1-12

0220   B. Marconcini, "Tradizione e redazione in Mt. 3,1-12," *RBib* 19 (1971): 165-86.

0221   B. Marconcini, "La predicazione del Battista in Marco e Luca confrontata con la redazione di Matteo," *RBib* 20 (1972): 451-66.

0222   B. Marconcini, "La predicazione del Battista," *BibO* 15 (1973): 49-60.

3:1-5

0223   Jean Doignon, "L'Argumentation d'Hilaire de Poitiers dans l'Exemplum de la Tentation de Jesus (In Matthaeum, 3,1-5)," *BT* 29/1 (1978): 126-28.

3:4

0224   Hans Windisch, "Die Notiz über Tracht und Speise des Taufers Johannes und ihre Entsprechungen in der Jesusüberlieferung," *ZNW* 32 (1933): 65-87.

3:7-10

0225   Carl Kazmierski, "The Stones of Abraham: John the Baptist and the End of Torah (Matt. 3,7-10 Par. Luke 3,7 - 9)," *Bib* 68/1 (1987): 22-40.

3:9

0226   R. Menahem, "A Jewish Commentary on the New Testament: A Sample Verse," *Immanuel* 21 (1987): 43-54.

3:10

0227   John Pairman Brown, "The Ark of the Covenant and the Temple of Janus," *BZ* 30/1 (1986): 20-35.

3:11-12

0228   G. Schwarz, "To de Achuron Katakausei," *ZNW* 72/3 (1981): 264-71.

0229   Harry Fleddermann, "John and the Coming One (Matt. 3:11-12–Luke 3:16-17)," *SBLSP* 23 (1984): 377-84.

0230   J. D. Charles, " 'The Coming One'/'Stronger One' and His Baptism: Matt. 3:11-12, Mark 1:8, Luke 3:16-17," *Pneuma* 11 (1989): 37-50.

3:11

0231   N. Krieger, "Barfuss Busse Tun," *NovT* 1 (1956): 227-28.

0232   L. W. Barnard, "A Note on Matt. 3.11 and Luke 3.16," *JTS* 8 (1957): 107.

0233   P. G. Bretscher, "Whose Sandals? (Matt. 3,11)," *JBL* 86 (1967): 81-87.

3:12

0234   James S. Alexander, "A Note on the Interpretation of the Parable of the Threshing Floor at the Conference at Carthage of A.D. 411," *JTS* 24/2 (1973): 512-19.

3:13-4:25

0235   Mark McVann, "The Making of Jesus the Prophet: Matthew 3:13-4:25," *List* 24/3 (1989): 262-77.

3:13-4:11

0236   Benno Przybylski, "The Role of Mt. 3:13-4:11 in the Structure and Theology of the Gospel of Matthew," *BTB* 4 (1974): 222-35.

3:13-17

0237   M. Dutheil, "Le Baptême de Jésus. Éléments d'interprétation," *SBFLA* 6 (1955-1956): 85-124.

0238   Placide Roulin and Giles Carton, "Le Baptême du Christ," *BVC* 25 (1959): 39-48.

0239   G. Saldarini and L. Moraldi, "Battesimo di Cristo," in L. Moraldi and S. Lyonnet, eds., *I Vangelini (Introduzione alla Bibbia)*. Torino: Marietti, 1960. Pp. 493-501.

0240   G. Strecker, "Die Taufe," in *Der Weg der Gerechtigkeit: Untersuchung zur Theologie des Matthäus*. Göttingen: Vandenhoeck & Ruprecht, 1962. Pp. 178-81.

0241   A. Viard, "Baptême du Seigneur," *EV* 85 (1975): 2-3.

0242   S. Johnson Samuel, "Communalism or Commonalism: A Study of Matthew's Account of Jesus' Baptism," *ITS* 25 (1988): 344-47.

3:13-15
0243   Harold L. Kitzmann, "The Fulfilling of Righteousness: Matthew 3:13-15: A Redactional Study," doctoral dissertation, Lutheran School of Theology, Chicago IL, 1985.

3:15
0244   Anton Fridrichsen, "Accomplir toute justice," in P.-L. Counchoud, *Congrès d'historie du Christianisme: Jubilé Alfred Loisy*. 3 vols. Paris: Rieder, 1928. 1:167-77.

0245   F. D. Coggan, "Note on St. Matthew 3:15," *ET* 60 (1949): 258.

0246   J. M. Ross, "St. Matthew 3:15," *ET* 61 (1949): 30-31.

0247   R. T. France, "The Servant of the Lord in the Teaching of Jesus," *TynB* 19 (1968): 26-52.

0248   Otto Eissfeldt, "πληρῶσαι πᾶσαν δικαιοσύνην in Matthäus 3:15," *ZNW* 61/3 (1970): 209-15.

0249   Robert G. Bratcher, " 'Righteousness' in Matthew," *BT* 40/2 (1989): 228-35.

4:1-19
0250   C. Jaeger, "Remarques philologiques sur quelques passages des Synoptiques," *RHPR* 16 (1936): 246-49.

4:1-11
0251   J. J. Pelikan, "The Temptation of the Church: A Study of Matthew 4:1-11," *CTM* 22 (1951): 251-59.

0252   J. M. Bover, "Diferente género literario de los evangelistas en la narración de las tendaciones de Jesús en el Desierto," in *En torno al problema de la escatología individual del Antiguo Testamento*. Madrid: Científica Medinaceli, 1955. Pp. 213-19.

0253   Birger Gerhardsson, *The Testing of God's Son (Matt. 4:1-11 & Par.): An Analysis of an Early Christian Midrash.* Lund: Gleerup, 1966.

0254   C. U. Wolf, "The Continuing Temptation of Christ in the Church. Searching and Preaching on Matthew 4:1-11," *Int* 20 (1966): 288-301.

0255   William R. Stegner, "Wilderness and Testing in the Scrolls and in Matthew 4:1-11," *BR* 18 (1967): 18-27.

0256   P. Pokorny, "The Temptation Stories and their Intention," *NTS* 20 (1974): 115-27.

0257   Balmer Kelly, "An Exposition of Matthew 4:1-11," *Int* 29/1 (1975): 57-62.

0258   K. Grayston, "The Temptations," *ET* 88 (1977): 143-44.

0259   Dieter Zeller, "Die Versuchungen Jesu in der Logienquelle," *TTZ* 89 (1980): 61-73.

0260   Wilhelm Wilkens, "Die Versuchung Jesu Hach Matthaus," *NTS* 28/4 (1982): 479-89.

0261   Walter Wink, "Matthew 4:1-11," *Int* 37/4 (1983): 392-97.

0262   Lamar Williamson, "Matthew 4:1-11," *Int* 38/1 (1984): 51-55.

0263   A. Hunter, "Rite Passage: The Implications of Matthew 4:11 for an Understanding of the Jewishness of Jesus," *ChJR* 19 (1986): 7-22.

0264   Klaus-Peter Koppen, "The Interpretation of Jesus' Temptations (Mt. 4,1-11; Mk. 1,12f; Lk. 4,1-3) by the Early Church Fathers," *PatByzR* 8/1 (1989): 41-43.

0265   O. J. McTernan, *A Call to Witness: Reflections on the Gospel of St. Matthew.* Collegeville: Liturgical Press, 1989.

0266   William R. Stegner, "Early Jewish Christianity—A Lost Chapter?" *ATJ* 44/2 (1989): 17-29.

0267   William R. Stegner, "The Temptation Narrative: A Study in the Use of Scripture by Early Jewish Christians," *BR* 35 (1990): 5-17.

0268   Hugh M. Humphrey, "Temptation and Authority: Sapiential Narratives in Q," *BTB* 21 (1991): 43-50.

4:3

0269   R. L. Mowery, "Subtle Differences: The Matthean 'Son of God' References," *NovT* 32 (1990): 193-200.

4:4

0270   G. D. Kilpatrick, "Matthew iv.4," *JTS* 45 (1944): 176-77.

4:5-7

0271   N. Hyldahl, "Die Versuchung auf der Zinne des Tempelso," *ScanJT* 15 (1961): 113-27.

4:5

0272   J. Jeremias, "Die Zinne des Tempels (Mt. 4,5; Lk. 4,9)," *ZDPV* 59 (1936): 195-208.

4:6

0273   R. L. Mowery, "Subtle Differences: The Matthean 'Son of God' References," *NovT* 32 (1990): 193-200.

4:8

0274   G. D. Kilpatrick, "Three Problems of New Testament Text," *NovT* 21/4 (1979): 289-92.

0275   D. Durken, "Mountains and Matthew," *BibTo* 28 (1990): 304-307.

4:9-10

0276   D. Flusser, "Die Versuchung Jesu und ihr jüdischer Hintergrund," *Jud* 45 (1989): 110-28.

4:12-7:29

0277   F. Genuyt, "Evangile de Matthieu, chapitres 4,12-7,29," *SémBib* 62 (1991): 2-20.

4:12-23

0278   A. Duprez, "Le programme de Jesus, selon Matthieu," *AsSeign* N.S. 34 (1973): 9-18.

0279   T. Harley Hall, "An Exposition of Matthew 4:12-23," *Int*
               29/1 (1975): 63-67.

4:12-17
0280   F. Neirynck, "Apò tóte ērxato and the Structure of
               Matthew," *ETL* 64/1 (1988): 21-59.

4:12-16
0281   G. G. Gamba, "Gesù si stabilisce a Cafarnao (Mt.
               4,12-16)," *BibO* 16 (1974): 109-32.

4:14-16
0282   George M. Soares Prabhu, "Matthew 4:14-16: A Key to the
               Origin of the Formula Quotations of Matthew," *IJT* 20/1
               (1971): 70-91.

4:15
0283   H. Dixon Slingerland, "The Transjordanian Origin of St.
               Matthew's Gospel," *JSNT* 1/3 (1979): 18-28.

4:17
0284   K. Romaniuk, "Repentez-vous, car le Royaume des Cieux
               est tout proche (Matt. iv.17 par.)," *NTS* 12 (1965-1966):
               259-69.

4:18-22
0285   M. H. Franzmann, "Studies in Discipleship: I. The Calling
               of the Disciples (Mt. 4:18-22; 1:1-4:16)," *CTM* 31 (1960):
               607-25.

4:18-19
0286   J. D. M. Derrett, "Esan gar Halieis (Mark 1:16). Jesus'
               Fisherman and the Parable of the Net," *NovT* 22/2 (1980):
               108-37.

4:19
0287   L. Grollenberg, "Mensen 'Vangen' (Lk. 5,10): Hen Redden
               van de Dood," *TijT* 5 (1965): 330-36.

4:21
0288   G. Strecker, "Die Reflexionszitate in Mt. 4-21," in *Der
               Weg der Gerechtigkeit: Untersuchung zur Theologie des
               Matthäus*. Göttingen: Vandenhoeck & Ruprecht, 1962. Pp.
               63-76.

4:23-5:2
0289   Gerhard Lohfink, "Wem gilt die Bergpredigt? Eine redaktionskritische Untersuchung von Mt. 4,23-5,2 und 7,28f.," *TTQ* 163 (1983): 264-84.

4:23-25
0290   K.-S. Krieger, "Das Publikum ter Bergpredigt (Mt. 4.23-25)," *K* 28 (1986): 98-119.

5:1-7:29
0291   William R. Farmer, "The Sermon on the Mount: A Form-Critical and Redactional Analysis of Matt. 5:1-7:29," *SBLSP* 25 (1986): 56-87.

0292   N. Casalini, *Il vangelo di Matteo come racconto teologico. Analisi delle sequenze narrative.* Jerusalem: Franciscan Press, 1990.

5-7
0293   J. H. Farmer, "An Analysis of the Sermon on the Mount," *RevExp* 1 (1904): 71-80.

0294   Paul Fiebig, *Jesu Bergpredigt: Rabbinische Texte zum Verständnis der Bergpredigt, ins Deutsche übersetzt, in ihren Ursprachen dargeboten und mit Erlauterungen und Lesanen versehen.* Göttingen: Vandenhoeck & Ruprecht, 1924.

0295   O. Hammelsbeck, "Die Bergpredigt in Andacht und Unterricht," *EvT* 5 (1938): 212-21.

0296   F. C. Grant, "The Sermon on the Mount," *ATR* 24 (1942): 131-44.

0297   Ernest R. Pinson, "Some Revolutionary Teachings of Jesus in the Sermon on the Mount," doctoral dissertation, New Orleans Baptist Theological Seminary, New Orleans LA, 1945.

0298   P. Bonnard, "Le Sermon sur la montagne," *RTP* 3 (1953): 233-46.

0299   Martin Dibelius, "Die Bergpredigt," in *Botschaft und Geschichte*. Tübingen: Mohr, 1953. 1:79-174.

0300   C. Kopp, "Die Stäte der Bergpredigt und Brotvermehrung," *BK* 8/3 (1953): 10-16.

0301   A. M. Hunter, *Design for Life: An Exposition of the Sermon on the Mount, Its Making, Its Exegesis and Its Meaning*. London: SCM Press, 1954.

0302   Henlee Barnette, "The Ethic of the Sermon on the Mount," *RevExp* 53 (1956): 23-33.

0303   James A. Langley, "A Critique of the Contemporary Interpretations of the Sermon on the Mount, with Special Reference to Albert Schweitzer, Reinhold Niebuhr, and C. H. Dodd," dctoral dissertation, Southwestern Baptist Theological Seminary, Fort Worth TX, 1956.

0304   Conrad R. Willard, "The Sermon on the Mount in the Writing of the Ante-Nicene Fathers from New Testament Times to Origen," doctoral dissertation, Midwestern Baptist Theological Seminary, Kansas City KS, 1956.

0305   K. Schubert, "The Sermon on the Mount and the Qumran Texts," in K. Stendahl, ed., *The Scrolls and the New Testament*. New York: Harper & Brothers, 1957. Pp. 118-28.

0306   J. Staudinger, *Die Bergpredict*. Wien: Herder, 1957.

0307   I. W. Batdorf, "How Shall We Interpret the Sermon on the Mount?" *JBR* 27 (1959): 211-17.

0308   J. Kurzinger, "Zur Komposition der Bergpredigt nach Matthaus," in *Studia Biblica et Orientalia*. 3 vols. Rome: Pontifical Institute, 1959. 2:1-21.

0309   Arthur M. Norton, "Motives to which Christ Appealed in the Sermon on the Mount," master's thesis, Midwestern Baptist Theological Seminary, Kansas City KS, 1959.

0310   J. Jeremias, *The Sermon on the Mount*. London: Athlone Press, 1961.

0311 Huber L. Drumwright, Jr., "A Homiletic Study of the Sermon on the Mount: The Ethical Motif," *SouJT* 5 (1962): 65-76.

0312 J. Héring, "Le Sermon sur la Montagne dans la nouvelle traduction anglaise de la Bible," *RHPR* 42 (1962): 122-12.

0313 W. D. Davies, *The Setting of the Sermon on the Mount*. Cambridge: University Press, 1964.

0314 W. K. Grossouw, "La moraledu Sermon sur la montagne," in *Spiritualité du Nouveau Testament*. Paris: Cerf, 1964. Pp. 45-58.

0315 J. Schmid, "Ich aber sage euch: Der Anruf der Bergpredigt," *BK* 19 (1964): 75-79.

0316 G. Eichholz, "Die Aufgabe einer Auslegung der Bergpredigt" in *Tradition und Interpretation*. Munich: Kaiser, 1965. Pp. 35-56.

0317 G. Eichholz, *Auslegung der Bergpredigt*. Neukirchen: Verlag des Erziehungsvereins, 1965.

0318 W. D. Davies, *The Sermon on the Mount*. Cambridge: University Press, 1966.

0319 J. Jeremias, "Die Bergpredigt," in *Abba: Studien zur neutestamentlichen Theologie und Zeitgeschichte*. Göttingen: Vandenhoeck & Ruprecht, 1966. Pp. 171-89.

0320 M. Laconi, "Il discorso della montagna," in *Il Messaggio della salvezza*. 5 vols. Torino: Leumann, 1966-1970. Pp. 281-363.

0321 K. Grayston, "Sermon on the Mount," in *Bibel und Qumran*. Berlin: Evangelische Haupt-Bibelgesellschaft, 1968. 4:279-89.

0322 N. Walter, "Die Bearbeitung der Seligpreisungen durch Matthäus," in F. Cross, ed., *Studia Evangelica IV*: Papers Presented to the Third International Congress on New Testament Studies, Christ Church, Oxford, 1965. (Part

I—The New Testament Scriptures). Berlin:
Akademie-Verlag, 1968. Pp. 246-58.

0323   H.-T. Wrege, *Die Überlieferungsgeschichte der Bergpredigt*.
Tübingen: Mohr, 1968.

0324   P. Hoffman, "Die Stellung der Bergpredigt im
Mattäusevangelium. Auslegung der Bergpredigt," *BibL* 10
(1969): 57-65, 111-12, 175-89, 264-75.

0325   P. Hoffman, "Die Stellung der Bergpredigt im
Mattäusevangelium. Auslegung der Bergpredigt," *BibL* 11
(1970): 89-104.

0326   E. Lerle, "Realisierbare Forderungen der Bergpredigt?" *KD*
16 (1970): 32-40.

0327   J. Fuillet, "Le discours sur lamontagne," in *Jésus devant
sa vie et sa mort*. Paris: Aubier, 1971. Pp. 83-95.

0328   Morris A. Inch, "Matthew and the House-Churches," *EQ*
43/4 (1971): 196-202.

0329   P. Pokorny, "The Core of the Sermon on the Mount," in
E. A. Livingston, ed., *Studia Evangelica VI*: Papers
Presented to the Fourth International Congress on New
Testament Studies, Christ Church, Oxford, 1969. Berlin:
Akademie-Verlag, 1973. Pp. 429-33.

0330   G. Schmahl, "Gültigkeit und Verbindlichkeit der
Bergpredigt," *BibL* 14 (1973): 180-87.

0331   J. Bligh, *The Sermon on the Mount*. Slough: St. Paul
Publications, 1975.

0332   G. Menestrina, "Matteo 5-7 e Luca 6,20-49 nell'Evangelo
di Tommaso," *BibO* 18 (1976) 65-67.

0333   F. Neirynck, "The Sermon on the Mount in the Gospel
Synopsis," *ETL* 52 (1976): 350-57.

0334   Karlmann Beyschlag, "Zur Geschichte der Bergpredigt in
der Alten Kirche," *ZTK* 74/3 (1977): 291-322.

0335   G. Bornkamm, "Der Aufbau der Bergpredigt," *NTS* 24 (1978): 419-32.

0336   Jacques Dupont, "Le message des Béatitudes," *CE* 24 (1978): 215-31.

0337   R. M. Grant, "The Sermon on the Mount in Early Christianity," *Semeia* 12 (1978): 215-31.

0338   Samuel Tobias Lachs, "Some Textual Observations on the Sermon on the Mount," *JQR* 69/2 (1978): 98-111.

0339   M. Bouttier, "Hesiode et le sermon sur la montagne," *NTS* 25 (1978-1979): 129-30.

0340   A.-L. Descamps, "Le Discours sur la montagne: Esquisse de théologie biblique," *RTL* 12 (1981): 5-39.

0341   W. Egger, "I titoli delle pericope bibliche come chiave di lettura," *RBib* 29 (1981): 33-43.

0342   J. Moltmann, *Nachfolge und Bergpredigt*. Munich: Kaiser, 1981.

0343   R. A. Guelich, *The Sermon on the Mount: A Foundation for Understanding*. Waco: Word Books, 1982.

0344   C. J. A. Hickling, "Conflicting Motives in the Redaction of Matthew: Some Considerations on the Sermon on the Mount and Matthew 18:15-20," in E. A. Livingstone, ed., *Studia Evangelica VII*: Papers Presented to the Fifth International Congress on New Testament Studies, Oxford, 1973. Sheffield: JSOT Press, 1982. Pp. 247-60.

0345   E. Bader, "Bergpredigt, sozialphilosophische Aspekte," *BL* 56 (1983): 144-49.

0346   H. Frankemölle, "Neue Literatur zur Bergpredigt," *TR* 79 (1983): 177-98.

0347   F. Montagnini, "Echi del discorso del monte nella Didaché," *BibO* 25 (1983): 137-43.

0348   Daniel T. W. Chow, "A Study of the Sermon on the Mount: With Special Reference to Matthew 5:21-48," *EAJT* 2/2 (1984): 312-14.

0349   J. Nagórny, "Kazanie na górze (Mt. 5-7) jako moralne oredize nowego przymierza," *RoczTK* 32 (1985): 5-21.

0350   C. Burchard, "Le thème du Sermon sur la Montogne," *ÉTR* 62 (1987): 1-17.

0351   Karin Bornkamm, "Umstrittener 'spiegel eines Christlichen lebens': Luthers Auslegung der Bergpredigt in seinen Wochenpredigten von 1530 bis 1532," *ZTK* 85 (1988): 409-54.

0352   C. E. Carlston, "Betz on the Sermon on the Mount: A Critique," *CBQ* 50 (1988): 47-57.

0353   Stanley Hauerwas, "The Sermon on the Mount, Just War and the Quest for Peace," *Conci* 195 (1988): 36-43.

0354   R. J. Miller, "The Lord's Prayer and Other Items from the Sermon on the Mount," *Forum* 5 (1989): 177-86.

0355   R. E. Strelan, "The Gospel in the Sermon on the Mount," *LTJ* 23 (1989): 19-26.

0356   A. Wright, "The Gospel in the Sermon on the Mount: A Jewish View," *NewBlack* 70 (1989): 182-89.

0357   J. G. Williams, "Paraenesis, Excess, and Ethics: Matthew's Rhetoric in the Sermon on the Mount," *Semeia* 50 (1990): 163-87.

0358   Hans Dieter Betz, "The Sermon on the Mount: In Defense of a Hypothesis," *BR* 36 (1991): 74-80.

0359   I. A. Massey, *Interpreting the Sermon on the Mount in the Light of Jewish Tradition as Evidenced in the Palestinian Targums of the Pentateuch.* Lewiston: Mellen Press, 1991.

0360   Ernest W. Saunders, "A Response to H. D. Betz on the Sermon on the Mount," *BR* 36 (1991): 81-87.

0361   Klyne Snodgrass, "A Response to H. D. Betz on the Sermon on the Mount," *BR* 36 (1991): 88-94.

0362   Loyd Allen, "The Sermon on the Mount in the History of the Church," *RevExp* 89 (1992): 245-62.

0363   William B. Tolar, "The Sermon on the Mount from an Exegetical Perspective," *SouJT* 35 (1992): 4-12.

5:1-20

0364   E. Nellesen, "Aufbruch und Vollendung der Königsherrschaft: Eine Meditation zu den Perikopen des Allerheiligenfestes," *BibL* 9 (1968): 222-29.

0365   J. Salguero, "Las Bienaventuranzas evangélicas," *CuBi* 29 (1972): 73-90.

0366   W. J. Dumbrell, "The Logic of the Role of the Law in Matthew 5:1-20," *NovT* 23 (1981): 1-21.

5:1-12

0367   J. W. Bowman, "An Exposition of the Beatitudes," *JBR* 15 (1947): 162-70.

0368   F. Buchholz, "Predigt über Matthäus 5,1-12," *EvT* 14 (1954): 97-104.

0369   E. Neuhäusler, "Die Seligpreisungen," in *Anspruch und Antwort Gottes: Zur Lehre von den Weisungen innerhalb der synoptischen Jesusverkündigun*. Düsseldorf, Patmos, 1962. Pp. 141-69.

0370   H. Frankemölle, "Die Makarismen (Mt. 5,1-12; Lk. 6,20-23)," *BZ* 15 (1971): 52-75.

0371   R. Kieffer, "Un exemple concret, les béatitudes (Mt. 5,1-12; Lc. 6,20-26)," in *Essais de méthodologie néo-testamentaire*. Lund: Gleerup, 1972. Pp. 26-50.

0372   P.-E. Jacquemin, "Les béatitudes selon saint Matthieu," *AsSeign* N.S. 66 (1973): 50-63.

0373   A. Viard, "Les béatitudes," *EV* 85 (1975): 5-6.

0374   R. A. Guelich, "The Matthean Beatitudes: 'Entrance-Requirements' of Eschatological Blessings," *JBL* 95 (1976): 415-34.

0375   O. J. McTernan, *A Call to Witness: Reflections on the Gospel of St. Matthew.* Collegeville: Liturgical Press, 1989.

0376   W. R. Domeirs, " 'Blessed Are You . . . " *JTSA* 73 (1990): 67-76.

5:1-10
0377   A. Paul, "Béatitudes," *Chr* 22 (1975): 326-29.

0378   Julie A. Luscomb, "The Hebraic Background of Jesus' Beatitudes (Matthew 5:1-10)," master's thesis, Oral Roberts University, Tulsa OK, 1987.

5:1-8
0379   Barclay M. Newman, "Some Translational Notes on the Beatitudes," *BT* 26/1 (1975): 106-20.

5:1-2
0380   Dale C. Allison, "Jesus and Moses (Mt. 5:1-2)," *ET* 98/7 (1987): 203-204.

5:1
0381   J. Manek, "On the Mount - On the Plain (Mt. 5:1 - Lk. 6:17)," *NovT* 9 (1967): 124-31.

5:2-5a
0382   D. Squillaci, "Il mistero di Betlem nel profeta Michea (5,2-5a)," *PalCI* 41/15 (1962): 763-66.

5:2
0383   Joseph Sickenberger, "Zwei neue Aüsserungen zur Ehebruchklausel bei Matthäus," *ZNW* 42 (1949): 202-209.

5:3-7:29
0384   A. M. Perry, "The Framework of the Sermon on the Mount," *JBL* 54 (1935): 103-15.

5:3-47
0385   S. Légasse, *Les pavvres en esprit.* Paris: Cerf, 1974.

5:3-16

0386   M. Du Buit, "Les Béatitudes," in *En tous les temps Jésus-Christ*. Mulhouse: Salvator, 1974-1977. 3:17-56.

5:3-12

0387   E. Percy, "Die Seligpreisungen der Bergpredigt (Mt. 5,3-12; Lk. 6,20-23)," in *Die Botschaft Jesu: Eine traditionskritische und exegetische Untersuchung*. Lund: Gleerup, 1953. Pp. 40-108.

0388   G. Braumann, "Zum traditionsgeschichtlichen Problem der Seligpreisungen Mt. 5:3-12," *NovT* 4 (1960-1961): 253-60.

0389   C. H. Dodd, "The Beatitudes: A Form-Critical Study," in *More New Testament Studies*. Manchester: University Press, 1968. Pp. 1-10.

0390   W. Trilling, "Heilsverheissung und Lebenslehre des Jüngers," in *Vielfalt und Einheit im Neuen Testament: Zur Exegese und Verkündigung des Neuen Testaments*. Einsiedeln: Benziger, 1968. Pp. 64-85.

0391   G. Strecker, "Die Makarismen der Bergpredigt," *NTS* 17 (1970-1971): 255-75.

0392   G. Strecker, "Les macarismes du discours sur la montagne," in *L'Évangile selon Matthieu*. Gembloux: Duculot, 1972. Pp. 185-208.

0393   R. Kieffer, "Wisdom and Blessing in the Beatitudes of St. Matthew and St. Luke," in E. A. Livingston, ed., *Studia Evangelica VI*: Papers Presented to the Fourth International Congress on New Testament Studies, Christ Church, Oxford, 1969. Berlin: Akademie-Verlag, 1973. Pp. 291-95.

0394   J. Coppens, "Les Béatitudes," *ETL* 50 (1974): 256-60.

0395   Jacques Dupont, "Introduction aux Béatitudes," *NRT* 98 (1976): 97-108.

0396   Hans Dieter Betz, "Die Makarismen der Bergpredigt (Matthaus 5:3-12)," *ZTK* 75/1 (1978): 3-19.

0397   G. Bleickert, "Die Seligpreisungen: Eine meditative Erschliessung," *GeistL* 51 (1978): 326-38.

0398   D. Flusser, "Some Notes to the Beatitudes," *Immanuel* 8 (1978): 37-47.

0399   N. J. McEleney, "The Beatitudes of the Sermon on the Mount/Plain," *CBQ* 43/1 (1981): 1-13.

0400   George J. Brooke, "The Wisdom of Matthew's Beatitudes," *ScrB* 19 (1988): 35-41.

0401   J. Pantelis, "Los Pobres en espíritu. Bienaventurados en el Reino de Dios. Mateo 5,3-12," *RevB* 51 (1989): 1-9.

0402   K. Stock, "Der Gott der Freude: Die acht Seligpreisungen (II)," *GeistL* 62 (1989): 433-46.

0403   K. Stock, "Der Weg der Freude: Die acht Seligpreisungen (I)," *GeistL* 62 (1989): 360-73.

5:3-10

0404   Rudolf Bultmann, "Matthaus 5,3-10," in *Marburger Predigten*. Tübingen: Mohr, 1956. Pp. 180-88.

0405   H. Spämann, "Die acht Seligkeiten: Eine Meditation zu Mt. 5,3-10," *BibL* 5 (1964): 131-36.

0406   George W. Buchanan, "Matthean Beatitudes and Traditional Promises," in W. R. Farmer, ed. *New Synoptic Studies*. Macon GA: Mercer University Press, 1983. Pp. 161-84.

5:3-6

0407   C. Michaelis, "Die π Alliteration der Subjektsworte der ersten 4 Seligpreisungen in Mt. V 3-6 und ihre Bedeutung für den Aufbau der Seligpreisungen bei Mt., Lk. und in Q," *NovT* 10 (1968): 148-61.

5:3-5

0408   D. Flusser, "Blessed Are the Poor in Spirit," *IEJ* 10 (1960): 1-13.

0409   Felix Böhl, "Die Demut ('nwh) als höchste der Tugenden: Bemerkungen zu Mt. 5,3,5," *BZ* 20/2 (1976): 217-23.

5:3

0410   M. Knepper, "Die 'Armen' der Bergpredigt-Jesu," *BK* 8/1 (1953): 19-27.

0411   Ernest Best, "Matthew 5:3," *NTS* 7 (1961): 255-58.

0412   V. Rodzianko, "The Meaning of Matthew 5,3," in F. Cross, ed., *Studia Evangelica II*: Papers Presented to the Second International Congress on New Testament Studies, Christ Church, Oxford, 1961. (Part I--The New Testament Scriptures). Berlin: Akademie-Verlag, 1964. Pp. 229-35.

0413   S. Légasse, "Les Pauvres en Esprit et les 'Volontaires' de Qumran," *NTS* 8 (1961-1962): 336-45.

0414   C. H. Dodd, "New Testament Translation Problems I," *BT* 27/3 (1976): 301-11.

0415   G. Schwarz, " 'Ihenn gehört das Himmelreich' (Matthäus V.3)," *NTS* 23/3 (1977): 341-43.

0416   Klaus Jörms, " 'Armut, zu der der Geist hilft' (Mt. 5:3) als *nota ecclesiae*," *TZ* 43 (1987): 59-70.

0417   A. M. Ambrozic, "Reflections on the First Beatitude," *CICR* 17 (1990): 95-104.

5:4

0418   P. Schempp, "Die zweite Seligpreisung," *EvT* I (1934-1935): 10-23.

0419   W. Tebbe, "Die zweite Seligpreisung (Matth. 5,4)," *EvT* 12 (1952-1953): 121-28.

5:6

0420   J. M. Bover, "Beati qui esurint et sitiunt iustitiam (Mt. 5,6)," *EE* 16 (1942): 9-26.

0421   Robert G. Bratcher, " 'Righteousness' in Matthew," *BT* 40/2 (1989): 228-35.

0422   Wiard Popkes, "Die Gerechtigkeitstradition im
            Matthäus-Evangelium," *ZNW* 80/1 (1989): 1-23.

0423   A. Sicari, "The Hunger and Thirst of Christ," *CICR* 18
            (1991): 590-602.

5:9

0424   B. W. Bacon, "The Blessing of the Peacemakers," *ET* 41
            (1929-1930): 58-60.

0425   Rudolf Schnackenburg, "Die Sellgpreisung der
            Friedensstifter (Mt. 5,9) im Mattäischen Kontext," *BZ* 26/2
            (1982): 161-78.

0426   J. Gnilka, "Selig, die Frieden stiften," *IKaZ* 18 (1989):
            97-103.

5:10

0427   Robert G. Bratcher, " 'Righteousness' in Matthew," *BT*
            40/2 (1989): 228-35.

0428   Wiard Popkes, "Die Gerechtigkeitstradition im
            Matthäus-Evangelium," *ZNW* 80/1 (1989): 1-23.

5:11-12

0429   W. Stenger, "Die Seligpreisungen der Geschmähtem (Mt.
            5,11-12; Lk. 6,22-23)," *K* 28 (1986): 33-60.

0430   P. J. Maartens, "Critical Dialogue in Theory and Practice
            of Literary Interpretation: A Study of Semiotic Relations in
            Matthew 5:11 and 12," *LB* 65 (1991): 5-24.

0431   V. H. Matthews and C. C. Benjamin, "The Stubborn and
            the Fool," *LB* 65 (1991): 5-24.

5:11

0432   Michael W. Holmes, "The Text of Matthew 5:11," *NTS*
            32/2 (1986): 283-86.

5:12

0433   Jacques Dupont, "Réjouissez-vous et exultez," in *Les
            Béatitudes*. Tome II: La bonne nouvelle. Paris: Gabalda,
            1969. 2:320-38.

0434 M. Corbin, "Votre récompense est grande dans les cieux," *Chr* 28 (1981): 65-77.

5:13-48

0435 O. J. McTernan, *A Call to Witness: Reflections on the Gospel of St. Matthew*. Collegeville: Liturgical Press, 1989.

5:13-26

0436 E. Schillebeeckx, "The Light of the Body Is the Eye," in *God Among Us: The Gospel Proclaimed*. London: SCM Press, 1983. Pp. 56-58.

5:13-16

0437 J. B. Soucek, "Salz der Erde und Licht der Welt. Zur Exegese von Matth. 5:13-16," *TZ* 19 (1962): 169-79.

0438 Rudolf Schnackenburg, "Ihr seid das Salz der Erde, das Licht der Welt," in *Evangelienforschung: Ausgewählte Aufsätze deutscher Exegeten*. Graz: Styria, 1968. Pp. 119-46.

0439 Helga Rusche, "Ihr, Salz der Erde, Licht der Welt!" *BibL* 14 (1973): 215-17.

0440 S. Légasse, "Les chrétiens 'sel de la terre', 'lumiere du monde'," *AsSeign* N.S. 36 (1974): 17-25.

0441 A. Viard, "Les disciples du Christ au service du monde," *EV* 85 (1975): 6-8.

0442 M. Krämer, "Ihr seid das Salz der Erde . . . Ihr seid das Licht der Welt," *MTZ* 28 (1977): 133-57.

5:13-14

0443 G. Schwarz, "Matthäus v. 13a und 14a: Emendation und Rückübersetzung," *NTS* 17 (1970-1971): 80-86.

5:13

0444 A. J. Mee, "Ye Are the Salt of the Earth (Mt. 5,13)," *ET* 46 (1934-1935): 476-77.

0445 J. H. Morrison, "Ye Are the Salt of the Earth! (Mt. 5,13)," *ET* 46 (1934-1935): 525.

0446   L. Köhler, "Salz, das dumm wird," *ZDPV* 59 (1936): 133-34.

0447   Oscar Cullmann, "Que signifie le sel la parabole de Jésus?" in *La foi et le culte dans l'église primitive*. Neuchâtel: Delachaux & Niestlé, 1958. Pp. 211-20.

0448   Helmut Thielicke, "The Salt, Not the Honey, of the World," *Lead* 4/1 (1983): 114-19.

0449   S. Hellestam, "Mysteriet med saltet," *SEÅ* 55 (1990): 59-63.

5:14

0450   K. M. Campbell, "The New Jerusalem in Matthew 5:14," *SJT* 31/4 (1978): 335-63.

0451   P.-R. Berger, "Die Stadt auf dem Berge: Zum kulturhistorischen Hintergrund von Mt. 5,14," in W. Haubeck and M. Bachmann, eds. *Wort in der Zeit*. Leiden: Brill, 1980. Pp. 82-85.

0452   J. D. M. Derrett, "The Light and the City: Mt. 5:14," *ET* 103 (1992): 174-75.

5:15

0453   J. Jeremias, "Die Lampe unter dem Scheffel," *ZNW* 39 (1940): 237-40.

0454   J. D. M. Derrett, "Light Under a Bushel: The Hanukkah Lamp?" *ET* 78 (1966-1967): 18.

5:17-48

0455   A.-L. Descamps, "Essai d'interprétation de Mt. 5,17-48. 'Formgeschichte' ou 'Redaktionsgeschichte'?" in Kurt Aland, et al., eds., *Studia Evangelica: Papers Presented to the International Congress on the Four Gospels, Christ Church, Oxford, 1957*. Berlin: Akademie-Verlag, 1959. Pp. 156-73.

5:17-37

0456   L. Deiss, "La loi nouvelle," *AsSeign* N.S. 37 (1971): 19-33.

5:17-20

0457   E. Schweizer, "Matth. 5,17-20. Anmerkungen zum Gesetzesverständnis des Matthäus," *TLZ* 77 (1952): 479-84.

0458   W. Trilling, "Die Gesetzefrage nach 5,17-20," in *Das wahre Israel: Studien zur Theologie des Matthäus-Evangeliums*. Munich: Kösel, 1964. Pp. 167-86.

0459   André Feuillet, "Morale Ancienne et Morale Chrétienne d'après Mt. 5.17-20; Comparaison avec la Doctrine de l'Épitre aux Romains," *NTS* 17 (1970-1971): 123-37.

0460   Robert Banks, "Matthew's Understanding of the Law: Authenticity and Interpretation in Matthew 5:17-20," *JBL* 93/2 (1974): 226-42.

0461   E. Schweizer, "Noch einmal Mt. 5,17-20." in *Matthäus und seine Gemeinde*. Stuttgart: KBW, 1974. Pp. 78-85.

0462   L. Sabourin, "Matthieu 5,17-20 et le rôle prophétique de la Loi," *SE* 30 (1978): 303-11.

0463   Ulrich Luz, "Die Erfüllung des Gesetzes bei Matthäus," *ZTK* (1978-1979): 398-435.

0464   C. Heubüly, "Mt. 5:17-20: Ein Beitrag zur Theologie des Evangelisten Matthäus," *ZNW* 71 (1980): 143-49.

0465   Christine Heutuot, "Mt. 5,17-20," *ZNW* 71/3 (1980): 143-49.

5:17-18

0466   W. D. Davies, "Matthew 5:17,18," in *Christian Origins and Judaism: A Collection of New Testament Studies*. London: Longman & Todd, 1962. Pp. 31-66.

0467   O. Hanssen, "Zum Verständnis der Bergpredigt. Eine missionstheologische Studie zu Mt. 5,17-18," in E. Lohse, et al., eds., *Der Ruf Jesu und die Antwort der Gemeinde*. Göttingen: Vandenhoeck & Ruprecht, 1970. Pp. 94-111.

0468   Warren Vanhetloo, "Indications of Verbal Inspiration," *CBTJ* 5/1 (1989): 63-85.

<u>5:17</u>

0469   S. Clive Thexton, "Jesus' Use of the Scriptures," *LQHR* 179 (1954): 102-108.

0470   Gerhard Barth, "Das Gesetzesverständnis des Evangelisten Matthäus," in G. Bornkamm, G. Barth, H. J. Held, eds., *Überlieferung und Auslegung im Matthäusevangelium,*. Neukirchen-Vluyn: Neukircher Verlag, 1961. Pp. 54-154.

0471   C. F. D. Moule, "Fulfillment-Words in the New Testament: Use and Abuse," *NTS* 14/3 (1968): 293-320.

0472   J. W. Deenick, "The Fourth Commandment and Its Fulfillment," *RTR* 28/2 (1969): 54-61.

0473   William R. Eichhorst, "The Issue of Biblical Inerrancy in Definition and Defense," *GTJ* 10/1 (1969): 3-17.

0474   James H. Burtness, "Lifestyle and Law: Some Reflections on Matthew 5:17," *Dia* 14/1 (1975): 13-20.

0475   H. W. M. van de Sandt, "An Explanation of Rom. 8:4a," *Bij* 37/4 (1976): 361-78.

0476   D. H. C. Read, " 'Thou Shalt Not!'—Says Who?" *ET* 88 (1977): 209-11.

0477   S. Clive Thexton, "The Word of God in the Old Testament," *ET* 93 (1981): 50-51.

<u>5:18</u>

0478   A. M. Honeyman, "Matthew 5:18 and the Validity of the Law," *NTS* 1 (1954-1955): 141-42.

0479   W. Auer, "Jota unum aut unus apex non praeteribit a lege," *BK* 14 (1959): 97-103.

0480   Robert G. Hamerton-Kelly, "Attitudes to the Law in Matthew's Gospel: A Discussion of Matthew 5:18," *BR* 17 (1972): 19-32.

0481   G. Schwarz, "ἰῶτα ἓν ἢ μία κεραία (Matthäus 5:18)," *ZNW* 66 (1975): 268-69.

0482 Meinrad Limbeck, "Die nichts bewegen wollen! Zum Gesetzesverständnis des Evangelisten Matthäus," *TTQ* 168 (1988): 299-320.

5:19-20

0483 B. T. Viviano, "Matthew, Master of Ecumenical Infighting," *CThM* 10/6 (1983): 325-32.

5:19

0484 H. Schürmann, " 'Wer daher eines dieser geringsten Gebote auflöst . . . ' Wo fand Matthäus das Logion Mt. 5,19?" in *Traditionsgeschichtliche Untersuchungen zu den synoptischen Evangelien*. Düsseldorf: Patmos, 1968. Pp. 126-36.

5:20-48

0485 J. P. Renard, "La Lectura Super Matthaeum 5:20-48 de Thomas d'Aquin," *RTAM* 50 (1983): 145-90.

5:20-22

0486 W. Trilling, "Die neue und wahre Gerechtigkeit (Mt. 5, 20-22)," in *Christusverkündigung in den synoptischen Evangelien*. Munich: Kösel, 1969. Pp. 86-107.

5:20

0487 H. Günther, "Die Gerechtigkeit des Himmelreiches in der Bergpredigt," *KD* 17 (1971): 113-26.

0488 Harvey Lange, "The Greater Righteousness," *CThM* 5/2 (1978): 116-21.

0489 Robert G. Bratcher, " 'Righteousness' in Matthew," *BT* 40/2 (1989): 228-35.

0490 Wiard Popkes, "Die Gerechtigkeitstradition im Matthäus-Evangelium," *ZNW* 80/1 (1989): 1-23.

5:21-48

0491 E. Percy, "Die Stellung Jesu zum Gesetz," in *Die Botschaft Jesu: Eine traditionskritische und exegetische Untersuchung*. Lund: Gleerup, 1953. Pp. 116-23.

0492 E. Percy, "Die Forderungen Jesu und das Gesetz. Die Antithesen der Bergpredigt. Mt. 5,21-48," in *Die Botschaft*

Jesu: Eine traditionskritische und exegetische Untersuchung. Lund: Gleerup, 1953. Pp. 123-64.

0493   V. Hasler, "Das Herzstuck der Bergpredigt," *TZ* 15 (1959): 90-106.

0494   B. Holtzclaw, "A Note on Matthew 5.21-48," in H. Barth and R. E. Cocroft, eds., *Festschrift to Honor F. Wilbur Gingrich.* Leiden: Brill, 1972. Pp. 161-63.

0495   R. A. Guelich, "The Antitheses of Matthew V. 21-48: Traditional and/or Redactional?" *NTS* 22/4 (1976): 444-57.

0496   Daniel T. W. Chow, "A Study of the Sermon on the Mount: With Special Reference to Matthew 5:21-48," *EAJT* 2/2 (1984): 312-14.

0497   John R. Levison, "Responsible Initiative in Matthew 5:21-48," *ET* 98/8 (1987): 231-34.

0498   D. J. Harrington, "Not to Abloish, but to Fulfill," *BibTo* 27 (1989): 333-37.

5:21-32

0499   T. van Eupen, "De Onverbreekbaarheid van de Huwelijksbandd Een Eenstemmige Traditie?" *TijT* 10/3 (1970): 291-303.

5:21-22

0500   C. F. D. Moule, "Matthew 5,21-22," *ET* 50 (1938-1939): 189-90.

0501   H.-J. Iwand, "Du sollst nicht töten," *EvT* 10 (1950-1951): 145-53.

5:21f.

0502   C. F. D. Moule, "The Angry Word: Mt. 5:21f.," *ET* 81 (1969-1970): 10-13.

0503   M. Weise, "Mt. 5:21f.—ein Zeugnis sakraler Rechtsprechung in der Urgemeinde," *ZNW* 49 (1958): 116-23.

5:21

0504   C. Jaeger, "À propos de deux passages du sermon sur la montagne (Matthieu 6,13; 5,21 et 33)," *RHPR* 18 (1938): 415-18.

0505   S. Clive Thexton, "Jesus' Use of the Scriptures," *LQHR* 179 (1954): 102-108.

0506   M. McNamara, " 'You Have Heard That It Was Said . . .': Mt. 5,21 and Tgs Gn 9.60," in *The New Testament and the Palestinian Targum to the Pentateuch*. Rome: Biblical Institute Press, 1966. Pp. 126-31.

0507   C. F. D. Moule, "Uncomfortable Words. Part I. The Angry Word: Matthew 5:21f.," *ET* 81/1 (1969): 10-13.

5:22

0508   E. C. Colwell, "Has *Raka* a Parallel in the Papyri?" *JBL* 53 (1934): 351-54.

0509   P. Wernberg-Moller, "A Semitic Idiom in Matt. v.22," *NTS* 3 (1956-57): 71-73.

0510   F. Bussby, "Note on Matthew 5:22 and Matthew 6:7 in the Light of Qumran," *ET* 76 (1964-1965): 26.

0511   R. A. Guelich, "Mt. 5,22: Its Meaning and Integrity," *ZNW* 64 (1973): 39-52.

5:22a

0512   David A. Black, "The Text of Matthew 5:22a Revisited," *NovT* 30/1 (1988): 1-8.

5:23f.

0513   J. Jeremias, "Lass allda deine Gabe (Mt. 5,23f.)," *ZNW* 36 (1937): 150-54.

5:25-26

0514   Ernest Lussier, "The Biblical Theology on Purgatory," *AmER* 142 (1960): 225-33.

0515   G. B. Caird, "Expouding the Parables: The Defendant," *ET* 77 (1965-1966): 36-39.

5:27-32

0516   Heinrich Baltensweiler, "Matthäusevangelium (Kap. 19,1-12; 5,27-32)," in *Die Ehe im Neuen Testament: Exegetische Untersuchungen über Ehe, Ehelosigkeit und Ehescheidung.* Stuttgart: Zwingle, 1967. Pp. 82-119.

0517   Will Deming, "Mark 9:42-10:12, Matthew 5:27-32, and b. Nid, 13b: A First Century Discussion of Male Sexuality," *NTS* 36/1 (1990): 130-41.

5:27-28

0518   H. Ordon, "Jezusowa interpretatacja zakazu cudzolóstwa," *RoczTK* 31 (1984): 81-90.

5:28

0519   Klaus Haacker, "Der Rechtssatz Jesu zum Thema Ehebruch," *BZ* 21/1 (1977): 113-16.

5:29-30

0520   Herbert W. Basser, "The Meaning of 'Shtuth', Gen. 4.11 in Reference to Matthew 5.29-30 and 18.8-9," *NTS* 31/1 (1985): 148-51.

5:29

0521   Henry Clavier, "Matthieu 5,29 et la non-résistance," *RHPR* 37 (1957): 44-57.

5:30a

0522   S. D. Currie, "Matthew 5:30a: Resistance or Protest?" *HTR* 57 (1964): 140-45.

5:31

0523   G. J. Wenham, "Matthew and Divorce: An Old Crux Revisited," *JSNT* 22 (1984): 95-107.

0524   Phillip H. Wiebe, "Jesus' Divorce Exception," *JETS* 32 (1989): 327-33.

5:31-32

0525   Augustine Stock, "Matthean Divorce Texts," *BTB* 8/1 (1978): 24-33.

0526   Charles C. Ryrie, "Biblical Teaching on Divorce and Remarriage," *GTJ* 3/2 (1982): 177-92.

0527 B. N. Wambacq, "Matthieu 5,31-32: Possibilite de Divorce ou Obligation de Rompre une Union Illigitime," *NRT* 104/1 (1982): 34-49.

0528 Gerhard Lohfink, "Jesu Verbot der Ehescheidung und eine Adressaten," *TTQ* 167 (1987): 144-46.

5:32

0529 A. Allgeier, "Die crux interpretum im neutestamentlichen Ehescheidungs-verbot. Eine philologische Untersuchung zu Mt. 5,32 und 19,9," in *Reverendissimo Patri Iacobo Mariae Vosté*. Roma: Salita del Grillo, 1943. Pp. 128-42.

0530 J. M. Gonzalez Ruiz, "El divorcio en Mt. 5,32 y 19,9," in *La enciclica Humani Generis*. Madrid: Científica Medinaceli, 1952. Pp. 511-28.

0531 Heinrich Baltensweiler, "Die Ehebruchsklausein bei Matthaeus: zu Matth. 5:32; 19:9," *TZ* 15 (1959): 340-56.

0532 John J. O'Rourke, "A Note on an Exception: Mt. 5:32 (19:9) and 1 Cor 7:12 Compared," *HeyJ* 5 (1964): 299-302.

0533 A. Isaksson, "The Synoptic Logion on Divorce," in *Marriage and Ministry in the New Temple: A Study with Special Reference to Mt. 19,3-12 and 1 Cor. 11,3-16*. Lund: Gleerup, 1965. Pp. 66-74.

0534 A. Isaksson, "The Origin of the Clause on Unchastity," in *Marriage and Ministry in the New Temple: A Study with Special Reference to Mt. 19,3-12 and 1 Cor. 11,3-16*. Lund: Gleerup, 1965. Pp. 75-92.

0535 J. B. Bauer, "Die matthaische Ehescheidungsklausel," in *Evangelienforschung: Ausgewählte Aufsätze deutscher Exegeten*. Graz: Styria, 1968. Pp. 147-58.

0536 H. G. Coiner, "Those 'Divorce and Remarriage' Passages," *CTM* 39/6 (1968): 367-84.

0537 Richard N. Soulen, "Marriage and Divorce: A Problem in New Testament Interpretation," *Int* 23/4 (1969): 439-50.

0538   G. Giavini, "Nuove e vecchie vie per la lettura delle
                 clausole di Matteo sul divorzio," *SuC* 99 (1971): 83-93.

0539   G. Schneider, "Jesu Wort über die Ehescheidung in der
                 Überlieferung des Neuen Testaments," *TTZ* 80 (1971):
                 65-87.

0540   Tarcision Stramare, "Matteo Divorzista?" *Div* 15/2 (1971):
                 213-35.

0541   Henri Crouzel, "Le Texte Patristique de Matthieu V.32 et
                 XIX.9," *NTS* 19/1 (1972): 98-119.

0542   A. Vargas-Machuca, "Los casos de 'divorcio' admitidos
                 por San Mateo (5,32 y 19,9). Consecuencias para la
                 teologia actual," *EE* 50 (1975): 5-54.

0543   Mark Geldard, "Jesus' Teaching on Divorce: Thoughts on
                 the Meaning of Porneia in Matthew 5:32 and 19:9," *Ch* 92
                 (1978): 134-43.

0544   John J. Kilgallen, "To What Are the Matthean
                 Exception-Texts (5,32 and 19,9) An Exception?" *Bib* 61/1
                 (1980): 102-105.

0545   William A. Heth, "Another Look at the Erasmian View of
                 Divorce and Remarriage," *JETS* 25/3 (1982): 263-72.

0546   Ben Witherington, "Matthew 5.32 and 19.9—Exception or
                 Exceptional Situation?" *NTS* 31/4 (1985): 571-76.

0547   Markus N. A. Bockmuehl, "Matthew 5.32; 19.9 in the
                 Light of Pre-Rabbinic Halakhah," *NTS* 35/2 (1989): 291-95.

0548   Don T. Smith, "The Matthean Exception Clauses in the
                 Light of Matthew's Theology and Community," *SBT* 17/1
                 (1989): 55-82.

0549   Michael W. Holmes, "The Text of the Matthean Divorce
                 Passages: A Comment on the Appeal to Harmonization in
                 Textual Decisions," *JBL* 109 (1991): 651-54.

5:33

0550 C. Jaeger, "À propos de deux passages du sermon sur la montagne (Matthieu 6,13; 5,21 et 33)," *RHPR* 18 (1938): 415-18.

5:33-37

0551 Paul S. Minear, "Yes or No: The Demand for Honesty in the Early Church," *NovT* 13 (1971): 1-13.

0552 Gerhard Dautzenberg, "Ist das Schwurverbot Mt. 5,33-37; Jak 5,12 ein Beispiel für die Torakritik Jesu?" *BZ* 25/1 (1981): 47-66.

0553 J. Blank, "Schwört überhaupt nicht," *Orient* 53 (1989): 97-99.

5:34-37

0554 G. Stahlin, "Zum Gebrauch von Beteuerungsformeln im Neuen Testament," *NovT* 5 (1962): 115-43.

5:35

0555 Dennis C. Duling, " 'Do Not Swear . . . by Jerusalem Because It Is the City of the Great King," *JBL* 110 (1991): 291-309.

5:37

0556 Paul S. Minear, "Let Your Yes Be Yes," in A. Jirku, ed. *Von Jerusalem nach Ugarit*. Graz: Akademische Verlag, 1966. Pp. 30-46.

0557 Lucile L. Brandt, "The Christian Yea and Nay," *BLT* 22/4 (1977): 245-50.

5:38-48

0558 Jerome Rausch, "The Principle of Nonresistance and Love of Enemy in Mt. 5,38-48," *CBQ* 28/1 (1966): 31-41.

0559 Fritz Neugebauer, "Die Dargebotene Wange und Jesu Gebot der Feindesliebe: Erwgungen zu Lk. 6,27-36/Mt. 5,38-48," *TLZ* 110/12 (1985): 865-76.

0560 D. Gill, "Socrates and Jesus on Non-Retaliation and Love of Enemies," *Horizons* 18 (1991): 246-62.

5:38-42

0561   Harald Sahlin, "Traditionskritische Bemerkungen zu Zwei Evangelienperikopen," *ScanJT* 33/1 (1979): 6

0562   Markus Rathey, "Talion im NT? Zu Mt. 5,38-42," *ZNW* 82 (1991): 264-66.

5:38-39

0563   H. E. Bryant, "Matthew 5,38.39," *ET* 48 (1936-37): 236-37.

5:38f.

0564   David Daube, "Matthew v.38f," *JTS* 45 (1944): 177-87.

5:39-47

0565   Edgar V. McKnight and Charles H. Talbert, "Can the Griesbach Hypothesis Be Falsified?" *JBL* 91/3 (1972): 338-68.

5:39-42

0566   Harald Sahlin, "Ett svart stlle i Bergspredikan (Mt. 5:39-42)," *SEÅ* 51/52 (1986-1987): 214-218.

5:39-41

0567   Lewis Donelson, " 'Do Not Resist Evil' and the Question of Biblical Authority," *HBT* 10 (1988): 33-46.

5:39

0568   E. W. Archer, "Matthew v. 39," *ET* 42 (1930-1931): 190-91.

0569   H. E. Bryant, "Matthew 6,13 and 5,39," *ET* 47 (1935-1936): 93-95.

5:39b

0570   Marcus Borg, "A New Context for Romans XIII," *NTS* 19/2 (1973): 205-18.

0571   Klaus Krieger, "Fordert Mt. 5:39b das passive Erdulden von Gewalt? Ein kleiner Beitrag zur Redaktionskritik der 5 Antithese," *BibN* 54 (1990): 28-32.

5:43-48

0572　O. Bayer, "Sprachbewegung und Weltveränderung. Ein systematischer Versuch als Auslegung von Mt. 5,43-48," *EvT* 35 (1975): 309-21.

0573　Bonnie B. Thurston, "Matthew 5:43-48," *Int* 41/2 (1987): 170-73.

5:43-44

0574　O. J. F. Seitz, "Love your Enemies," *NTS* 16 (1969-1970): 39-54.

5:43

0575　M. Smith, "Mt. 5.43: 'Hate Thine Enemy'," *HTR* 45 (1952): 71-73.

0576　Olof Linton, "St. Matthew 5,43," *ScanJT* 18 (1964): 66-80.
0577　G. Molin, "Matthäus 5,43 und das Schrifttum von Qumran," in *Bibel und Qumran*. Berlin: Evangelische Haupt-Bibelgesellschaft, 1968. Pp. 150-52.

5:44

0578　Marcus Borg, "A New Context for Romans XIII," *NTS* 19/2 (1973): 205-18.

5:46

0579　E. M. Sidebottom, " 'Reward' in Matthew v.46, etc.," *ET* 67 (1955-1956): 219-20.

0580　Marcus Borg, "A New Context for Romans XIII," *NTS* 19/2 (1973): 205-18.

5:48

0581　E. Fuchs, "Die volkommene Gewisshdt zur Auslegung von Matthäus 5,48," in *Neutestamentliche Studien für Rudolf Bultmann*. Berlin: Töpelmann, 1957. Pp. 130-36.

0582　H. Bruppacher, "Was sagte Jesus in Matthäus 5,48?" *ZNW* 58 (1967): 145.

0583　E. Yarnold, "*Teleios* in St. Matthew's Gospel," in F. Cross, ed., *Studia Evangelica IV*: Papers Presented to the Third International Congress on New Testament Studies,

Christ Church, Oxford, 1965. (Part I—The New Testament Scriptures). Berlin: Akademie-Verlag, 1968. Pp. 269-73.

0584   L. Sabourin, "Why Is God Called 'Perfect' in Mt. 5:48?" *BZ* 24/2 (1980): 266-68.

6:1-18
0585   E. Schweizer, "Zu Röm. 2,28f und Mt. 6,1-18," in *Matthäus und seine Gemeinde*. Stuttgart: KBW, 1974. Pp. 86-97.

0586   Christian Dietzfelbinger, "Die Frommigkeitsregeln von Mt. 6,1-18 als Zeugnisse Fruchristlicher Geschichte," *ZNW* 75/3 (1985): 184-201.

0587   O. J. McTernan, *A Call to Witness: Reflections on the Gospel of St. Matthew*. Collegeville: Liturgical Press, 1989.

6:1-6
0588   A. George, "La justice à faire le secret (Matthieu 6,1-6 et 16-18)," in *Studia Biblica et Orientalia*. 3 vols. Rome: Pontifical Institute, 1959. 2:22-30.

0589   Birger Gerhardsson, "Geistiger Opferdienst nach Matth. 6,1-6, 16-21," in H. Baltensweiler and Bo Reicke, eds., *Neues Testament und Geschichte* (festschrift for Oscar Cullmann). Zürich: Theologischer Verlag, 1972. Pp. 69-77.

6:1
0590   Robert G. Bratcher, " 'Righteousness' in Matthew," *BT* 40/2 (1989): 228-35.

0591   Wiard Popkes, "Die Gerechtigkeitstradition im Matthäus-Evangelium," *ZNW* 80/1 (1989): 1-23.

6:2-18
0592   Paul S. Minear, "Keep It Secret," in A. Jirku, ed., *Von Jerusalem nach Ugarit*. Graz: Akademische Verlag, 1966. Pp. 47-68.

6:2
0593   E. Klostermann, "Zum Verstandnis von Mt. 6,2," *ZNW* 47 (1956): 280-81.

0594   N. J. McEleney, "Does the Trumpet Sound or Resound? An Interpretation of Matthew 6,2," *ZNW* 76/1 (1985): 43-46.

6:4

0595   P. Ellingworth, " 'In Secret' (Matthew 6.4, 6, 18)," *BT* 40 (1989): 446-47.

0596   Günther Schwarz, "ὁ βλέτων ἐν τῷ κρυπτῶι," *BibN* 54 (1990): 38-41.

6:5-15

0597   Scott L. Tatum, "Great Prayers of the Bible," *SouJT* 14 (1972): 29-42.

0598   Philip B. Harner, "Matthew 6:5-15," *Int* 41/2 (1987): 173-78.

6:5-13

0599   Richard J. Dillon, "On The Christian Obedience Of Prayer (Matthew 6:5-13)," *Worship* 59/5 (1985): 413-26.

6:6

0600   S. Clive Thexton, "Jesus' Use of the Scriptures," *LQHR* 179 (1954): 102-108.

0601   P. Ellingworth, " 'In Secret' (Matthew 6.4, 6, 18)," *BT* 40 (1989): 446-47.

0602   Günther Schwarz, "ὁ βλέτων ἐν τῷ κρυπτῶι," *BibN* 54 (1990): 38-41.

6:7

0603   F. Bussby, "Note on Matthew v.22 and Matthew vi.7 in the Light of Qumran," *ET* 76 (1964-1965): 26.

6:9-15

0604   E. Lohmeyer, *Das Vater-Unser*. Zürich: Zwingli Verlag, 1952.

0605   W. Stiller, "*Vaterunser,* Biblische Erwägungen," *TGI* 42 (1952): 49-52.

0606   T. W. Manson, "The Lord's Prayer," *BJRL* 38
              (1955-1956): 99-113, 436-48.

0607   H. Schürmann, *Das Gebet des Herrn aus der Verkündigung
              Jesu erläutert*. Freiburg: Herder, 1957.

0608   W. Fresenius, "Beobachtungen und Gedanken zum Gebet
              des Herrn," *EvT* 20 (1960): 235-39.

0609   G. G. Willis, "The Lord's Prayer in Irish Gospel
              Manuscripts," in F. Cross, ed., *Studia Evangelica III*:
              Papers Presented to the Second International Congress on
              New Testament Studies, Christ Church, Oxford, 1961 (Part
              II—The New Testament Message) Berlin: Akademie-
              Verlag, 1964. Pp. 282-88.

0610   J. Jeremias, "Das Vater-Unser im Lichte der neuren
              Forschung," in *Abba: Studien zur neutestamentlichen
              Theologie und Zeitgeschichte*. Göttingen: Vandenhoeck &
              Ruprecht, 1966. Pp. 152-71.

0611   C. M. Laymon, *The Lord's Prayer in Its Biblical Setting*.
              Nashville: Abingdon Press, 1966.

0612   P. Bonnard, J. DuPont, and F. Refoulé, eds., *Notre Père qui
              es aux cieu*. Paris: Cerf, 1968.

0613   G. Casalis, "Das Vater Unser und die Weltlage," *EvT* 29
              (1969): 357-71.

0614   Andrew Bandstra, "The Original Form of the Lord's
              Prayer," *CalTJ* 16/1 (1981): 15-37.

0615   Andrew Bandstra, "The Lord's Prayer and Textual
              Criticism: A Response," *CalTJ* 17/1 (1982): 88-97.

6:9-13
0616   Johannes Herrmann, "Der alttestamentamentliche Urgund
              des Vaterunsers," in *Festschrift Otto Procksch*. Leipzig:
              Deicherts'sche, 1934. Pp. 71-98.

0617   O. Schäfer, "Das Vaterunser, das Gebet des Christen," *TGI*
              35 (1943): 1-6.

0618   J. Jeremias, "The Lord's Prayer in Modern Research," *ET* 71 (1959-1960): 141-46.

0619   Raymond E. Brown, "The Pater Noster as an Eschatological Prayer," in *New Testament Essays*. Milwaukee: Bruce, 1965. Pp. 217-53.

0620   D. W. Shriver, "The Prayer That Spans the World. An Exposition: Social Ethics and the Lord's Prayer," *Int* 21 (1967): 274-88.

0621   C. W. F. Smith, "The Lord's Prayer," in *Bibel und Qumran*. Berlin: Evangelische Haupt-Bibelgesellschaft, 1968. 3:154-58.

0622   G. Schwarz, "Matthäus vi.9-13, Lukas xi.2-4," *NTS* 15 (1968-1969): 233-47.

0623   J. Carmignac, *Recherches sur le 'Notre Père'*. Paris: Letouzey et Ané, 1969.

0624   Danile C. Arichea, "Translating the Lord's Prayer (Matthew 6.9-13)," *BT* 31/2 (1980): 219-23.

0625   L. Gil, "Versiones del *Pater noster* al castellano en el Siglo de Oro," *FilN* 1 (1988): 175-91.

0626   W. M. Buchan, "Research on the Lord's Prayer," *ET* 100 (1989): 336-39.

0627   R. J. Miller, "The Lord's Prayer and Other Items from the Sermon on the Mount," *Forum* 5 (1989): 177-86.

0628   D. Templeton, "The Lord's Prayer as Eucharist in Daily Life," *IBS* 11 (1989): 133-40.

0629   H.-M. Barth, "Das Vaterunser als ökumenisches Gebet," *UnSa* 45 (1990): 99-109, 113.

0630   S. Schroer, "Konkretionen zum Vaterunser," *UnSa* 45 (1990): 110-13.

0631   D. Baumgardt, "Kaddish and the Lord's Prayer," *JBQ* 19 (1991): 164-69.

0632   R. G. Kratz, "Die Gnade de täglichen Brots: Späte Psalmen
            auf dem Weg zum Vaterunser," *ZTK* 89 (1992): 1-40.

0633   F. Urbanek, " 'Vater im Himmel': das alte Vaterunser in
            sprachlicher Neuauflage," *LB* 66 (1992): 39-54.

6:9-11

0634   F. Hauck, "ἄρτος ἐπιούσιος," *ZNW* 33 (1934): 199-202.

6:9

0635   W. Marchel, "Les aspects théologiques de la prière
            chrétienne 'Abba, Père' (Gal 4,6; Rom 8,15)," in *Abba,
            Pere! La prière du Christ et des chrétiens*. Rome: Biblical
            Institute Press, 1963. Pp. 213-43.

0636   W. Marchel, "Notre Père (Mt. 6,9; Lc 11,2)," in *Abba,
            Pere! La prière du Christ et des chrétiens*. Rome: Biblical
            Institute Press, 1963. Pp. 191-202.

0637   J. Swetnam, "Hallowed Be Thy Name," *Bib* 52 (1971):
            556-63.

0638   David J. Clark, "Our Father in Heaven," *BT* 30/2 (1979):
            210-13.

0639   L. Brož, "Theology of the First Petition," *CVia* 31 (1988):
            243-51.

0640   Monsengwo Pasinya, "Lokola biso tokolimbisaka baninga
            (Mt. 6,9 par.): Incidence théologique d'une traduction,"
            RAfT 12 (1988): 15-21

0641   Willem A. VanGemeren, " 'Abba' in the Old Testament?"
            JETS 31 (1988): 386-98.

6:10

0642   Martin Dibelius, "Die dritte Bitte des Vaterunsers," in
            Botschaft und Geschichte. Tübingen: Mohr, 1953. Pp.
            175-77.

0643   Kair A. Syreeni, "Between Heaven and Earth: On the
            Structure of Matthew's Symbolic Universe," *JSNT* 40
            (1990): 9-13.

0644 Marc Philonenko, "La troisème demande du 'Notre Père et l'hymne de Nabuchodonosor," *RHPR* 72 (1992): 23-31.

6:11

0645 Matthew Black, "The Aramaic of τὸν ἄρτον ἡμῶν τὸν ἐπιούσιον, Matt. vi.11 Luke xi.3," *JTS* 42 (1941): 186-89.

0646 G. H. P. Thompson, "Thy Will Be Done in Earth as It Is in Heaven (Matthew vi. II)," *ET* 70 (1959-1960): 379- 81.

0647 J. Starcky, "La Quatrième Demande du Pater," *HTR* 64 (1971): 401-409.

0648 B. Hemmerdinger, "Un élément pythagoricien dans le Pater," *ZNW* 63 (1972): 121.

0649 Bernard Orchard, "The Meaning of τὸν ἐπιούσιον (Mt. 6:11 = Lk. 11:3)," *BTB* 3 (1973): 274-82.

0650 R. ten Kate, "Geef ons Heden ons 'Dagelijks Brood'," *NedTT* 32/2 (1978): 125-39.

0651 Henri Bourgoin, "Epiousios Explique par la Notion de Prefixe Vide," *Bib* 60/1 (1979): 91-96.

0652 Delores Aleixandre, "En torno a la cuarta peticion del Padrenuestro [Matt. 6:11, Lk. 11:3l]," *EB* 45 (1987): 325-36.

0653 H. Heinen, "Göttliche Sitometrie: Beobachtungen zur Brotbitte des Vaterunsers," *TTZ* 99 (1990): 72-79.

0654 Arland J. Hultgren, "The Bread Petition of the Lord's Prayer," *ATR* 11 (1990): 41-54.

0655 L. Ramaroson, " 'Notre part de nourriture'," *ScE* 43 (1991): 87-115.

0656 R. G. Kratz, "Die Gnade de täglichen Brots: Späte Psalmen auf dem Weg zum Vaterunser," *ZTK* 89 (1992): 1-40.

6:12f.

0657 E. Sjöberg, "Das Licht in dir. Zur Deutung von Matth. 6,12f. Par.," *ScanJT* 5 (1952): 89-105.

6:12

0658 F. C. Burkitt, " 'As We Have Forgiven' (Matt. 6:12)," *JTS* 33 (1932): 253-55.

0659 F. C. Fensham, "The Legal Background of Mt. 6:12," *NovT* 4 (1960-1961): 1-2.

0660 J. M. Ford, "The Forgiveness Clause in the Matthean Form of the Our Father," *ZNW* 59 (1968): 127-31.

0661 Samuel Tobias Lachs, "On Matthew 6:12," *NovT* 17/1 (1975): 6-8.

6:13

0662 H. E. Bryant, "Matthew 6,13 and 5,39," *ET* 47 (1935-1936): 93-95.

0663 C. Jaeger, "À propos de deux passages du sermon sur la montagne (Matthieu 6,13; 5,21 et 33)," *RHPR* 18 (1938): 415-18.

0664 J. N. Hoare, "Lead us not into Temptation," *ET* 50 (1938-1939): 333.

0665 A. J. B. Higgins, " 'Lead Us Not into Temptation': Some Latin Variants," *JTS* 46 (1945): 179-83.

0666 W. Powell, "Lead Us Not into Temptation," *ET* 67 (1955-1956): 177-78.

0667 J. B. Bauer, "Liberia nos a malo," *VD* 34 (1956): 12-15

0668 M. H. Sykes, "And Do Not Bring Us to the Test," *ET* 73 (1961-1962): 189-90.

0669 M. B. Walker, "Lead Us Not Into Temptation," *ET* 73 (1961-1962): 287.

0670 J. Carmignac, "La portée d'une négation devant un verbe au causatif," *RB* 72 (1965): 218-26.

0671 G. Smith, "Matthaean 'Additions' to Lord's Prayer," *ET* 82 (1970-1971): 54-55.

0672   Buetubela Balembo, "Et ne now sournets pas à la tentation. La difficile actualisation de Mt. 6,13," *RAfT* 10 (1986): 5-13.

0673   Pierre Grelot, "L'épreuve de la Tentation," *EV* 99 (1989): 280-84.

0674   Wiard Popkes, "Die letzte Bitte des Vater-Unser. Formgeschichte Beobachtungen zum Gebet Jesu," *ZNW* 81 (1990): 1-20.

0675   S. E. Porter, "Mt. 6:13 and Lk. 11:4: 'Lead Us not into Temptation'," *ET* 101 (1990): 359-62.

0676   E. Moore, "Lead Us Not into Temptation," *ET* 102 (1991): 171-72.

6:13a

0677   Davis McCaughey, "Matthew 6.13a: The Sixth Petition in the Lord's Prayer," *ABR* 33 (1985): 31-40.

6:14

0678   Jacques Dupont, "Dieu ou Mammon," *CrNSt* 5/3 (1984): 441-61.

6:16-21

0679   Birger Gerhardsson, "Geistiger Opferdienst nach Matth. 6,1-6, 16-21," in H. Baltensweiler and Bo Reicke, eds., *Neues Testament und Geschichte* (festschrift for Oscar Cullmann). Zürich: Theologischer Verlag, 1972. Pp. 69-77.

6:18

0680   P. Ellingworth, " 'In Secret' (Matthew 6.4, 6, 18)," *BT* 40 (1989): 446-47.

0681   Günther Schwarz, "ὁ βλέτων ἐν τῷ κρυπτῶι" *BibN* 54 (1990): 38-41.

6:19-34

0682   H. Riesenfeld, "Vom Schätzesammeln und Sorgen: ein Thema urchristlicher Paränese. Zu Mt. vi.19-34)," in *Neotestamentica et Patristica* (festschrift for Oscar Cullmann). Leiden: Brill, 1962. Pp. 47-58.

0683　　　E. Neuhäusler, "Allem Besitz entsagen," in *Anspruch und Antwort Gottes: Zur Lehre von den Weisungen innerhalb der synoptischen Jesusverkündigun,*. Düsseldorf, Patmos, 1962. Pp. 170-85.

6:22-23
0684　　　C. Edlung, *Das Auge der Einfalt: Eine Untersuchung zu Matth. 6,22-23 und Luk. 11,34-35.* Lund: Gleerup, 1952.

0685　　　Dale C. Allison, "The Eye is the Lamp of the Body (Matthew 6.22-23 = Luke 11.34-36)," *NTS* 33/1 (1987): 61-83.

0686　　　Marc Philonenko, "La parabole sur la lampe (Luc 11:33-36) et le horoscopes qoumãniens," *ZNW* 79/1-2 (1988): 145-51.

6:24-34
0687　　　K. Barth, "Predigt über Matth. 6,24-34," *EvT* 2 (1935): 331-38.

0688　　　P.-E. Jacquemin, "Les options du chretien," *AsSeign* N.S. 39 (1972): 18-27.

0689　　　C. E. Carlston, "Matthew 6:24-34," *Int* 41/2 (1987): 179-83.

6:24
0690　　　H. P. Rüger, "Μαμωνας," *ZNW* 64 (1973): 127-31.

6:25-34
0691　　　Hans Dieter Betz, "Kosmogonie und Ethik in der Bergpredigt," *ZTK* 81/2 (1984): 139-71.

0692　　　J. D. M. Derrett, "Birds of the Air and Lilies of the Field," *DR* 105 (1987): 181-92.

0693　　　C. Lejeune, "Les oiseaux et les lis. Lecture 'écologique' de Matthieu 6,25-34," *Hokhma* 44 (1990): 3-20.

0694　　　J. J. Bartolomé, "Los pájaros y los lirios: Una aproximación a la cuestión ecológica desde Mt. 6,25-34," *EB* 49 (1991): 165-90.

6:25-33

0695   Rudolf Bultmann, "Matthäus 6,25-33," in *Marburger Predigten*. Tübingen: Mohr, 1956. Pp. 14-25.

6:25

0696   D. Dormeyer, "Das Verstandnis von Arbeit in Neuen Testament im Horizont der Naherwartung," *HTS* 45/4 (1989): 801-14.

6:26

0697   E. Fuchs, "Die Verkündigung Jesu. Der Spruch von den Raben," in H. Ristow and K. Matthiae, eds., *Der historische Jesus und der kerygmatische Christus*. Berlin: Evangelische Verlagsanstalt, 1962. Pp. 385-88.

0698   J. F. Healey, "Models of Behavior: Matt. 6:26," *JBL* 108 (1989): 497-98.

6:27

0699   Patrick P. Saydon, "Some Biblico-Liturgical Passages Reconsidered," *MeliT* 18/1 (1966): 10-17.

0700   G. Schwarz, "Prostheinae epi teen Helikian autou Pechun hena," *ZNW* 71/3 (1980): 244-47.

6:28-30

0701   M. E. Irwin, "Considering the Lilies," *McMJT* 2 (1991): 20-28.

6:28

0702   P. Katz, "πῶς αὐξάνουσιν, Matt. VI. 28," *JTS* 5 (1954): 207-209.

0703   J. Enoch Powell, "Those 'Lilies of the Field' Again," *JTS* 33/2 (1982): 490-92.

6:29

0704   J. P. Hyatt, "Solomon in All His Glory," *JBR* 8 (1940): 27-30.

6:33

0705   W. H. P. Hatch, "A Note on Matthew 6:33," *HTR* 38 (1945): 270-72.

0706   F. Nötscher, "Das Reich (Gottes) und seine Gerechtigkeit,"
             in *Vom Alten zum Neuen Testament*. Bonn: Hanstein, 1962.
             Pp. 226-30.

0707   Jacques Dupont, "La justice qui donne accès au
             Royaume," in *Les Béatitudes*. Tome II: *La bonne nouvelle*.
             Paris: Gabalda, 1969. 2:245-72.

0708   Jacques Dupont, "Chercher le Royaume et la justice," in
             Les Béatitudes. Tome III: *Les évangélistes*. Paris: Gabalda,
             1973. 3:272-304.

0709   Thomas Schmidt, "Burden, Barrier, Blasphemy: Wealth in
             Matt. 6:33, Luke 14:33, and Luke 16:15," *TriJ* 9/2 (1988):
             171-89.

0710   Robert G. Bratcher, " 'Righteousness' in Matthew," *BT*
             40/2 (1989): 228-35.

0711   Wiard Popkes, "Die Gerechtigkeitstradition im
             Matthäus-Evangelium," *ZNW* 80/1 (1989): 1-23.

<u>7:1</u>

0712   Franz Steinmetz and Friedrich Wulf, "Richtet Nicht,"
             GeistL 42/1 (1969): 71-75.

0713   George S. Hendry, "Judge Not: A Critical Test of Faith,"
             TT 40/2 (1983): 113-29.

0714   J. D. M. Derrett, "Christ and Reproof (Matthew 7.1-5/Luke
             6.37-42)," *NTS* 34/2 (1988): 271-81.

<u>7:2</u>

0715   M. McNamara, " 'With What Measure You Mete It Shall
             Be Measured to You . . . ,' Mt. 7,2; Mk. 4,24; Lk. 6,38 and
             PT Gn 38,26," in *The New Testament and the Palestinian
             Targum to the Pentateuch*. Rome: Biblical Institute Press,
             1966. Pp. 138-42.

0716   H. P. Rüger, "Mit welchem Mass ihr messt, wird euch
             gemessen werden," *ZNW* 60 (1969): 174-82.

0717   D. Bivin, "A Measure of Humility," *JeruP* 4 (1991):
             13-14.

7:3-5

0718   G. B. King, "A Further Note on the Mote and the Beam (Matt. 7:3-5; Luke 6:41-42)," *HTR* 26 (1933): 73-76.

7:5

0719   C. Daniel, " 'Faux Prophete': Surnom des Esseniens dans le Sermon sur la Montagne," *RevQ* 7/25 (1969): 45-79.

7:6

0720   A. M. Perry, "Pearls before Swine," *ET* 46 (1934-1935): 381-82.

0721   T. F. Glasson, "Chiasmus in St. Matthew vii.6," *ET* 68 (1956-1957): 302.

0722   Thomas J. Bennett, "Matthew 7:6—A New Interpretation," *WTJ* 49/2 (1987): 371-86.

0723   Hermann von Lips, "Schweine futtert man, Hunde nicht ein Versuch, das Ratsel von Matthäus 7:6 zu losen," *ZNW* 79/3 (1988): 165-86.

7:6a

0724   J. Jeremias, "Matthäus 7,6a," in *Abba: Studien zur neutestamentlichen Theologie und Zeitgeschichte* Göttingen: Vandenhoeck & Ruprecht, 1966. Pp. 83-87.

0725   G. Schwarz, "Matthäus vii 6a. Emendation und Rückübersetzung," *NovT* 14 (1972): 18-25.

0726   Stephen Llewelyn, "Mt. 7:6a: Mistranslation or Interpretation," *NovT* 31/2 (1989): 97-103.

7:7-8

0727   Dominic Crossan, "Aphorism in Discourse and Narrative," *Semeia* 43 (1988): 121-40.

7:7

0728   Otto A. Piper, "In Search of Christ's Presence," *Int* 12 (1958): 16-27.

0729   N. Brox, "Suchen und Finden. Zur Nachgeschichte von Mt. 7,7b, Lk. 11,9b," in *Orientierung an Jesus: Zur Theolohie* *der Synoptiker* (festschrift for Josef Schmid). Freiburg: Herder, 1973. Pp. 17-36.

7:8

0730   David Hellholm, "En textgrammatisk konstruktion I Matteusevangeliet," *SEÅ* 51 (1986-1987): 80-89.

0731   Willem A. VanGemeren, " 'Abba' in the Old Testament? *JETS* 31 (1988): 386-98.

7:12

0732   H.-W. Bartsch, "Traditionsgeschichtliches zur 'Goldenen Regel' und zum Aposteldekret," *ZNW* 75/1 (1984): 128-32.

0733   W. Wolbert, "Die Goldene Regel und das ius talioni," *TTZ* 95 (1986): 169-81.

0734   Bruce Waltke, "Relating Human Personhood to the Health Sciences: An Old Testament Perspective," *Crux* 25/3 (1989): 2-10.

0735   M. Collin and P. Lenhardt, *Évangile et tradition d'Israël.* Paris: Cerf, 1990.

0736   P. Ricoeur, "The Golden Rule: Exegetical and Theological Perplexities," *NTS* 36 (1990): 392-97.

7:13-14

0737   J. D. M. Derrett, "The Merits of the Narrow Gate," *JSNT* 15 (1982): 20-29.

0738   E. P. Nacpil, "The Way To Life: Matt. 7:13-14," *EAJT* 11/1 (1983): 130-32.

0739   Martino Conti, "La via della beatitudine e della rovina secondo il Salmo I," *Ant* 61/1 (1986): 3-39.

7:13

0740   R. Parrott, "Entering the Narrow Door: Matt. 7:13/Luke 13:22-24," *Forum* 5 (1989): 111-20.

7:13a

0741   G. Schwarz, "Matthäus vii.13a," *NovT* 12 (1970): 229-32.

7:14

0742 David A. Black, "Remarks on the Translation of Matthew 7:14" *FilN* 2 (1989): 193-95.

0743 G. H. R. Horsley, "τί at Matthew 7:14: 'Because' not 'How'," *FilN* 3 (1990): 141-43.

7:14b

0744 A. J. Mattill, Jr., " 'The Way of Tribulation'," *JBL* 98/4 (1979): 531-46.

7:15-23

0745 David Hill, "The False Prophets and Charismatics: Structure and Interpretation in Matthew 7:15-23," *Bib* 57 (1976): 327-48.

7:15

0746 Otto Böcher, "Wölfe in Schafspelzen. Zum religionsgeschichtlichen Hintergrund von Matth. 7,15," *TZ* 24 (1968): 405-26.

7:21-27

0747 A. Ornella, "Les chrétiens seront jugés," *AsSeign* N.S. 40 (1973): 16-27.

7:21-23

0748 Hans Dieter Betz, "Eine Episode im Jungsten Gericht," *ZTK* 78/1 (1981): 1-30.

0749 Alberto Maggi, "Nota sull'uso τῷ σῷ ονοματι e ανομια in Mt. 7:21-23" *FilN* 3 (1990): 145-49.

7:22

0750 E. Schweizer, "Observance of the Law and Charismatic Activity in Matthew," *NTS* 16/3 (1970): 213-30.

7:23

0751 Norbert Lohfink, "Psalm 6: Beobachtung beim Versuch, ihn 'kanonisch' auszulegen," *TTQ* 167/4 (1987): 277-88.

7:24-27

0752 Walter Magass, " 'Er aber Schlief' (Mt. 8,24)," *LB* 29/30 (1973): 55-59.

7:27

0753   George Howard, "A Note on Codex Sinaiticus and Shem-Tob's Hebrew Matthew," *NTS* 38 (1992): 187-204.

7:28f.

0754   Gerhard Lohfink, "Wem gilt die Bergpredigt? Eine redaktionskritische Untersuchung von Mt. 4,23-5,2 und 7,28f," *TTQ* 163 (1983): 264-84.

7:29

0755   A. Houtepen, "Eigentijds Leergezag: Een Oecumenische Discussie," *TijT* 18/1 (1978): 26-47.

8:1-11:1

0756   Irenee Fransen, "La Charte de l'Apotre," *BVC* 37 (1961): 34-45.

8-9

0757   William G. Thompson, "Reflections on the Composition of Mt. 8:1-9:34," *CBQ* 33 (1971): 365-88.

0758   B. F. Drewes, "The Composition of Matthew 8-9," *SEAJT* 12 (1972): 92-101.

0759   C. Burger, "Jesu Taten nach Matthäus 8 und 9," *ZTK* 70 (1973): 272-87.

0760   Jack Dean Kingsbury, "Observations on the 'Miracle Chapters' of Matthew 8-9," *CBQ* 40/4 (1978): 559-73.

0761   Jeremy Moiser, "The Structure of Matthew 8-9: A Suggestion." *ZNW* 76/1 (1985): 117-18.

8:1-13

0762   Marcel Bastin, "Jesus Worked Miracles: Texts from Mt. 8," *LV* 39/2 (1984): 131-39.

8:1-4

0763   John J. Pilch, "Understanding Biblical Healing: Electing the Appropriate Model," *BTB* 18 (1988): 60-66.

0764   Jack Dean Kingsbury, "Retelling the 'Old, Old Story': The Miracle of the Cleansing of the Leper as an Approach to the Theology of Matthew," *CThM* 4/6 (1977): 342-49.

0765 Marcel Bastin, "Jesus Worked Miracles: Texts from Mt. 8," *LV* 39/2 (1984): 131-39.

8:5-13

0766 H. F. D. Sparks, "The Centurion's παῖς," *JTS* 42 (1941): 179-80.

0767 Rudolf Schnackenburg, "Zur Traditionsgeschichte von Joh, 4, 46-54," *BZ* 8 (1964): 58-88.

0768 E. F. Siegman, "St. John's Use of the Synoptic Material," *CBQ* 30/2 (1968): 182-98.

0769 F. Schnider and W. Stenger, "Der Hauptmann von Kapharnaum: die Heilung des Sohnes des Koniglichen," in *Johannes und die Synoptiker: Verleich ihrer Parallelen.* Munich: Kösel, 1971. Pp. 54-88.

0770 G. Zuntz, "The 'Centurion' of Capernaum and His Authority (Matt. viii.5-13)," in *Opuscula Selecta: Classica, Hellenistica, Christiana.* Manchester: University Press, 1972. Pp. 181-88.

0771 J. D. M. Derrett, "Law in the New Testament: The Syro-Phoenician Woman and the Centurion of Capernaum," *NovT* 15 (1973): 161-86.

8:9

0772 M. Frost, "I Also Am a Man under Authority," *ET* 45 (1933-1934): 477-78.

0773 C. F. Hogg, "The Lord's Pleasure in the Centurion's Faith," *ET* 47 (1935-1936): 44-45.

8:11-12

0774 Dale C. Allison, "Who Will Come from East and West," *IBS* 11 (1989): 158-70.

0775 Dieter Zeller, "Das Logion Mt. 8,11f., Lk. 13,28f., und das Motiv der 'Völkerwallfahrt'," *BZ* 15 (1971): 222-37; 16 (1972): 84-93.

0776 W. Grimm, "Zum Hintergrund von Mt. 8,11f., Lk. 13,28f.," *BZ* 16 (1972): 255-56.

8:12

0777   B. Schwank, "Dort wird Heulen und Zähneknirschen sein,"
            BZ 16 (1972): 121-22.

8:13

0778   E. Haenchen, "Faith and Miracle," in Kurt Aland, et al.,
            eds., *Studia Evangelica*: Papers Presented to the
            International Congress on the Four Gospels, Christ Church,
            Oxford, 1957. Berlin: Akademie-Verlag, 1959. Pp. 495-98.

8:14-15

0779   É. Charpentier, "Un miracle, trois récits: guérison de la
            bellemère de Pierre," *CE* N.S. 8 (1974): 45-48.

0780   Marcel Bastin, "Jesus Worked Miracles: Texts from Mt.
            8," *LV* 39/2 (1984): 131-39.

8:16-22

0781   Marcel Bastin, "Jesus Worked Miracles: Texts from Mt.
            8," *LV* 39/2 (1984): 131-39.

8:16-17

0782   Alva J. McClain, "Was Christ Punished for Our Diseases?"
            GTJ 6 (1965): 3-6.

8:17

0783   Victor J. Eldridge, "Typology: The Key to Understanding
            Matthew's Formula Quotations?" *Coll* 15 (1982): 43-51.

8:18-22

0784   Jack Dean Kingsbury, "On Following Jesus: The 'Eager'
            Scribe and the 'Reluctant' Disciple (Matthew 8:18-22),"
            NTS 34/1 (1988): 45-59.

0785   Jarmo Killunen, "Der Nnachfolgewillige Schriftgelehrte:
            Matthäus 8:19-20 im verständnis des Evangelisten," *NTS*
            37 (1991): 268-79.

8:20

0786   P. M. Casey, "The Son of Man Problem," *ZNW* 67/3
            (1976): 147-54.

0787   Maurice Casey, "The Jackals and the Son of Man (Matt.
            8.20//Luke 9.58)," *JSNT* 23 (1985): 3-22.

0788 Mahlon H. Smith, "No Place for a Son of Man," *Forum* 4/4 (1988): 83-107.

8:21-22
0789 A. Ehrhardt, "Lass die Toten ihre Toten begraben," *ScanJT* 6 (1953): 128-64.

0790 Byron McCane, "Let the Dead Bury Their Own Dead: Secondary Burial and Matthew 8:21-22," *HTR* 83 (1990): 31-43.

8:21f.
0791 Roy A. Harrisville, "Jesus and the Family," *Int* 23/4 (1969): 425-38.

8:22
0792 F. Perles, "Zwei Übersetzungsfehler im Text der Evangelien," *ZNW* 19 (1919-1920): 96.

0793 F. Perles, "Noch einmal Mt. 8:22," *ZNW* 25 (1926): 286.

0794 H. G. Klemm, "Das Wort von der Selbstbestattung der Toten," *NTS* 16 (1969-1970): 60-75.

0795 G. Schwarz, "Aphes tous Nekrous Thapsai tous heauton nekrous," *ZNW* 72/3 (1981): 272-76.

8:23-27
0796 G. Bornkamm, "Die Sturmstillung im Matthäus-evangelium," in G. Bornkamm, G. Barth, H. J. Held, eds. *Überlieferung und Auslegung im Matthäusevangelium.* Neukirchen-Vluyn: Neukircher Verlag, 1961. Pp. 48-53.

0797 J. Duplacy, "Et il y eut un grand calme . . . La tempête apaisée (Matthieu 8:23-27)," *BVC* 74 (1967): 15-28.

0798 Paul F. Feiler, "The Stilling of the Storm in Matthew: A Response to Gunther Bornkamm," *JETS* 26/4 (1983): 399-406.

8:23-24
0799 E. Hilgert, "Symbolismus und Heilsgeschichte in den Evangelien," in F. Christ, ed., *Oikonomia: Heilsgeschichte*

als Thema der Theologie (festschrift for Oscar Cullmann). Hambug: Reich, 1967. Pp. 51-56.

8:24

0800   R. Pesch, "Die matthäische Fassung der Erzählung Mt. 8,24," in *Jesu ureigene Taten? Ein Beitrag zur Wunderfrage.* Freiburg: Herder, 1970. Pp. 87-98.

0801   Walter Magass, " 'Er aber Schlief' (Mt. 8,24)," *LB* 29/30 (1973): 55-59.

8:28-34

0802   A. Vögtle, "Die historische und theologische Tragweite der heutigen Evangelienforschung," *ZKT* 86 (1964): 385-417.

0803   R. Pesch, *Der Besessene von Gerasa: Entstehung und Überlieferung einer Wundergeschichte.* Stuttgart: Katholisches Bibelwerk, 1972.

8:28

0804   Tjitze Baarda, "Gadarenes, Gerasenes, Gergesenes and the 'Distessaron' Tradition," in E. E. Ellis and M. Wilcox, eds., *Neotestamentica et Semitica* (festschrift for Matthew Black). London: T. &. T. Clark, 1969. Pp. 181-97.

8:29

0805   R. L. Mowery, "Subtle Differences: The Matthean 'Son of God' References," *NovT* 32 (1990): 193-200.

9-27

0806   G. D. Kilpatrick, "The Historic Present in the Gospels and Acts," *ZNW* 68/3 (1977): 258-62.

9:1-8

0807   F. Neirynck, "Les accords mineurs et la rédaction des évangiles L'épisode du paralytique (Mt., IX,1-8; Lc. V,17-26 pa.r; Mc., II,1-12)," *ETL* 50 (1974): 215-30.

9:2

0808   Robert H. Thouless, "Miracles and Physical Research," *Theology* 72 (1969): 253-58.

9:8

0809   W. Schenk, "Den Menschen, Mt. 9:8," *ZNW* 54 (1963): 272-75.

0810   Juan Leal, " 'Qui Dedit Potestatem Talem Hominibus' (Mt. 9,8)," *VD* 44 (1966): 53-59.

9:9-26

0811   F. Genuyt, "Evangile de Matthieu 9,9-26," *SémBib* 64 (1991): 3-14.

9:9-13

0812   R. Pesch, "Manifestation de la miséricorde de Dieu (Mt. 9)," *AsSeign* N.S. 41 (1971): 15-24.

0813   M. Theobald, "Der Primat der Synchronie vor der Diachronie als Grundaxiom der Literaturkritik: Methodische Erwagungen an Hand von Mk. 2,13-17, Mt. 9,9-13," *BZ* 22/2 (1978): 161-86.

0814   Mark Kiley, "Why 'Matthew' in Matt. 9, 9-13?" *Bib* 65/3 (1984): 347-51.

9:9

0815   B. Lindars, "Matthew, Levi, Lebbaeus and the Value of the Western Text," *NTS* 4 (1957-1958): 220-22.

0816   R. Pesch, "Levi-Matthäus (Mc. 2,14/Mt. 9,9; 10,3): Ein Beitrag zur Lösung eines alten Problems," *ZNW* 59 (1968): 40-56.

9:13-14

0817   José O'Callaghan, "Tres casos de armonización en Mt. 9," *EB* 47 (1989): 131-34.

9:13

0818   David Hill, "On the Use and Meaning of Hosea vi.6 in Matthew's Gospel," *NTS* 24 (1977): 107-19.

9:14-17

0819   J. Fernández, "La cuestion de ayuno (Mt. 9,14-17; Mc. 2,18-22; Lu. 5,33-39)," *CuBi* 19 (1962): 162-69.

0820   Philippe Rolland, "Les Predecesseurs de Marc: Les Sources Presynoptiques de Mc II,18-22 et Paralleles," *RB* 89/3 (1982): 370-405.

0821   George J. Brooke, "The Feast of New Wine and the Question of Fasting," *ET* 95/6 (1984): 175-76.

9:14-15
0822   J. C. O'Neill, "The Source of the Parables of the Bridegroom and the Wicked Husbandman," *JTS* 39 (1988): 485-89.

9:17
0823   A. E. Harvey, "New Wine in Old Skins: II. Priest," *ET* 84/7 (1973): 200-203.

9:18-26
0824   E. Galbiati, "Gesù guarisce l'emorroissa e risuscita la figlia di Giairo (Matt. 9,18-26)," *BibO* 6 (1964): 225-30.

0825   W. Marxsen, "Bibelarbeit über Mk. 5,21-43, Mt. 9,18-26," in *Der Exeget als Theologe*. Gütersloh: Mohn, 1968. Pp. 171-82.

0826   Everett R. Kalin, "Matthew 9:18-26: An Exercise in Redaction Criticism," *CThM* 15/1 (1988): 39-47.

9:18-25
0827   Roger Omanson, "A Question of Harmonization—Matthew 9:18-25," *BT* 42 (1991): 241.

9:18
0828   José O'Callaghan, "La Variante eis/Elthon en Mt. 9,18," *Bib* 62/1 (1981): 104-106.

9:20-22
0829   Manfred Hutter, "Ein Altorientalischer Bittegestus in Mt. 9,20-22," *ZNW* 75/1 (1984): 133-35.

9:20
0830   José O'Callaghan, "Reflexions critiques sobre Mt. 9,20 i 13,4," *RCT* 10 (1985): 319-22.

9:24

0831   R. C. Fuller, "The Healing of Jairus' Daughter," *Scr* 3 (1948): 53.

9:27-31

0832   A. Fuchs, "Mt. 9,27-31 (20,29-34)," in *Sprachliche Untersuchungen zu Matthäus und Lukas: Ein Beitrag zur Quellenkritik*. Rome: Biblical Institute Press, 1971. Pp. 18-37, 45-170.

9:28

0833   Angelo Lancellotti, "La Casa Pietro a Cafarnao nel Vangeli Sinottici: Redazione   e Tradizione," *Ant* 58/1 (1983): 48-69.

9:32-34

0834   Pierre Guillemette, "La Forme des Recits d'Exorcisme de Bultmann: Un Dogme a Reconsiderer," *ÉgT* 11/2 (1980): 177-93.

0835   R. F. Collins, "Jesus' Ministry to the Deaf and Dumb," *MeliT* 35/1 (1984): 12-36.

9:35-11:1

0836   J. A. Grassi, "The Last Testament-Succession Literary Background of Matthew 9:35-11:1 and Its Significance," *BTB* 7/4 (1977): 172-76.

0837   Schuyler Brown, "The Mission to Israel in Matthew's Central Section (Mt. 9:35-11:1)," *ZNW* 69/1 (1978): 73-90.

0838   Robert E. Morosco, "Matthew's Formation of a Commissioning-Type Scene Out of the Story of Jesus' Commissioning of the Twelve," *JBL* 104/4 (1984): 539-56.

0839   Roman Bartnicki, "Die Jünger Jesu in Mt. 9,35-11,1," *ColIT* 58 (1988): 39-56.

0840   Dorothy J. Weaver, *Matthew Missionary Discourse: A Literary Critical Analysis*. Sheffield: JSOT Press, 1990.

9:35-38

0841   O. Weber, "Predigt über Matth. 9,35-38," *EvT* 8 (1948-1949): 117-23.

0842   C. Rene Padilla, "Bible Studies," *Miss* 10/3 (1982): 319-38.

9:36

0843   François Martin, "The Image of Shepherd in the Gospel of St. Matthew," *ScE* 27 (1975): 261-301.

9:37-38

0844   C. H. Talbert, *Literary Patterns, Theological Themes and the Genre of Luke-Acts*. Missoula: Scholars Press, 1974.

0845   R. A. Edwards, *A Theology of Q*. Philadelphia: Fortress, 1976.

9:37f.

0846   B. Charette, "A Harvest for the People? An Interpretation of Matthew 9:37f.," *JSNT* 38 (1990): 29-35.

10:1-42

0847   F. Genuyt, "Evangile de Matthieu 10,1-42," *SémBib* 65 (1992): 3-17.

10:1-16

0848   F. W. Beare, "The Mission of the Disciples and the Mission Charge: Matthew 10 and Parallels," *JBL* 89/1 (1970): 1-13.

0849   A. Kretzer, "Die Ersten und die Letzten in der Ordnung der Basileia: Mt. 10,1-16," in *Der Herrschaft der Himmel und die Söhne des Reiches: Eine redaktionsgeschichte Untersuchung zum Base' eiabegriff und Basileiaverständnis im Matthäusevangelium*. Stuttgart: KBW, 1971. Pp. 272-302.

10:3

0850   R. Pesch, "Levi-Matthäus (Mc 2,14 / Mt. 9,9; 10,3): Ein Beitrag zur Lösung eines alten Problems," *ZNW* 59 (1968): 40- 56.

10:5-6

0851   Morna D. Hooker, "Prohibition of Foreign Missions in Mt. 10,5-6," *ET* 82 (1970-1971): 361-65.

0852   Morna D. Hooker, "Uncomfortable Words: X. The Prohibition of Foreign Missions," *ET* 82/12 (1971): 361-65.

10:5b-6

0853   W. Trilling, "Die Sendung zu Israel: 10,5b-6; 15,24," in *Das wahre Israel: Studien zur Theologie des Matthäus-Evangeliums*. Munich: Kösel, 1964. Pp. 99-105.

0854   H. Schürmann, "Mt. 10,5b-6 und die Vorgeschichte des synoptischen Aussendungsberichtes," in *Traditionsgeschichtliche Untersuchungen zu den synoptischen Evangelien*. Düsseldorf: Patmos, 1968. Pp. 137-49.

0855   Yoshito Anno, "The Mission to Israel in Matthew: The Intention of Matthew 10:5b-6 Considered in the Light of the Religio-Political Background," doctoral dissertation, Lutheran School of Theology, Chicago IL, 1984.

0856   Roman Bartnicki, "Der Bereich der Tätigkeit der Jünger nach Mt. 10,5b-6," *BZ* 31 (1987): 250-56.

10:7-42

0857   M. Laconi, "Il discorso missionario," in *Il Messaggio della salvezza*. 5 vols. Torino: Leumann, 1966-1970. 5:365-91.

10:7-8

0858   Martino Conti, "Il mandato di Cristo (Mt. 10.7-8.11-15),' *Ant* 47 (1972): 17-68.

10:9-10

0859   Martino Conti, "Fondamenti biblici della poverti nel ministero apostolico (Mt. 10,9-10)," *Ant* 46 (1971): 393-426.

10:10

0860   J. Andrew Kirk, "Did 'Officials' in the New Testament Church Receive a Salary?" *ET* 84/4 (1973): 105-108.

0861   José O'Callaghan, "Dos retoques antioquenos: Mt. 10,10; Mc. 2,20," *Bib* 68/4 (1987) 564-67.

0862   G. Schwarz, "προφῆς αὐτοῦ oder τῆς μισθο˜υ αὐτοῦ?" *BibN* 56 (1991): 25.

10:11-15

0863 Martino Conti, "Il mandato di Cristo (Mt. 10.7-8.11-15),' *Ant* 47 (1972): 17-68.

10:13

0864 J. A. Montgomery, "New Testament Notes," *JBL* 56 (1937): 51-52.

10:14

0865 Edouard Delebecque, " 'Secouez la Poussiere de vos Pieds ...... sur l'Hellenisme de Luc IX,5," *RB* 89/2 (1982): 177-84.

0866 Bruce A. Stevens, "Jesus as the Divine Warrior," *ET* 94/1 (1983): 326-29.

10:15

0867 R. M. Grant, "Like Children," *HTR* 39 (1946): 71-73.

10:16

0868 Warren Vanhetloo, "The Incarnate Shepherd," *CBTJ* 1/1 (1985): 20-34.

0869 Paul de Vries, "The Taming of the Shrewd," *CT* 34/5 (1990): 14-17.

10:17-19

0870 Matthew Mahoney, "Luke 21:14-15: Editorial Rewriting or Authenticity?" *ITQ* 47/3 (1980): 220-38.

10:19

0871 Ragnar Leivestad, "An Interpretation of Matt. 10:19," *JBL* 71 (1952): 179-81.

10:21

0872 Pierre Grelot, "Miche 7,6 dans les evangiles et dans la littrature rabbinique," *Bib* 67/3 (1986): 363-77.

10:23

0873 Jacques Dupont, "Vous n'aurez pas achevé les villes d'Israël avant que le fils de l'homme ne vienne (Mat. X 23)," *NovT* 2 (1957-1958): 228-44.

0874 E. Bammel, "Matthäus 10,23," *ScanJT* 15 (1961): 79-92.

0875   Royce Clark, "Eschatology and Matthew 10:23," *RQ* 6 (1963): 73-81.

0876   Royce Clark, "Matthew 10:23 and Eschatology (II)," *RQ* 8 (1965): 53-69.

0877   H. Schürmann, "Zur Traditions- und Redaktionsgeschichte von Mt. 10,23," in *Traditionsgeschichtliche Untersuchungen zu den synoptischen Evangelien.* Düsseldorf: Patmos, 1968. Pp. 150-56.

0878   M. Künzi, *Das Naherwartungslogion Matthäus 10,23: Geschichte seiner Auslegung.* Tübingen: Mohr, 1970.

0879   S. McKnight, "Jesus and the End-Time. Matthew 10:23," *SBLSP* 25 (1986): 501-20.

0880   Roman Bartnicki, "Das Trostwort an die Juenger in Matth. 10,23," *TZ* 43/4 (1987): 311-19.

0881   Volker Hampel, " 'Ihr werdet mit den Stadten Israels nicht zu Ende kommen'," *TZ* 45/1 (1989): 1-31.

10:23b

0882   Charles H. Giblin, "Theological Perspective and Matthew 10:23b," *TS* 29/4 (1968): 637-61.

10:24-31

0883   Edward May, et al., "Outlines on the Swedish Gospels (Alternate Series)," *CTM* 29 (1958): 277-91.

10:25

0884   W. C. B. MacLaurin, "Beelzeboul," *NovT* 20/2 (1978): 156-60.

10:26-31

0885   Dale C. Allison, "Matthew 10:26-31 and the Problem of Evil," *SVTQ* 32/4 (1988): 293-308.

10:28

0886   I. H. Marshall, "Uncomfortable Words. VI. 'Fear Him Who Can Destroy both Soul and Body in Hell'," *ET* 81/9 (1970): 276-82.

0887   A. Fernández, "No temáis a los que matan el cuerpo, pero no pueden matar el alma, Interpretación patristica de Mt. 10,28," *Burgense* 28 (1987): 85-108.

0888   Chaim Milikowsky, "Which Gehenna: Retribution and Eschatology in the Synoptic Gospels and in Early Jewish Texts," *NTS* 34/2 (1988): 238-49.

10:29
0889   T. Hirunuma, "ἄνευ τοῦ πατρός 'Without (of) the Father'," *FilN* 3 (1990): 53-62.

10:30
0890   Dale C. Allison, "The Hairs on Your Head Are Numbered," *ET* 101 (1990): 334-36.

10:32-33
0891   G. W. H. Lampe, "St. Peter's Denial," *BJRL* 55/2 (1973): 346-68.

10:32
0892   B. Lindars, "Jesus as Advocate: A Contribution to the Christology Debate," *BJRL* 62/2 (1980): 476-97.

10:34-39
0893   M. Vidal, "Seguimiento de Cristo y evangelización. Variación sobre un tema de moral neotestamentaria (Mt. 10,34-39)," *Sale* 18 (1971): 289-312.

10:34-36
0894   T. A. Roberts, "Some Comments on Matthew x.34-36 and Luke xii.51-53," *ET* 69 (1957-1958): 304-306.

10:34
0895   Matthew Black, "The Violent Word," *ET* 81 (1969-1970): 115-18.

0896   Matthew Black, "Uncomfortable Words: III. The Violent Word," *ET* 81/4 (1970): 115-18.

0897   Karen A. Barta, "Mission and Discipleship in Matthew: A Redaction-Critical Study of Mt. 10:34," doctoral dissertation, Marquette University, Milwaukee WI, 1979.

10:35f.

0898
Bo Reicke, "Mik. 7 søsom 'messiansk' text, med särskild hänsyn till Matt. 10:35 f. och Luk. 12:53," in *Professor Johannes Lindblom: på hans 65-,35 årsdag den 7 juni 1947*. Uppsala: Wretmans, 1948. Pp. 263-84.

10:37-39

0899
Tomas Arvedson, "Bakgrunden till Mt. 10, 37-39 et parr.," in *Erling Eidem: Theologiae doctori, summo suo praedidi, sexagenario, pie ac reverenter obtulit hunc fasciculum societas exegetica upsaliensis*. Uppsala: Wretmans, 1940. Pp. 74-82.

10:38

0900
E. Dinkler, "Jesu Wort vom Kreuztragen," in *Neutestamentliche Studien für Rudolf Bultmann*. Berlin: Töpelmann, 1957. Pp. 110-29.

10:39

0901
Tomas Arvedson, "Phil. 2,6 und Mt. 10,39," *ScanJT* 5 (1952): 49-51.

10:40-42

0902
Savas Agourides, " 'Little Ones' in Matthew," *BT* 35/3 (1984): 329-34.

10:40

0903
James L. Price, "Christ in Every Man," *RL* 27 (1958): 577-82.

0904
H. K. Stothard, "Apostolic Authority," *CT* 14/3 (1969): 116-19.

10:42

0905
S. Légasse, "Le logion sur le 'verre d'eau'," in *Jésus et l'enfant: 'Enfants', 'Petis' et 'simples' dans la tradition synoptique*. Paris: Gabalda, 1969. Pp. 76-85.

0906
José O'Callaghan, "Dissensio critica in Mt. 10,42," *Era* 86 (1988): 163-64.

10:46-52

0907   W. Trilling, "Die Zeichen der Messiaszeit (Mt. 10, 46-52)," in *Christusverkündigung in den synoptischen Evangelien*. Munich: Kösel, 1969. Pp. 146-64.

11:1-14:13a

0908   R. Doyle, "Matthew's Wisdom: A Redaction-Critical Study of Matthew 11.1-14.13a," doctoral dissertation, University of Melbourne, Melbourne, Australia, 1984.

11:1

0909   David Hellholm, "En textgrammatisk konstruktion I Matteusevangeliet," *SEÅ* 51 (1986-1987): 80-89.

11:2-26

0910   Selma Hirsch, "Studien zu Matthäus 11,2-26," *TZ* 5 (1949): 241-60.

11:2-19

0911   P. Hoffmann, "Johannes und der Menschensohn Jesus," in *Studien zur Theologie der Logienquelle*. Münster: Aschendorff, 1972. Pp. 190-233.

0912   John P. Meier, "John the Baptist in Matthew's Gospel," *JBL* 99 (1980): 383-405.

11:2-15

0913   Marianne Sawicki, "How to Teach Christ's Disciples: John 1:19-37 and Matthew 11:2-15," *LexTQ* 21/1 (1986): 14-26.

0914   Walter Vogels, "Performers and Receivers of the Kingdom: A Semiotic Analysis of Matthew 11:2-15," *ScE* 42 (1991): 335-36.

11:2-6

0915   Rudolf Bultmann, "Matthäus 11,2-6," in *Marburger Predigten*. Tübingen: Mohr, 1956. Pp. 87-97.

0916   A. Vögtle, "Wort und Wunder in der urkirchlichen Glaubenswerbung (Mt. 11,2-6, Lk. 7,18-23)," in *Das Evangelium und die Evangelien*. Düsseldorf: Patmos, 1971. Pp. 219-42.

0917   Jan Lambrecht, " 'Are You the One Who Is to Come, or Shall We Look for Another?' The Gospel Message of Jesus Today," *LouvS* 8/2 (1980): 115-18.

0918   Martin Cawley, "Health of the Eyes: Gift of the Father: In the Gospel Tradition 'Q'," *WS* 3 (1981): 41-70.

0919   R. F. Collins, "Jesus' Ministry to the Deaf and Dumb," *MeliT* 35/1 (1984): 12-36.

0920   Walter Wink, "Jesus' Reply to John: Matt. 11:2-6/Luke 7:18-23," *Forum* 5 (1989): 121-28.

11:3
0921   A. Strobel, "Die Täuferanfrage (Mt. 11,3/Luk. 7,19)," in *Untersuchungen zum eschatologischen Verzögerungsproblem auf Grund der spätjüdischurchristlichen Geschichte von Habakuk 2,2 ff.* Leiden: Brill, 1961. Pp. 265-77.

0922   Carroll Simcox, "Is Anybody Good Enough to Be Antichrist?" *CT* 102/20 (1985): 582-85.

0923   A. George, "Paroles de Jésus sur ses miracles (Mt. 11,5.21; 12,27.28 et par.)," in J. DuPont, et al., eds., *Jésus aux origines de la christologie.* Louvain: University Press, 1975. Pp. 283-301.

11:5-21
0924   R. Pesch, "Jesu Antwort auf die Täuferanfrage (Mt. 11,5, Lk. 7,22)," in *Jesu ureigene Taten? Ein Beitrag zur Wunderfrage.* Freiburg: Herder, 1970. Pp. 36-44.

0925   A. George, "Paroles de Jésus sur ses miracles (Mt. 11,5.21; 12,27.28 et par.)," in J. DuPont, et al., eds., *Jésus aux origines de la christologie.* Louvain: University Press, 1975. Pp. 283-301.

11:6
0926   C. L. Mitton, "Stumbling Block Characteristics of Jesus," *ET* 82 (1970-1971): 168-72.

11:7-15
0927   J. A. T. Robinson, "Elijah, John and Jesus," *NTS* 4 (1958): 263-81.

11:7-8

0928   C. Daniel, "Les Esséniens et 'Ceux qui sont dans les maisons des rois'," *RevQ* 6 (1967): 261-77.

11:10

0929   W. C. Kaiser, "The Promise of the Arrival of Elijah in Malachi and the Gospels," *GTJ* 3/2 (1982): 221-33.

11:12-13

0930   P. W. Barnett, "Who Were the 'Biastai'?" *RTR* 36/3 (1977): 65-70.

11:12

0931   G. Braumann, "Dem Himmelreich wird Gewalt angetan (Mt. 11,12 par.)," *ZNW* 52 (1961): 104-109.

0932   W. E. Moore, "Biazō, arpazō and Cognates in Josephus," *NTS* 21 (1975): 519-43.

0933   B. E. Thiering, "Are the 'Violent Men' False Teachers?" *NovT* 21/4 (1979): 293-97.

0934   Sharon Karam, "Flannery O'Connor: A Modern Apocalyptic," *BibTo* 18/3 (1980): 182-86.

0935   Peter S. Cameron, *Violence and the Kingdom: The Interpretation of Matthew 11:12*. 2d ed. Frankfurt: Lang, 1988.

0936   W. E. Moore, "Violence to the Kingdom: Josephus and the Syrian Churches," *ET* 100/5 (1989): 174-77.

0937   Paolo Papone, "Il regno dei cieli soffre violenza? (Mt. 11:12)," *RBib* 38 (1990): 375-76.

11:14

0938   W. C. Kaiser, "The Promise of the Arrival of Elijah in Malachi and the Gospels," *GTJ* 3/2 (1982): 221-33.

11:16-19

0939   F. Mussner, "Der nicht erkannte Kairos (Mt. 11,16-19 = Lk. 7,31-35)," in *Studia Biblica et Orientalia*. 3 vols. Rome: Pontifical Institute, 1959. Pp. 2:31-44.

0940   S. Légasse, "La parabole des enfants sur la place," in *Jésus et l'enfant: 'Enfants', 'Petis' et 'simples' dans la tradition synoptique*. Paris: Gabalda, 1969. Pp. 289-317.

0941   F. Christ, "Das Rechtfertigungswort," in *Jesus Sophia: Die Sophia-Christologie bei den Synoptikern*. Zürich: Zwingli, 1970. Pp. 63-80.

0942   Olof Linton, "The Parable of the Children's Game," *NTS* 22/2 (1976): 159-79.

0943   Harald Sahlin, "Traditionskritische Bemerkungen zu Zwei Evangelienperikopen," *ScanJT* 33/1 (1979): 6.

11:16-17
0944   José O'Callaghan, "La variante 'se gritan . . . diciendo', de Mt. 11,16-17," *EE* 61 (1986): 67-70.

11:18-19
0945   M. H. Franzmann, "Of Food, Bodies, and the Boundless Reign of God in the Synoptic Gospels," *Pacifica* 5 (1992): 17-31.

11:19
0946   P. M. Casey, "The Son of Man Problem," *ZNW* 67/3 (1976): 147-54.

0947   C. Deutsch, "Wisdom in Matthew: Transformation of a Symbol," *NovT* 32 (1990): 13-47.

11:20-24
0948   Joseph A. Comber, "The Composition and Literary Characteristics of Matt. 11:20-24." *CBQ* 39/4 (1977): 497-504.

11:20
0949   S. Clive Thexton, "Jesus' Use of the Scriptures," *LQHR* 179 (1954): 102-108.

11:24-30
0950   W. D. Davies, " 'Knowledge' in the Dead Sea Scrolls and Matthew 11:24-30," *HTR* 46 (1953): 113-39.

<u>11:25-30</u>

0951   Johannes Weiss, "Das Logion Mt. 11,25-30," in Hans Windisch, ed., *Neutestamentliche Studien Georg Heinrici zu seinem 70. Geburtstag.* Leipzig: Hinrichs'sche, 1914. Pp. 120-29.

0952   Tomas Arvedson, *Das Mysterium Christi: Eine Studie zu Mt. 11,25-30.* Uppsala: Wretmans, 1937.

0953   K. G. Steck, "Über Matthäus 11,25-30," *EvT* 15 (1955): 343-49.

0954   A. M. Hunter, "Crux Criticorum. Matt. xi.25-30: A Re-appraisal," *NTS* 8 (1961-1962): 241-49.

0955   W. D. Davies, " 'Knowledge' in the Dead Sea Scrolls and Matthew 11:25-30," in *Christian Origins and Judaism: A Collection of New Testament Studies.* London: Longman & Todd, 1962. Pp. 119-44.

0956   S. Légasse, "La revélation aux 'simples' et l'appel aux 'accables'," in *Jésus et l'enfant: 'Enfants', 'Petis' et 'simples' dans la tradition synoptique.* Paris: Gabalda, 1969. Pp. 231-46.

0957   André Feuillet, "Comparaison avec les synoptiques: L'hymne de jubilation (Mt. 11, 25-30; Lc 10, 21-22)," in *Le mystère de l'amour divin dans la théologie johannique.* Paris: Gabalda, 1972. Pp. 133-77.

0958   R. Beauvery, "La sagesse se rend justice," *AsSeign* (1974): 17-24.

0959   L. Randellini, "L'inno di giubulo: Mt. 11,25-30; Lc. 10,20-24)," *RBib* 22 (1974): 183-235.

0960   A. M. Hunter, "The Great Thanksgiving (Matt. 11.25-30)," in *Gospel and Apostle.* London: SCM Press, 1975. Pp. 60-67.

0961   Kenneth O. Gangel, "Leadership: Coping with Cultural Corruption," *BSac* 144 (1987): 450-60.

0962   Dale C. Allison, "Two Notes on a Key Text: Matthew 11:25-30," *JTS* 39 (1988): 477-85.

0963   C. Deutsch, "Wisdom in Matthew: Transformation of a Symbol," *NovT* 32 (1990): 13-47.

11:25-27
0964   Harold A. Guy, "Matthew 11,25-27; Luke 10,21-22," *ET* 49 (1937-1938): 236-37.

0965   W. Grundmann, "Die *ēpiois* in der Urchristlichen Paränese," *NTS* 5 (1958-1959): 188-205.

0966   F. Christ, "Der Jubelruf," in *Jesus Sophia: Die Sophia-Christologie bei den Synoptikern*. Zürich: Zwingli, 1970. Pp. 81-99.

0967   W. Grimm, "Der Dank fur die empfangene Offenbarung bei Jesus und Josephus," *BZ* 17 (1973): 249-56.

11:25-26
0968   W. Marchel, "Le terme 'Abba', expression des aspects originaux de la priere de Jésus au Père (Mt. 11,25.26; Lc. 10,21)," in *Abba, Pere! La prière du Christ et des chrétiens*. Rome: Biblical Institute Press, 1963. Pp. 150-71.

0969   Jacques Dupont, "La révélation aux tout-petits," in *Les Béatitudes*. Tome II: *La bonne nouvelle*. Paris: Gabalda, 1969. 2:181-215.

11:27-31
0970   M. Collin and P. Lenhardt, *Évangile et tradition d'Israël*. Paris: Cerf, 1990.

11:27
0971   E. Percy, "Der Vater und der Sohn (Mt. 11,27; Lk. 10,22)," in *Die Botschaft Jesu: Eine traditionskritische und exegetische Untersuchung*. Lund: Gleerup, 1953. Pp. 259-71.

0972   Paul Winter, "Matthew 11:27 and Luke 10:22 from the First to the Fifth Century. Reflections on the Development of the Text," *NovT* 1 (1956): 112-48.

0973   B. M. F. van Iersel, "Mt. 11,27-Lk. 10:22," in *"Der Sohn" in der synoptischen Jesusworten.* Leiden: Brill, 1961. Pp. 146-61.

0974   W. Grundmann, "Matth. xi.27 und die Johanneischen 'Der Vater-Der Sohn'-Stellen," *NTS* 12 (1965-66): 42-49.

0975   P. Hoffmann, "Die Apokalypsis des Sohnes," in *Studien zur Theologie der Logienquelle.* Münster: Aschendorff, 1972. Pp. 102-42.

0976   Jesse Sell, "Johannine Traditions in Logion 61 of the Gospel of Thomas," *PRS* 7/1 (1980): 24-37.

0977   Barry W. Henaut, "Matthew 11:27: The Thunderbolt in Corinth?" *TJT* 3 (1987): 282-300.

11:28-30

0978   Theodor Haering, "Matth. 11,28-30," in *Aus Schrift und Geschichte. Theologische Abhandlungen, Adolf Schlatter zu seinem 70. Geburtstag.* Stuttgart: Calwer, 1922. Pp. 3-15.

0979   Rudolf Bultmann, "Matthäus 11,28-30," in *Marburger Predigten.* Tübingen: Mohr, 1956. Pp. 71-78.

0980   J. B. Bauer, "Das milde Joch und die Ruhe, Matth. 11, 28-30," *TZ* 17 (1961): 99-106.

0981   Hans Dieter Betz, "The Logion of the Easy Yoke and of Rest," *JBL* 86 (1967): 10-24.

0982   Graham N. Stanton, "Salvation Proclaimed: X. Matthew 11:28-30: Comfortable Words?" *ET* 94/1 (1982): 3-9.

0983   Samuele Bacchiocchi, "Matthew 11:28-30: Jesus' Rest and the Sabbath.," *AUSS* 22/3 (1984): 289-316.

0984   M. Hengel, "Die Einladung Jesu (Mt. 11,28-30)," *TBe* 18 (1987): 113-19.

0985   B. Charette, " 'To Proclaim Liberty to the Captives': Matthew 11:28-30 in the Light of OT Prophetic Expectation," *NTS* 38 (1992): 290-97.

11:28

0986   G. N. Curnock, "A Neglected Parallel (Mt. 11,28 and Ex. 33,14)," *ET* 44 (1932-1933): 141.

0987   James J. C. Cox, "Bearers of Heavy Burdens: A Significant Textual Variant," *AUSS* 9/1 (1971): 1-15.

11:29

0988   E. Dinkler, "Jesu Wort vom Kreuztragen," in *Neutestamentliche Studien für Rudolf Bultmann.* Berlin: Töpelmann, 1957. Pp. 110-29.

0989   M. Maher, " 'Take My Yoke upon You' (Matt. xi.29)," *NTS* 22 (1975-1976): 97-103.

11:29b

0990   K. Luke, "The Syriac Text of Matthew 11:29b and John 1:32-33," *BB* 16 (1990): 177-91.

12:1-14

0991   John Mark Hicks, "The Sabbath Controversy in Matthew: An Exegesis of Matthew 12:1-14," *RQ* 27/2 (1984): 79-91.

12:1-8

0992   P. Benoit, "Les épis arrachés (Mt. 12,1-8 et par.)," *SBFLA* 13 (1962-1963): 76-92.

0993   J. A. Grassi, "The Five Loaves of the High Priest," *NovT* 7 (1964-1965): 119-22.

0994   Edgar V. McKnight and Charles H. Talbert, "Can the Griesbach Hypothesis Be Falsified?" *JBL* 91/3 (1972): 338-68.

0995   Matty Cohen, "La Controverse de Jésus et des Pharisiens à Propos de la Cueillette des Epis, selon l'Évangile de Saint Matthieu," *MSR* 34/1 (1977): 3-12.

12:7

0996   Kenneth A. Michael, " 'It Is Mercy I Desire and Not Sacrifice. Reflections on Matthew 12:7," *Diakonia* (1988): 111-20.

12:18-21

0997   E. Lohmeyer, "Matth. 12,18-21," in *Gottesknecht und Davidssohn*. 2nd ed. Göttingen: Vandenhoeck & Ruprecht, 1953. Pp. 8-14.

0998   Victor J. Eldridge, "Typology: The Key to Understanding Matthew's Formula Quotations?" *Coll* 15 (1982): 43-51.

12:18

0999   C. Tassin, "Matthieu 'targumiste?' L'exemple de Mt. 12,18 (= Is 42,1)," *EB* 48 (1990): 199-214.

12:22-37

1000   L. R. Fisher, "Can This Be the Son of David?" in F. T. Trotter, ed., *Jesus and the Historian* (festschrift for Ernest Cadman Colwel). Philadelphia: Westminster Press, 1968. Pp. 82-97.

1001   Roland Meynet, "Qui Donc Esr 'Le Plus Fort'? Analyse Rhetorique de Mc. 3,22-30; Mt. 12,22-37; Luc. 11,14-26," *RB* 90/3 (1983): 334-50.

12:22-32

1002   David Peel, "Missing the Signs of the Kingdom," *ET* 99 (1988): 114-15.

12:22-30

1003   R. F. Collins, "Jesus' Ministry to the Deaf and Dumb," *MeliT* 35/1 (1984): 12-36.

12:22-24

1004   Pierre Guillemette, "La forme des récits d'exorcisme de Bultmann: Un dogme à reconsidérer," *ÉgT* 11/2 (1980): 177-93.

12:24

1005   W. C. B. MacLaurin, "Beelzeboul," *NovT* 20/2 (1978): 156-60.

12:25-32

1006   Chrys C. Caragounis, "Kingdom of God, Son of Man and Jesus' Self-Understanding," *TynB* 40 (1989): 3-23.

12:27-28

1007 A. George, "Paroles de Jésus sur ses miracles (Mt. 11,5.21; 12,27.28 et par.)," in J. DuPont, et al., eds., *Jésus aux origines de la christologie*. Louvain: University Press, 1975. Pp. 283-301.

12:28

1008 C. S. Rodd, "Spirit or Finger," *ET* 72 (1960-1961): 157-58.

1009 Robert G. Hamerton-Kelly, "A Note on Matthew 12:28 Par. Luke 11:20," *NTS* 11/2 (1965): 167-69.

1010 T. Lorenzmeier, "Zum Logion Mt. 12,28; Lk. 11,20," in D. D. Betz and L. Schottroff, eds., *Neues Testament und christliche Existenz* (festschrift for Herbert Braum). Tübingen: Mohr, 1973. Pp. 289-304.

1011 Chrys C. Caragounis, "Kingdom of God, Son of Man and Jesus' Self-Understanding," *TynB* 40 (1989): 223-38.

12:30-31

1012 J. G. Williams, "A Note on the 'Unforgivable Sin' Logion," *NTS* 12 (1965): 75-77.

12:31-32

1013 E. Lövestam, *Spiritus Blasphemia. Eine Studie zu Mk. 3, 82f par. Mt. 12,31f,, Lk. 12,10*. Lund: Gleerup, 1968.

1014 Eugene Boring, "The Unforgivable Sin Logion Mark 3:28-29/Matt. 12:31-32/Luke 12:10: Formal Analysis and History of the Tradition," *NovT* 18/4 (1976): 258-79.

12:31

1015 John P. Oaks, "An Analytical and Definitional Approach to the Problem of the Unpardonable Sin," doctoral dissertation, New Orleans Baptist Theological Seminary, New Orleans LA, 1953.

1016 Gerhard L. Miller, "Purgatory," *TD* 33/4 (1986): 31-36.

12:32

1017   Jan Lambrecht, "Ware Verwantshasp en Eeuwige Zonde: Onstaan en Structuur van Mc. 3:20-35," *Bij* 29/2 (1968): 114-50.

1018   R. Schippers, "The Son of Man in Matt. 12.32 Lk. 12.10, compared with Mk. 3.28," in F. Cross, ed., *Studia Evangelica IV*: Papers Presented to the Third International Congress on New Testament Studies, Christ Church, Oxford, 1965 (Part I—The New Testament Scriptures). Berlin: Akademie-Verlag, 1968. Pp. 231-35.

1019   P. M. Casey, "The Son of Man Problem," *ZNW* 67/3 (1976): 147-54.

1020   Chrys C. Caragounis, "Kingdom of God, Son of Man and Jesus' Self-Understanding," *TynB* 40 (1989): 223-38.

12:38-42

1021   P. Seidelin, "Das Jonaszeichen," *ScanJT* 5 (1952): 119-31.

1022   Otto Glombitza, "Das Zeichen des Jona (Zum Verständnis von Matth. xii. 38-42)," *NTS* 8 (1961-1962): 359-66.

1023   John Howton, "The Sign of Jonah," *SJT* 15 (1962): 288-304.

1024   Edgar V. McKnight and Charles H. Talbert, "Can the Griesbach Hypothesis Be Falsified?" *JBL* 91/3 (1972): 338-68.

12:38

1025   A. K. M. Adam, "The Sign of Jonah: A Fish-Eye View," *Semeia* 51 (1990): 177-91.

12:39

1026   R. A. Edwards, *The Sign of Jonah in the Theology of the Evangelists and Q*. London: SCM, 1971.

12:40

1027   H. K. McArthur, " 'On the Third Day'," *NTS* 18/1 (1971): 81-86.

1028   Santiago Guijarro Oporto, "The Sign of Jonah," *TD* 32/1 (1985): 49-53.

12:41

1029   S. Clive Thexton, "Jesus' Use of the Scriptures," *LQHR* 179 (1954): 102-108.

12:44-45

1030   H. S. Nyberg, "Zum grammatischen Verständis von Matth. 12,44-45," in *Adolf Jülicher zum achtzigjährigen Geburtstag*. Uppsala: Das neutestamentliche Seminar zu Uppsala, 1936. Pp. 22-35.

12:44

1031   J. Leclercq, "*Scopis mundatam* (Matth. 12,44; Lc. 11,25): Le balai dans la Bible et dans la Liturgie d'après la tradition latine," in J. Fontaine and C. Kannengiesser, eds., *Epektasis. Mélanges patristiques* (festschrift for Cardinal Jean Daniélou). Paris: Beauchesne, 1972. Pp. 129-37.

12:46-50

1032   Roger Mercurio, "Some Difficult Marian Passages in the Gospels," *MarSt* 11 (1960): 104-22.

13-28

1033   F. D. Bruner, *Matthew: A Commentary:*. Vol. 2. *The Churchbook: Matthew 13-28*. Dallas: Word, 1990.

13-19

1034   André Feuillet, "Dans le sillage de Vatican II. Reflexions sur quelques versets de Jn. 6 (vv. 14-15 et 67-69) et sur le realisme historique du Quatrime vangile," *Div* 30/1 (1986): 3-52.

13:1-37

1035   Hugo Lattanzi, "Eschatologici Sermonis Domini Logica Interpretatio," *Div* 11/1 (1967): 71-92.

13:1-23

1036   J. Jeremias, "Palästinakundliches zum Gleichnis vom Säemann (Mark 4:3-8 Par.)," *NTS* 13 (1966): 48-53.

1037   Jacques Dupont, "Le semeur est sorti pour semer (Mt. 13)," *AsSeign* 46 (1974): 18-27.

1038   David Wenham, "The Interpretation of the Parable of the Sower," *NTS* 20 (1974): 299-319.

1039   Harvey H. Potthoff, "Homiletical Resources: The Sermon as Theological Event Interpretations of Parables," *QR* 4/2 (1984): 76-102.

1040   J. G. du Plessis, "Pragmatic Meaning in Matthew 13:1-23," *Neo* 21 (1987): 33-56.

1041   P. Mark Achtemeier, "Matthew 13:1-23," *Int* 44/1 (1990): 61-65.

13:1-3
1042   Barclay M. Newman, "To Teach or Not to Teach (A Comment on Matthew 13.1-3)," *BT* 34/1 (1983): 139-43.

13:3-23
1043   Gilbert Silverman and William B. Oglesby, Jr., "The New Birth Phenomenon during Imprisonment: Corrective Emotional Experience or Flight into Health?" *PPsy* 31/3 (1983): 179-83.

13:3-9
1044   L. Ramaroson, " 'Parole-semence' ou 'peuple-semence' dana la Parabole du Semeur?" *ScE* 40 (1988): 91-101.

1045   M. Laconi, "Il discorso delle parabole," in *Il Messaggio della salvezza*. 5 vols. Torino: Leumann, 1966-1970. 4:393-402.

13:4-7
1046   José O'Callaghan, "Dos variantes en la parábola del sembrador," *EB* 48 (1990): 267-70.

13:4
1047   José O'Callaghan, "Reflexions critiques sobre Mt. 9,20 i 13,4," *RCT* 10 (1985): 319-22.

13:5-6
1048   J. Horman, "The Source of the Version of the Parable of the Sower in the Gospel of Thomas," *NovT* 21/4 (1979): 326-43.

13:7

1049   José O'Callaghan, "La Variante 'Ahogaron' en Mt. 13,7," *Bib* 68/3 (1987): 402-403.

13:8

1050   J. Bernardi, "Cent, soixante et trente," *RB* 36 (1991): 398-402.

13:11

1051   Lucien Cerfaux, "La connaissance des secrets du Royaume d'après Matt. xiii. 11 et par.," *NTS* 2 (1955-1956): 238-49.

13:12

1052   G. Linkeskog, "Logia-Studien," *ScanJT* 4 (1951-1952): 129-89.

13:13-15

1053   Dan O. Via, "Matthew on the Understandability of the Parables," *JBL* 84 (1965): 430-32.

13:15

1054   David S. New, "The Occurrence of Auton in Matthew 13:15 and the Process of Text Assimilation," *NTS* 37 (1991): 478-80.

13:20-23

1055   W. Link, "Die Geheimnisse des Himmelreichs," *EvT* 2 (1935): 115-27.

13:21a

1056   Jan Joosten, "The Text of Matthew 13:21a and Parallels in the Syriac Tradition," *NTS* 37 (1991): 153-59.

13:24-30

1057   C. E. Carlston, "A Positive Criterion of Authenticity?" *BR* 7 (1962): 33-44.

1058   William G. Doty, "An Interpretation: Parable of the Weeds and Wheat," *Int* 25 (1971): 185-93.

1059   Domenico Ellena, "Thematische Analyse der Wachstumsgleichnisse," *LB* 23 (1973): 48-62.

1060   David R. Catchpole, "John the Baptist, Jesus and the Parable of the Tares," *SJT* 31/6 (1978): 557-71.

1061   Gilbert Silverman and William B. Oglesby, Jr., ''The New Birth Phenomenon during Imprisonment: Corrective Emotional Experience or Flight into Health?'' *PPsy* 31/3 (1983): 179-83.

13:24
1062   Harvey H. Potthoff, ''Homiletical Resources: The Sermon as Theological Event Interpretations of Parables,'' *QR* 4/2 (1984): 76-102.

13:31-32
1063   O. Kuss, ''Zur Senfkornparabel,'' *TGl* 41 (1951): 40-49.

1064   B. Schultze, ''Die ekklesioklogische Bedeutung des Gleichnisses vom Senfkorn,'' *OCP* 27 (1961): 362-86.

1065   H. K. McArthur, ''The Parable of the Mustard Seed,'' *CBQ* 33/2 (1971): 198-210.

1066   John A. Sproule, ''The Problem of the Mustard Seed,'' *GTJ* 1/1 (1980): 37-42.

13:32
1067   W. Harold Mare, ''The Smallest Mustard Seed: Matthew 13:32,'' *GTJ* 9 (1968): 3-9.

13:33
1068   R. W. Funk, ''Beyond Criticism in Quest of Literacy: The Parable of the Leaven,'' *Int* 25 (1971): 149-70.

1069   Domenico Ellena, ''Thematische Analyse der Wachstumsgleichnisse,'' *LB* 23 (1973): 48-62.

1070   Elizabeth Waller, ''The Parable of the Leaven: A Sectarian Teaching and the Inclusion of Women,'' *USQR* 35 (1980): 99-109.

1071   J. M. Bassler, ''The Parable of the Loaves,'' *JR* 66 (1986): 157-72.

13:35
1072   S. del Paramo, ''El fin de las parabolas de Cristo y el Salmo 77,'' in *Valoración sobrenatural del ''cosmos'': La*

inspiración bíblica. Madrid: Científica Medinaceli, 1954. Pp. 341-64.

13:39

1073   Raymond E. Gingrich, "Adumbrations of Our Lord's Return: Political Alignments," *GTJ* 9/1 (1968): 3-14.

13:44-52

1074   Delmar Jacobson, "An Exposition of Matthew 13:44-52," *Int* 29/3 (1975): 277-82.

1075   Harvey H. Potthoff, "Homiletical Resources: The Sermon as Theological Event Interpretations of Parables," *QR* 4/2 (1984): 76-102.

13:44-46

1076   Charles W. Hedrick, "The Treasure Parable in Matthew and Thomas," *Forum* 2/2 (1986): 41-56.

1077   Jeffrey A. Gibbs, "Parables of Atonement and Assurance: Matthew 13:44-46," *CTQ* 51/1 (1987): 19-40.

1078   Norbert Lohfink, "Die Not der Exegese mit der Reich-Gottes-Verkündigung Jesu," *TTQ* 168/11 (1988): 1-15.

1079   Paul W. Meyer, "Context as a Bearer of Meaning in Matthew," *USQR* 42/1 (1988): 69-72.

13:44

1080   J. D. M. Derrett, "Law in the New Testament: The Treasure in the Field," *ZNW* 54 (1963): 31-42.

1081   Walter Magass, " 'Der Schatz im Acker' (Mt. 13, 44): Von der Kirche als einem Tauschphanomen-Paradigmatik und Transformation," *LB* 21 (1973): 2-18.

1082   John W. Sider, "Interpreting the Hidden Treasure," *CSR* 13/4 (1984): 360-72.

1083   George Howard, "A Note on Codex Sinaiticus and Shem-Tob's Hebrew Matthew," *NTS* 38 (1992): 187-204.

<u>13:47-50</u>
1084   Domenico Ellena, ''Thematische Analyse der Wachstumsgleichnisse,'' *LB* 23 (1973): 48-62.

1085   W. G. Morrice, ''The Parable of the Dragnet and the Gospel of Thomas,'' *ET* 95/9 (1984): 269-73.

<u>13:47-49</u>
1086   J. D. M. Derrett, ''Esan gar Halieis (Mark 1:16). Jesus' Fisherman and the Parable of the Net,'' *NovT* 22/2 (1980): 108-37.

<u>13:52</u>
1087   J. Becker, ''Erwagungen zu Fragen der Neutestamentlichen Exegese,'' *BZ* 13/1 (1969): 99-102.

1088   Dieter Zeller, ''Zu Einer Judischen Vorlage von Mt. 13, 52,'' *BZ* 20/2 (1976): 223-26.

<u>13:53-18:35</u>
1089   David W. Gooding, ''Structure littéraire de Matthieu 13:53 à 18:35,'' *RB* 85 (1978): 227-52.

<u>13:53</u>
1090   David Hellholm, ''En textgrammatisk konstruktion I Matteusevangeliet,'' *SEÅ* 51 (1986-1987): 80-89.

<u>13:55</u>
1091   George W. Buchanan, ''Jesus and the Upper Class,'' *NovT* 7/3 (1965): 195-206.

<u>14:1-2</u>
1092   Philippe Rolland, ''La question synoptique demande-t-elle une response compliquee?'' *Bib* 70/2 (1989): 217-23.

<u>14:3-12</u>
1093   John P. Meier, ''John the Baptist in Matthew's Gospel,'' *JBL* 99 (1980): 383-405.

<u>14:3</u>
1094   Lamar Cope, ''The Death of John the Baptist in the Gospel of Matthew; or, the Case of the Confusing Conjunction,'' *CBQ* 38/4 (1976): 515-19.

14:6

1095   José O'Callaghan, "Sobre tres variants de Mt. 14,6.15.18," *RCT* 11 (1986): 27-30.

14:13-21

1096   J. A. Grassi, *Loaves and Fishes: The Gospel Feeding Narratives*. Collegeville: Liturgical Press, 1991.

14:13-14

1097   F. Neirynck, "The Matthew-Luke Agreements in Matt. 14:13-14 and Lk. 9:10-11 (par. Mk. 6:30-34): The Two-Source Theory behind the Impasse," *ETL* 60/1 (1984): 25-44.

14:15

1098   José O'Callaghan, "Sobre tres variants de Mt. 14,6.15.18," *RCT* 11 (1986): 27-30.

14:16

1099   Jerome Murphy-O'Connor, "The Structure of Matthew XIV-XVII." *RB* 82/3 (1975): 360-84.

1100   J. A. Grassi, " 'You Yourselves Give Them to Eat': An Easily Forgotten Command of Jesus," *BibTo* 97 (1978): 1704-09.

14:18

1101   José O'Callaghan, "Sobre tres variants de Mt. 14,6.15.18," *RCT* 11 (1986): 27-30.

14:22-24

1102   Edward J. Kilmartin, "A First Century Chalice Dispute," *SE* 12 (1960): 403-408.

14:22-33

1103   Charles R. Carlisle, "Jesus' Walking on the Water: A Note on Matthew 14.22-33," *NTS* 31/1 (1985): 151-55.

1104   R. Strunk, "In der Nachfolge des königlichen Menschen: Die Gemeinde des Vertrauens," *ZDT* 2 (1986): 204-18.

1105   David Hill, "The Walking on the Water: A Geographic or Linguistic Answer?" *ET* 99 (1988): 267-69.

<u>14:23</u>

1106   D. Durken, "Mountains and Matthew," *BibTo* 28 (1990): 304-307.

<u>14:28-33</u>

1107   J. D. M. Derrett, "Der Wasserwandel in christilicher und buddhistischer Perspektive," *ZRGG* 41/3 (1989): 193-214.

<u>14:28-31</u>

1108   E. Lövestam, "Wunder und Symbolhandlung: Eine Studie über Matthaus 14:28-31," *KD* 8 (1962): 124-35.

<u>14:28</u>

1109   Ralph Stehley, "Boudhisme et Nouveau Testament: Apropos de la Marche de Pierre sur l'Eau," *RHPR* 57/4 (1977): 433-37.

<u>15:1-20</u>

1110   S. Clive Thexton, "Jesus' Use of the Scriptures," *LQHR* 179 (1954): 102-108.

1111   Gregory Murray, "What Defiles a Man?" *DR* 106 (1988): 297-98.

<u>15:4-6</u>

1112   J. D. M. Derrett, "KORBAN, HO ESTIN ŌRON," *NTS* 16/4 (1970): 364-68.

<u>15:5</u>

1113   Joseph A. Fitzmyer, "The Aramaic Qorbān Inscription from Jebel Hallet el-Ṭûri and Mark 7:11/Matt. 15:5," *JBL* 78 (1959): 60-65.

1114   Z. W. Falk, "On Talmudic Vows," *HTR* 59 (1966): 309-12.

1115   Albert I. Baumgarten, "Korban and the Pharisaic Paradosis," *JNES* 16-17 (1984-1985): 5-17.

<u>15:6</u>

1116   José O'Callaghan, "La variante 'palabra' o 'precepto' en Mt. 15,6," *EE* 61 (1986) 421-23.

15:13-26
>
> **1117**   Howard Horton, "The Gates of Hades Shall Not Prevail Against It," *RQ* 5 (1961): 1-5.

15:17
>
> **1118**   C. Jaeger, "Remarques philologiques sur quelques passages des Synoptiques," *RHPR* 16 (1936): 246-49.

15:21-28
>
> **1119**   J. I. Hasler, "The Incident of the Syro-Phoenician Woman (Mt. 15,21-28, Mk. 7,14-30)," *ET* 45 (1933-1934): 459-61.
>
> **1120**   P. D. Hamilton, "The Syro-Phoenician Woman: Another Suggestion," *ET* 46 (1934-1935): 477-78.
>
> **1121**   C. E. Garritt, "The Syro-Phoenician Woman," *ET* 47 (1935-1936): 43.
>
> **1122**   J. D. Smart, "Jesus, the Syro-Phoenician Woman and the Disciples," *ET* 50 (1938-1939): 469-72.
>
> **1123**   Roy A. Harrisville, "The Woman of Canaan. A Chapter in the History of Exegesis," *Int* 20 (1966): 274-87.
>
> **1124**   P. E. Scherer, "A Gauntlet with a Gift in It. From Text to Sermon on Matthew 15:21-28 and Mark 7:24-30," *Int* 20 (1966): 387-99.
>
> **1125**   W. Storch, "Zur Perikope von der Syrophonizierin," *BZ* 14/2 (1970): 256-57.
>
> **1126**   T. Lovison, "La pericopa della Cananea Mt. 15,21-28," *RBib* 19 (1971): 273-305.
>
> **1127**   K. Gatzweiler, "Un pas vers l'universalisme: la Cananéenne (Mt. 15)," *AsSeign* 51 (1972): 15-24.
>
> **1128**   S. Légasse, "L'épisode de la Cananéenne d'après Mt. 15,21-28," *BLE* 73 (1972): 21-40.
>
> **1129**   Scott L. Tatum, "Great Prayers of the Bible," *SouJT* 14 (1972): 29-42.

1130   J. D. M. Derrett, "Law in the New Testament: The
             Syro-Phoenician Woman and the Centurion of Capernaum,"
             NovT 15 (1973): 161-86.

1131   Mark C. Thompson, "Matthew 15:21-28," *Int* 35/3 (1981):
             279-84.

1132   Alice Dermience, "La pericope de la Cananeenne (Matt.
             15:21-28): redaction et theologie," *ETL* 58/1 (1982): 25-49.

1133   C. Fullkrug-Weitzel, "Die kanaanäische Frau und die
             Verheissung Israels, Mt. 15,21-28," *TexteK* 31/32 (1986):
             40-60.

1134   John P. Meier, "Matthew 15:21-28," *Int* 40 (1986):
             397-402.

1135   C. M. Martini, *Women in the Gospels*. New York:
             Crossroad, 1990.

15:22
1136   G. Schwarz, "Syrophoinikissa - Cananaia," *NTS* 30/4
             (1984): 626-28.

15:24
1137   Warren Vanhetloo, "The Incarnate Shepherd," *CBTJ* 1/1
             (1985): 20-34.

15:29-31
1138   Thomas J. Ryan, "Matthew 15:29-31: An Overlooked
             Summary," *Horizons* 5/1 (1978): 31-42.

1139   R. F. Collins, "Jesus' Ministry to the Deaf and Dumb,"
             MeliT 35/1 (1984): 12-36.

15:29
1140   D. Durken, "Mountains and Matthew," *BibTo* 28 (1990):
             304-307.

15:32-39
1141   J. Knackstedt, "Die beiden Brotvermehrungen im
             Evangelium," *NTS* 10 (1963-1964): 309-35.

15:33-41
1142

W. Trilling, "Der Tod Jesu, Ende der alten Weltzeit (Mk. 15,33-1)," in *Christusverkündigung in den synoptischen Evangelien*. Munich: Kösel, 1969. Pp. 191-211.

15:35-36a
1143

José O'Callaghan, "Consideraciones críticas sobre Mt. 15,35-36a," *Bib* 67 (1986): 360-62.

16:1-20
1144

L. Perrin, "Interpréter, c'est recevoir un 'plus': la révélation et la filiation. Une lecture de Mt. 16,1-20," *SémBib* 55 (1989): 19-28.

16:1-19
1145

B. Willaert, "La connexion litteraire entre la premiere prediction de la passion et la confession de Pierre chez les synoptiques," *ETL* 32 (1956): 24-45.

16:1-8
1146

Nikolaus Walter, "Eine Vormatthaische Schilderung derr Auferstehung Jesus," *NTS* 19/4 (1973): 415-29.

16:1-4
1147

A. K. M. Adam, "The Sign of Jonah: A Fish-Eye View," *Semeia* 51 (1990): 177-91.

1148

X. Quinzá Lleó, "La reflexión bíblica sobre los signos de los tiempos," *EB* 48 (1990): 317-34.

16:4
1149

R. A. Edwards, *The Sign of Jonah in the Theology of the Evangelists and Q*. London: SCM, 1971.

16:7-19
1150

A. Legault, "L'authenticité de Mt. 16,17-19 et le silence de Marc et de Luc," in *L'Église dans la Bible*. Bruges: Desclée de Brouwer, 1962. Pp. 35-52.

16:13-18:35
1151

Larry A. Vigen, "To Think the Things of God: A Discoursive Reading of Matthew 16:13-18:35," doctoral dissertation, Vanderbilt University, Nashville TN, 1985.

16:13-17:23
1152

Oscar H. Hirt, "Interpretation in the Gospels: An Examination of the Use of Redaction Criticism in Mark 8:27-9:32," doctoral dissertation, Dallas Theological Seminary, Dallas TX, 1985.

16:13-23
1153

A. Vögtle, "Messiasbekenntnis und Petrusverheissung. Zur Komposition Mt. 16,13-23 par.," *BZ* 1 (1957): 252-72; 2 (1958): 85-103.

1154

William J. Tobin, "The Petrine Primacy Evidence of the Gospels," *LV* 23/1 (1968): 27-70.

1155

André Feuillet, "Chercher à prsuader Dieu," *NovT* 12 (1970): 350-60.

1156

H. Thyen, "Das Petrus bekenntnis von Caesarea-Philippi. Mk. 8,27-9,1 parr.," in *Studie zur Sündenvergebung im Neuen Testament und seinen alttestamentlichen und jüdischen Voraussetzungen*. Göttingen: Vandenhoeck & Ruprecht, 1970. Pp. 218-36.

1157

Edgar V. McKnight and Charles H. Talbert, "Can the Griesbach Hypothesis Be Falsified?" *JBL* 91/3 (1972): 338-68.

1158

Bruce T. Dahlberg, "The Topological Use of Jeremiah 1:4-19 in Matthew 16:13-23," *JBL* 94/1 (1975): 73-80.

1159

Jean Galot, "La première profession de foi chrétienne," *EV* 97 (1987): 593-99.

16:13-20
1160

M. S. Enslin, "The Date of Peter's Confession," in R. P. Casey, et al. *Quantulacumque* (festschrift for Kirsopp Lake). London: Christophers, 1937. Pp. 117-22.

1161

W. Marxsen, "Der Fels der Kirche, Bibelarbeit über Matth. 16,13-20," in *Der 'Frühkatholizismus' im Neuen Testament*. Neukirchen: Neukirchener Verlag, 1956. Pp. 39-54.

1162   Frank A. Rice, "A History of Interpretation of Matthew 16:13-20," master's thesis, Golden Gate Baptist Theological Seminary, Mill Valley CA, 1960.

1163   Lyle O. Bristol, "Jesus and Peter at Caesarea Philippi," *Found* 5 (1962): 198-205.

1164   David H. David, "An Exegesis of Matt. 16:13-20," *Found* 5 (1962): 217-25.

1165   Leander E. Keck, "An Exegesis of Matt. 16:13-20," *Found* 5 (1962): 226-37.

1166   Bernard L. Ramm, "The Exegesis of Matt. 16:13-20 in the Patristic and Reformation Period," *Found* 5 (1962): 206-16.

1167   J. Guillet, "La confession de Cesaree," in *Jésus devant sa vie et sa mort.* Paris: Aubier, 1971. Pp. 117-35.

1168   G. Gaide, " 'Tu es le Christ' . . . 'Tu es Pierre' (Mt. 16)," *AsSeign* 52 (1974): 16-26.

1169   Paul S. Berge, "An Exposition of Matthew 16:13-20," *Int* 29/3 (1975): 283-88.

1170   M. J. Suggs, "Matthew 16:13-20," *Int* 39/3 (1985): 291-95.

16:13-19

1171   Tord Forberg, "Peter: The High Priest of the New Covenant?" *EAJT* 4/1 (1986): 113-21.

16:13-16

1172   E. Thurneysen, "Predigt über Matthäus 16,13-16, 21-28," *EvT* 3 (1936): 127-35.

16:13

1173   Simone Frutiger, "Les lectures d'Evangile ou les textes disjoints: Matthieu 16:13 à 25:46," *FV* 82 (1983): 59-75.

16:14

1174   J. Carmignac, "Pourquoi Jérémie est-il mentionné en Matthieu 16,14?" in G. Jeremias, et al., eds., *Tradition und Glaube: Das frühe Christentum in seiner Unwelt* (festschrift for Karl Georg Kuhn). Göttingen: Vandenhoeck & Ruprecht, 1971. Pp. 283-98.

1175　　　M. J. J. Menken, "The References of Jeremiah in the Gospel According to Matthew (Mt. 2,17; 16,14; 27,9)," *ETL* 60/1 (1984): 5-24.

1176　　　Benjamin G. Wright, III, "A Previously Unnoticed Greek Variant of Matt. 16:14: 'Some Say John the Baptist . . .'," *JBL* 105 (1986): 694-97.

16:15
1177　　　Pierre Ganne, "La Personne du Christ: 'Qui Dites-Vous que je Suis?'," *NRT* 104/1 (1982): 3-21.

16:16-19
1178　　　J. Hadzega, "Mt. 16,16-19 in der neueren Literatur des Orthodoxen," *TGl* 26 (1934): 458-64.

1179　　　Oscar Cullmann, "L'apôtre Pierre instrument du diable et instrument de Dieu: la place de Matt. 16:16-19 dans la tradition primitive," in A. J. B. Higgins, ed., *New Testament Essays* (festschrift for T. W. Manson). Manchester: Manchester University Press, 1959. Pp. 94-105.

1180　　　Julius R. Mantey, "What of Priestly Absolution," *CT* 13/9 (1969): 233-391.

1181　　　Jan Lambrecht, " 'Du bist Petrus': Mt. 16,16-19 und das Papsttum," *SNTU/A* 11 (1986): 5-32.

16:16-18
1182　　　J. K. Elliott, "Kēphas: Simōn Petros, o Petros: An Examination of New Testament Usage," *NovT* 14 (1972): 241-56.

16:16-17
1183　　　Jean Doignon, "Pierre 'Fondement de l'Eglise et Foi de la Confession de Pierre 'Base de l'Eglise' chez Hilaire de Poitiers," *RSPT* 66/3 (1982): 417-25.

1184　　　François Refoulé, "Le parallèle Matthieu 16/16-17—Galates 1/15-16 réxaminé," *ÉTR* 67/2 (1992): 161-75.

16:16

1185   Charles Boyer, "Apropos of a Statement by Karl Barth," *Unitas* 12 (1960): 223-26.

16:17-19

1186   H. Hirschberg, "Simon Bariona and the Ebionites," *JBL* 61 (1942): 171-91.

1187   R. Marcus, "A Note on *Bariona*," *JBL* 61 (1942): 281.

1188   A. Oepke, "Der Herrnspruch über die Kirche Mt. 16,17-19 in der Neuesten Forschung," *ScanJT* 2 (1948): 110-65.

1189   O. J. F. Seitz, "Upon This Rock: A Critical Re-examination of Matt. 16,17-19," *JBL* 69 (1950): 329-40.

1190   E. L. Allen, "On This Rock," *JTS* 5 (1954): 59-62.

1191   Otto Betz, "Felsenmann und Felsengemeinde," *ZNW* 48 (1957): 49-77.

1192   Dan O. Via, "Jesus and His Church in Matthew 16:17-19," *RevExp* 55 (1958): 22-39.

1193   Veselin Kesich, "The Problem of Peter's Primacy," *SVTQ* 4/2 (1961): 2-25.

1194   Peter Milward, "Prophetic Perspective and the Primacy of Peter," *AmER* 144 (1961): 122-29.

1195   Robert H. Gundry, "The Narrative Framework of Matthew 16:17-19," *NovT* 7/1 (1964): 1-9.

1196   M. Garcia Cordero, "Conceptión jerárquica de la Iglesia en el Nuevo Testamento," *Sale* 18 (1971): 233-87.

1197   A. Vögtle, "Zum Problem der Herkunft von Mt. 16,17-19," in *Orientierung an Jesus: Zur Theolohie der Synoptiker* (festschrift for Josef Schmid). Freiburg: Herder, 1973. Pp. 372-93.

1198   Max Wilcox, "Peter and the Rock: A Fresh Look at Matthew 16:17-19," *NTS* 22/1 (1975): 73-88.

1199   Christoph Kahler, "Zur From- und Traditionsgeschichte von Matth. 16:17-19," *NTS* 23/1 (1976): 36-58.

1200   Ian S. Kemp, "The Blessing, Power and Authority of the Church: A Study in Matthew 16:17-19," *ERT* 6/1 (1982): 9-22.

1201   Bernard P. Robinson, "Peter and His Successors: Tradition and Redaction in Matthew 16:17-19," *JSNT* 21 (1984): 85-104.

1202   J. Gnilka, " 'Tu es, Petrus'. Die Petrus-Verhei;ssung in Mt. 16,17-19," *MTZ* 38 (1987): 3-17.

1203   André Feuillet, "La primauté et l'humilité de Pierre. Leur attestation en Mt. 16,17-19, dans l'Evangile de Marc et dans le Première Epître de Pierre," *NovVet* 66/1 (1990): 3-24.

1204   Ulrich Luz, "Das Primatwort Matthaus 16:17-19 aus wirkungsgeschichtlicher Sicht," *NTS* 37 (1991): 415-33.

1205   C. Grappe, "Mt. 16,17-19 et le récit de la Passion," *RHPR* 72 (1992): 33-40.

16:17
1206   H. Lehman, "Du bist Petrus," *EvT* 13 (1953): 44-66.

16:18-20
1207   V. Burch, "The 'Stone' and the 'Keys' (Mt. 16,18ff.)," *JBL* 52 (1933): 147-52,

16:18-19
1208   F. Obrist, *Echtheitsfragen und Deutung der Primatsstelle Mt. 16,18f. in der deutschen protestantischen Theologie der letzten dreissig Jahre*. Münster: Aschendorff, 1961.

1209   K. L. Carroll, "Thou Art Peter," *NovT* 6 (1963-1964): 268-76.

1210   O. Da Spinetoli, "La Portata Ecclesiologica Di Mt. 16,18-19," *Ant* 42/3 (1967): 357-75.

1211   J. Schmid, "Petrus der Fels und die Petrusgestalt der Urgemeinde," in *Evangelienforschung: Ausgewählte Aufsätze deutscher Exegeten.* Graz: Styria, 1968. Pp. 159-75.

1212   J. Kahmann, "Die Verheissung an Petrus: Mt. 16:18-19 im Zusammenhang des Matthäusevangeliums," in *L'Évangile selon Matthieu.* Gembloux: Duculot, 1972. Pp. 261-80.

1213   Julius R. Mantey, "Distorted Translations in John 20:23; Matthew 16:18-19 and 18:18," *RevExp* 78/3 (1981): 409-16.

1214   B. T. Viviano, "Matthew, Master of Ecumenical Infighting," *CThM* 10/6 (1983): 325-32.

1215   Joel Marcus, "The Gates of Hades and the Keys of the Kingdom," *CBQ* 50/3 (1988): 443-55.

16:18

1216   Ferdinand Kattenbusch, "Die Vorzugstellung des Petrus und der Charakter der Urgemeinde zu Jerusalem," in *Festgabe von Fachgenossen und Freunden Karl Müller zum siebzigsten Geburtstag dargebracht.* Tübingen: Mohr, 1922. Pp. 322-51.

1217   J. E. L. Oulton, "An Interpretation of Matthew 16,18," *ET* 48 (1936-1937): 525-26.

1218   Henry Clavier, "*Petros kai petra,*" in *Neutestamentliche Studien für Rudolf Bultmann.* Berlin: Töpelmann, 1957. Pp. 94-109.

1219   B. M. Metzger, "The New Testament View of the Church," *TT* 19 (1962): 369-80.

1220   George Howard, "The Meaning of Petros-Petra," *RQ* 10/4 (1967): 217-21.

1221   Luther L. Grubb, "The Church Reaching Tomorrow's World," *GTJ* 12/3 (1971): 13-22.

1222   P. Glorieux, "Deux Eloges de la Sainte par Pierre d'Ailly," *MSR* 29/3 (1972): 113-29.

1223   J. W. Roberts, "The Meaning of Ekklesia in the New Testament," *RQ* 15/1 (1972): 27-36.

1224   D. Broughton Knox, "De-Mythologising the Church," *RTR* 32/2 (1973): 48-55.

1225   Peter Lampe, "Das Spiel mit dem Petrusnamen-Matt. xvi.18," *NTS* 25/2 (1979): 221-27.

1226   Carol Buzzetti, " 'You Are a Rock, Peter. . .' in Italy," *BT* 34/3 (1983): 308-11.

1227   Colin Brown, "The Gates of Hell: An Alternative Approach," *SBLSP* 26 (1987): 357-67.

1228   Augustine Stock, "Is Matthew's Presentation of Peter Ironic?" *BTB* 17/2 (1987): 64-69.

1229   J. D. M. Derrett, " 'Thou Art the Stone, and upon This Stone'," *DR* 106 (1988): 276-85.

1230   Raimund Lülsdorff, "Vom Stein zum Felsen: Anmerkungen zur biblischen Begruendung des Petrusamtes nach Mt. 16:18," *Cath* 44/4 (1990): 274-83.

1231   Ulrich Luz, "The Primacy Text (Mt. 16:18)," *PSB* 12/1 (1991): 41-55.

16:18b

1232   Robert Eppel, "L'interprétation de Matthieu 16.18b," in *Aux sources de la tradition chrétienne*. Paris: Delachaux & Niestlé, 1950. Pp. 71-73.

1233   Pierre Grelot, " 'Sur cette pierre je bâtirai mon Église' (Mt. 16,18b)," *NRT* 109/5 (1987): 641-59.

16:19

1234   H. J. Cadbury, "The Meaning of John 20,23, Matthew 16,19, and Matthew 18,18," *JBL* 58 (1939): 251-54.

1235   Julius R. Mantey, "The Mistranslation of the Perfect Tense in John 20,23, Mt. 16,19, and Mt. 18,18," *JBL* 58 (1939): 243-49.

1236   Julius Gross, "Die Schluesselgewalt nach Haimo von Auxerre," *ZRGG* 9 (1957): 30-41.

1237   S. V. McCasland, "Matthew Twists the Scriptures," *JBL* 80 (1961): 143-48.

1238   J. A. Emerton, "Binding and Loosing: Forgiving and Retaining," *JTS* 15 (1962): 325-31.

1239   Julius R. Mantey, "Evidence that the Perfect Tense in John 20:23 and Matthew 16:19 Is Mistranslated," *JETS* 16/3 (1973): 129-38.

1240   Paul Elbert, "The Perfect Tense in Matthew 16:19 and Three Charismata," *JETS* 17/3 (1974): 149-55.

1241   J. D. M. Derrett, "Binding and Loosing (Matt. 16:19; Matt. 18:18; John 20:23)," *JBL* 102 (1983): 112-17.

1242   Herbert W. Basser, "Derrett's 'Binding' Reopened," *JBL* 104 (1985): 297-300.

1243   Richard A. Hiers, " 'Binding' and 'Loosing': The Matthean Authorizations," *JBL* 104/2 (1985): 233-50.

1244   Dennis C. Duling, "Binding and Loosing: Matthew 16:19; Matthew 18:18; John 20:23," *Forum* 3 (1987): 3-31.

1245   G. Korting, "Binden oder lösen: Zun Verstockungs- und Befreiungstheologie in Mt. 16,19; 18:18-21:35 und Joh 15,1-17; 2,23," *SNTU-A* 14 (1989): 39-91.

1246   Kair A. Syreeni, "Between Heaven and Earth: On the Structure of Matthew's Symbolic Universe," *JSNT* 40 (1990): 9-13.

16:20

1247   Herbert W. Basser, "Marcus's 'Gates': A Response," *CBQ* 52 (1990): 307-308.

16:21-28

1248   E. Thurneysen, "Predigt über Matthäus 16,13-16, 21-28," *EvT* 3 (1936): 127-35.

16:21-27

1249   James M. Efird, "Matthew 16:21-27," *Int* 35/3 (1981): 284-89.

16:21-23

1250   B. Willaert, "La connexion litteraire entre la premiere prediction de la passion et la confession de Pierre chez les synoptiques," *ETL* 32 (1956): 24-45.

16:22

1251   Henry Clavier, "Notes sur un Motclef du Johannisme et de la Soteriologie Biblique: Hilasmos," *NovT* 10/4 (1968): 287-304.

16:26

1252   José O'Callaghan, "Nota Critica a Mc 8,36," *Bib* 64/1 (1983): 116-17.

17:1-13

1253   Sigfred Pedersen, "Die Proklamation Jesu als des Eschatologischen Offenbarungstragers," *NovT* 17/4 (1975): 241-64.

1254   Barbara E. Reid, "The Transfiguration: An Exegetical Study of Luke 9:28-36," doctoral dissertation, Catholic University of America, Washington DC, 1988.

17:1-9

1255   Heinrich Baltensweiler, *Die Verklärung Jesu: Historisches Ereignis und synoptische Berichte*. Zürich: Zwingli, 1959.

1256   F. Neirynck, "Minor Agreements: Matthew-Luke in the Transfiguration Story," in *Orientierung an Jesus: Zur Theologie der Synoptiker* (festschrift for Josef Schmid). Freiburg: Herder, 1973. Pp. 253-66.

1257   A. C. Winn, "Worship as a Healing Experience: An Exposition of Matthew 17:1-9," *Int* 29/1 (1975): 68-72.

17:1

1258   D. Durken, "Mountains and Matthew," *BibTo* 28 (1990): 304-307.

17:4

1259   José O'Callaghan, "Discusion Critica en Mt. 17,4," *Bib* 65/1 (1984): 91-93.

17:7

1260   José O'Callaghan, "Mt. 17,7: Revision Critica," *Bib* 66/3 (1985): 422-23.

17:10-13

1261   John P. Meier, "John the Baptist in Matthew's Gospel," *JBL* 99 (1980): 383-405.

17:11

1262   W. C. Kaiser, "The Promise of the Arrival of Elijah in Malachi and the Gospels," *GTJ* 3/2 (1982): 221-33.

17:17

1263   C. Jaeger, "Remarques philologiques sur quelques passages des Synoptiques," *RHPR* 16 (1936): 246-49.

17:20

1264   R. Merkelbach and D. Hagedorn, "Ein Neues Fragment aus Porphyrios 'Gegen die Christen'," *VC* 20/2 (1966): 86-90.

17:22

1265   J. Vara, "Dos conjeturas textuales sobre Mateo 25,21.23 y Mateo 26,32/17,22 y par.," *Salm* 33 (1986): 81-86.

17:24-27

1266   J. D. M. Derrett, "Peter's Penny: Fresh Light on Matthew 17:24-27," *NovT* 6/1 (1963): 1-15.

1267   Hugh Montefiore, "Jesus and the Temple Tax," *NTS* 11/1 (1964): 60-71.

1268   S. Légasse, "Jésus et l'impôt du Temple (Matthieu 17, 24-27)," *SE* 24 (1972): 361-77.

1269   N. J. McEleney, "Mt. 17:24-27: Who Paid the Temple Tax?" *CBQ* 38/2 (1976): 178-92.

1270   Richard J. Cassidy, "Matthew 17:24-27: A Word on Civil Taxes," *CBQ* 41/4 (1979): 571-80.

1271   David E. Garland, "Matthew's Understanding of the Temple Tax (Matt. 17:24-27)," *SBLSP* 26 (1987): 190-209.

1272   A. G. van Aarde, "Resonance and Reception: Interpreting Mt. 17:24-27 in Context," *ScrSA* 29 (1989): 1-12.

17:25

1273   José O'Callaghan, "Discusion Critica en Mt. 17:25," *FilN* 3 (1990): 151-53.

17:26

1274   Tjitze Baarda, "Geven als vreemdeling over de herkomst van een merkwaardige variant van ms 713 in Mattheus 17:26," *NedTT* 42 (1988): 99-113.

17:27

1275   H. A. Homeau, "On Fishing for Staters: Matthew 17:27," *ET* 85/11 (1974): 340-42.

1276   Günther Schwarz, "ΑΝΟΙΞΑΣ ΤΟ ΣΤΟΜΑ ΑΥΤΟΥ (Matthäus 17.27)," *NTS* 38 (1992): 138-41.

18-25

1277   Jose M. Casciaro Ramirez, "La encarnacion del verbo y la corporeidad humana," *ScripT* 18/3 (1986): 751-70.

18-23

1278   Daniel Patte, "Bringing Out of the Gospel-Treasure: What Is New and What Is Old: Two Parables in Matthew 18-23," *QR* 10 (1990): 79-108.

18:1-6

1279   David Wenham, "A Note on Mark 9:33-42/Matt. 18:1-6/Luke 9:46-50," *JSNT* 14 (1982): 113-18.

18:1-5

1280   S. Légasse, "Le debat sur 'le plus grand': Marc, ix.33-37 et paralleles," in *Jésus et l'enfant: 'Enfants', 'Petis' et 'simples' dans la tradition synoptique*. Paris: Gabalda, 1969. Pp. 17-36.

1281 Daniel Patte, "Jesus' Pronouncement about Entering the Kingdom Like a Child: A Structural Exegesis," *Semeia* 29 (1983): 3-42.

18:3

1282 Jacques Dupont, "Matthieu 18:3: ἐὰν μὴ στραφν˜τε καὶ γένησθε ὡς τὰ παιδία," in E. E. Ellis and M. Wilcox, eds., *Neotestamentica et Semitica* (festschrift for Matthew Black). London: T. &. T. Clark, 1969. Pp. 50-60.

1283 Daniel Patte, "Entering the Kingdom Like Children: A Structural Exegesis," *SBLSP* 21 (1982): 371-96.

1284 Vernon K. Robbins, "Pronouncement Stories and Jesus' Blessing of Children," *SBLSP* 21 (1982): 407-30.

1285 T. R. Hobbs, "Crossing Cultural Bridges: The Biblical World," *McMJT* 2 (1990): 1-21.

18:6

1286 J. D. M. Derrett, "Two Harsh Sayings Of Christ Explained," *DR* 103 (1985): 218-29.

18:8-14

1287 H. B. Kossen, "Quelques remarques sur l'ordre des paraboles dans Luc xv et sur la construction de Matthieu xviii.8-14," *NovT* 1 (1956): 75-80.

18:8-9

1288 Herbert W. Basser, "The Meaning of 'Shtuth', Gen. 4.11 in Reference to Matthew 5.29-30 and 18.8-9," *NTS* 31/1 (1985): 148-51.

18:10

1289 Jean Héring, "Un texte oublié: Matthieu 18:10. A propos des controverses recentes sur le pédobaptisme," in *Aux sources de la tradition chrétienne*. Paris: Delachaux & Niestlé, 1950. Pp. 85-102.

18:12-24

1290 Jacques Dupont, "La brebis et la drachme perdue," in *Les Béatitudes*. Tome II: La bonne nouvelle. Paris: Gabalda, 1969. 2:242-49.

18:12-13

1291   Warren Vanhetloo, "Two Ninety and Nines," *CBTJ* 2/1 (1986): 9-22.

18:12

1292   Jacques Dupont, "Les implications christologiques de la parabole de la brebis perdue," in J. DuPont, et al., eds., *Jésus aux origines de la christologie.* Louvain: University Press, 1975. Pp. 331-50.

18:14

1293   Savas Agourides, " 'Little Ones' in Matthew," *BT* 35/3 (1984): 329-34.

18:15-20

1294   C. J. A. Hickling, "Conflicting Motives in the Redaction of Matthew: Some Considerations on the Sermon on the Mount and Matthew 18:15-20," in E. A. Livingstone, ed., *Studia Evangelica VII*: Papers Presented to the Fifth International Congress on New Testament Studies, Oxford, 1973. Sheffield: JSOT Press, 1982. Pp. 247-60.

18:15-18

1295   Victor C. Pfitzner, "Purified Community-Purified Sinner: Explusion from the Communion According to Matthew 18:15-18 and 1 Corinthians 5:1-5," *ABR* 30 (1982): 34-55.

18:15-17

1296   G. Bornkamm, "Die Binde- und Lösegewalt in der Kirche des Matthaus," in *Geschichte und Glaube*: Band III. Munich: Kaiser, 1968; Band IV. Munich: Kaiser, 1971. 2:37-50.

1297   Jean Runzo, "Hutterite Communal Discipline, 1529-1565," *ARefG* 71 (1980): 160-79.

1298   Ghislain Lafont, "Fraternal Correction in the Augustinian Community: A Confrontation between the Praeceptum, IV, 6-9 and Matthew 18:15-17," *WS* 9 (1987): 87-91.

1299   David L. Burggraff, "Principles of Discipline in Matthew 18:15-17. Part I: A Contextual Study," *CBTJ* 4/2 (1988): 1-23.

1300   David L. Burggraff, "Principles of Discipline in Matthew 18:15-17. Part II: An Exegetical Study," *CBTJ* 5/1 (1989): 1-11.

1301   David L. Burggraff, "Principles of Discipline in Matthew 18:15-17. Part III: A Practical Study," *CBTJ* 5/2 (1989): 1-29.

1302   F. García Martínez, "La reprehensión fraterna en Qumran y Mt. 18,15-17," *FilN* 2/1 (1989): 23-40.

1303   G. Segalla, "Perdono 'cristiano' e correzione fraterna nella communità di 'Matteo' (Mt. 18,15-17, 21-35)," *StPa* 38 (1991): 499-518.

18:15
1304   Gerhard Barth, "Auseinandersetzungen im die Kirchenzucht im Umkreis des Matthausevangeliums," *ZNW* 69/3 (1978): 158-77.

18:17
1305   S. Hobhouse, "Let Him Be unto Thee as the Gentile and the Publican (Mt. 18,17)," *ET* 49 (1937-1938): 43-44.

18:18-21:35
1306   G. Korting, "Binden oder lösen: Zun Verstockungs- und Befreiungstheologie in Mt. 16,19; 18:18-21:35 und Joh 15,1-17; 2,23," *SNTU-A* 14 (1989): 39-91.

18:18
1307   H. J. Cadbury, "The Meaning of John 20,23, Matthew 16,19, and Matthew 18,18," *JBL* 58 (1939): 251-54.

1308   Julius R. Mantey, "The Mistranslation of the Perfect Tense in John 20,23, Mt. 16,19, and Mt. 18,18," *JBL* 58 (1939): 243-49.

1309   Julius R. Mantey, "What of Priestly Absolution," *CT* 13/9 (1969): 233-391.

1310   H. Thyen, "Mt. 18,18," in *Studie zur Sündenvergebung im Neuen Testament und seinen alttestamentlichen und jüdischen Voraussetzungen.* Göttingen: Vandenhoeck & Ruprecht, 1970. Pp. 236-43.

1311   Julius R. Mantey, "Distorted Translations in John 20:23; Matthew 16:18-19 and 18:18," *RevExp* 78/3 (1981): 409-16.

1312   J. D. M. Derrett, "Binding and Loosing (Matt. 16:19; Matt. 18:18; John 20:23)," *JBL* 102 (1983): 112-17.

1313   Herbert W. Basser, "Derrett's 'Binding' Reopened," *JBL* 104 (1985): 297-300.

1314   Richard A. Hiers, " 'Binding' and 'Loosing': The Matthean Authorizations," *JBL* 104/2 (1985): 233-50.

1315   Dennis C. Duling, "Binding and Loosing: Matthew 16:19; Matthew 18:18; John 20:23," *Forum* 3 (1987): 3-31.

1316   Kair A. Syreeni, "Between Heaven and Earth: On the Structure of Matthew's Symbolic Universe," *JSNT* 40 (1990): 9-13.

18:19-20
1317   E. C. Ratcliff, "The Prayer of St. Chrysostom: A Note on Cranmer's Rendering and Its Background," *ATR* 42 (1960): 1-9.

1318   J. Caba, "El poderde la petición comunitaria (Mt. 18,19-20)," Greg 54 (1973): 609-54.

1319   J. D. M. Derrett, "Where Two or Three Are Convened in My Name . . . .': A Sad Misunderstanding," *ET* 91/3 (1979): 83-86.

18:20
1320   Pietro Bolognesi, "Matteo 18:20 e la dottrina della Chiesa," *BibO* 29 (1987): 1671-77.

18:21-35
1321   Erhardt Guttgemanns, "Narrative Analyse Synoptischer Texte," *LB* 25 (1973): 50-73.

1322   Harvey H. Potthoff, "Homiletical Resources: The Sermon as Theological Event Interpretations of Parables," *QR* 4/2 (1984): 76-102.

1323   Donald Senior, "Matthew 18:21-35," *Int* 41/4 (1987): 403-407.

1324   G. Segalla, "Perdono 'cristiano' e correzione fraterna nella communità di 'Matteo' (Mt. 18,15-17, 21-35)," *StPa* 38 (1991): 499-518.

18:23-35

1325   L. G. Kelly, "Cultural Consistency in Translation," *BT* 21/4 (1970): 170-75.

1326   Christian Dietzfelbinger, "Das Gleichnis von der erlassenen Schuld. Eine theologische Untersuchung von Matthaus 18,23-35," *EvT* 32 (1972): 437-51.

1327   Martinus C. de Boer, "Ten Thousand Talents: Matthew's Interpretation and Redaction of the Parable of the Unforgiving Servant (Matt. 18:23-35)," *CBQ* 50 (1988): 214-32.

18:23-34

1328   B. B. Scott, "The King's Accounting: Matthew 18:23-34. *JBL* 104/3 (1985): 429-42.

18:23-25

1329   E. Fuchs, "The Parable of the Unmerciful Servant," in Kurt Aland, et al., eds., *Studia Evangelica*: Papers Presented to the International Congress on the Four Gospels, Christ Church, Oxford, 1957. Berlin: Akademie-Verlag, 1959. Pp. 487-94.

1330   A. Weiser, "Das Gleichnis vom unbarmhetzigen Knecht Mt. 18,23-35," in *Die Knechtsgleichnisse der synoptischen Evangelien*. Munich: Kösel, 1971. Pp. 75-104.

19:1-12

1331   Heinrich Baltensweiler, "Matthäusevangelium (Kap. 19,1-12; 5,27-32)," in *Die Ehe im Neuen Testament: Exegetische Untersuchungen über Ehe, Ehelosigkeit und Ehescheidung*. Stuttgart: Zwingle, 1967. Pp. 82-119.

<u>19:1-8</u>
>   **1332**
>
>   E. Lohmeyer, "Die Überlieferung der Werke Jesu," in *Gottesknecht und Davidssohn*. 2nd ed. Göttingen: Vandenhoeck & Ruprecht, 1953. Pp. 46-50.

<u>19:1</u>
>   **1333**
>
>   David Hellholm, "En textgrammatisk konstruktion I Matteusevangeliet," *SEÅ* 51 (1986-1987): 80-89.

<u>19:3-13</u>
>   **1334**
>
>   John J. Pilch, "Marriage in the Lord," *BibTo* 102 (1979): 2010-13.

<u>19:3-12</u>
>   **1335**
>
>   A. Isaksson, "The Origin of the Clause on Unchastity," in *Marriage and Ministry in the New Temple: A Study with Special Reference to Mt. 19,3-12 and 1 Cor. 11,3-16*. Lund: Gleerup, 1965. Pp. 75-92.

>   **1336**
>
>   J. D. M. Derrett, "The Teaching of Jesus on Marriage and Divorce," in *Law in the New Testament*. London: Longman & Todd, 1970. Pp. 363-88.

>   **1337**
>
>   David R. Catchpole, "The Synoptic Divorce Material as a Traditio-Historical Problem," *BJRL* 57/1 (1974): 92-127.

>   **1338**
>
>   Francis J. Moloney, "Matthew 19,3-12 and Celibacy. A Redactional and Form Critical Study," *JSNT* 1/2 (1979): 42-60.

>   **1339**
>
>   Charles C. Ryrie, "Biblical Teaching on Divorce and Remarriage," *GTJ* 3/2 (1982): 177-92.

>   **1340**
>
>   Craig L. Blomberg, "Marriage, Divorce, Remarriage, and Celibacy: An Exegesis of Matthew 19:3-12," *TriJ* 11 (1990): 161-96.

<u>19:3-9</u>
>   **1341**
>
>   David L. Dungan, "The Account of Jesus' Debate with the Pharisees Regarding Divorce (Matt. 19.3-9 = Mark 10.2-12)," in *The Sayings of Jesus in the Churches of Paul*. Oxford: Blackwell, 1971. Pp. 102-31.

1342 Augustine Stock, "Matthean Divorce Texts," *BTB* 8/1 (1978): 24-33.

1343 M. J. Molldrem, "A Hermeneutic of Pastoral Care and the Law/Gospel Paradigm Applied to the Divorce Texts of Scripture," *Int* 45 (1991): 43-54.

19:3f.

1344 C. Benton Kline, "Marriage Today: A Theological Carpet Bag," *JPC* 33/1 (1979): 24-37.

19:4-6

1345 Gladys Lewis, "A Christian Lifestyle for Families," *SouJT* 22/1 (1979): 74-83.

19:4

1346 David A. Black, "Conjectural Emendations in the Gospel of Matthew," *NovT* 31/1 (1989): 1-15.

19:9

1347 A. Allgeier, "Die crux interpretum im neutestamentlichen Ehescheidungs-verbot. Eine philologische Untersuchung zu Mt. 5,32 und 19,9," in *Reverendissimo Patri Iacobo Mariae Vosté*. Roma: Salita del Grillo, 1943. Pp. 128-42.

1348 J. M. Gonzalez Ruiz, "El divorcio en Mt. 5,32 y 19,9," in *La enciclica Humani Generis*. Madrid: Científica Medinaceli, 1952. Pp. 511-28.

1349 Heinrich Baltensweiler, "Die Ehebruchsklausein bei Matthaeus: zu Matth 5:32; 19:9," *TZ* 15 (1959): 340-56.

1350 Oral Collins, "Divorce in the New Testament," *GR* 7 (1964): 158-69.

1351 John J. O'Rourke, "A Note on an Exception: Mt. 5:32 (19:9) and 1 Cor 7:12 Compared," *HeyJ* 5 (1964): 299-302.

1352 J. B. Bauer, "Die matthäische Ehescheidungsklausel," in *Evangelienforschung: Ausgewählte Aufsätze deutscher Exegeten*. Graz: Styria, 1968. Pp. 147-58.

1353 H. G. Coiner, "Those 'Divorce and Remarriage' Passages," *CTM* 39/6 (1968): 367-84.

1354   Richard N. Soulen, "Marriage and Divorce: A Problem in New Testament Interpretation," *Int* 23/4 (1969): 439-50.

1355   L. Ramaroson, "Une nouvelle interprétation de la 'clausule' de Mt. 19, 9," *SE* 23 (1971): 247-51.

1356   Tarcision Stramare, "Matteo Divorzista?" *Div* 15/2 (1971): 213-35.

1357   A. Vargas-Machuca, "Los casos de 'divorcio' admitidos por San Mateo (5,32 y 19,9). Consecuencias para la teologia actual," *EE* 50 (1975): 5-54.

1358   Mark Geldard, "Jesus' Teaching on Divorce: Thoughts on the Meaning of Porneia in Matthew 5:32 and 19:9," *Ch* 92 (1978): 134-43.

1359   John J. Kilgallen, "To What Are the Matthean Exception-Texts (5,32 and 19,9) An Exception?" *Bib* 61/1 (1980): 102-05.

1360   Henri Crouzel, "Quelques remarques concernant le texte patristique de Mt. 19,9," *BLE* 82 (1981): 82-92.

1361   Carroll D. Osburn, "The Present Indicative in Matthew 19:9," *RQ* 24/4 (1981): 193-203.

1362   William A. Heth, "Another Look at the Erasmian View of Divorce and Remarriage," *JETS* 25/3 (1982): 263-72.

1363   G. J. Wenham, "Matthew and Divorce: An Old Crux Revisited," *JSNT* 22 (1984): 95-107.

1364   Ben Witherington, "Matthew 5.32 and 19.9—Exception or Exceptional Situation?" *NTS* 31/4 (1985): 571-76.

1365   G. J. Wenham, "The Syntax of Matthew 19.9," *JSNT* 28 (1986): 17-23.

1366   Markus N. A. Bockmuehl, "Matthew 5.32, 19.9 in the Light of Pre-Rabbinic Halakhah," *NTS* 35/2 (1989): 291-95.

1367   Don T. Smith, "The Matthean Exception Clauses in the Light of Matthew's Theology and Community," *SBT* 17/1 (1989): 55-82.

1368   Phillip H. Wiebe, "Jesus' Divorce Exception," *JETS* 32 (1989): 327-33.

1369   C. Marucci, "Clausole matteane e critica testuale. In merito alla teoria di H. Crouzel sul testo originale di Mt. 19,9," - *RBib* 38 (1990): 301-25.

19:10-12

1370   C. Daniel, "Esseniens et Eunuques (Matthieu 19,10-12)," *RevQ* 6 (1968): 353-90.

1371   J.-M. van Cangh, "Fondement Angelique de la Vie Religieuse," *NRT* 95/6 (1973): 635-47.

1372   Roger Balducelli, "The Decision for Celibacy," *TS* 36/2 (1975): 219-42.

1373   Thaddee Matura, "Le Celibat dans le Nouveau Testament," *NRT* 97/6 (1975): 481-500.

1374   G. G. Gamba, "La 'Eunuchia' per il Regno Deicieli. Annotazioni in Margineamatteo 19,10-12," *Sale* 42/2 (1980): 243-87.

1375   Christian Wolff, "Niedrigkeit und Verzicht in Wort und Weg Jesu und in der apostolischen Existenz des Paulus," *NTS* 34/2 (1988): 183-96.

19:12

1376   Walter Bauer, "Matth. 19,12 und die alten Christen," in Hans Windisch, ed., *Neutestamentliche Studien Georg Heinrici zu seinem 70. Geburtstag.* Leipzig: Hinrichs'sche, 1914. Pp. 235-44.

1377   D. W. Trautman, *The Eunuch Logion of Matthew 19,12: Historical and Exegetical Dimensions as Related to Celibacy.* Rome: Catholic Book Agency, 1966.

1378   Walter Bauer, "Matth. 19,12 und die alten Christen," in G. Strecker, ed., *Aufsätz und kleine Schriften*. Tübingen: Mohr, 1967. Pp. 253-62.

1379   Q. Quesnell, " 'Made Themselves Eunuchs for the Kingdom of Heaven'," *CBQ* 30/3 (1968): 335-58.

1380   J. Blinzler, " 'Zur Ehe unfähig . . .': Auslegung von Mt. 19,12," in *Aus der Welt und Umwelt des Neuen Testaments: Gesammelte Aufsätze 1*. Stuttgart: Katholisches Bibelwerk, 1969. Pp. 20-40.

1381   D. Heinrich Greeven, "Ehe nach dem Neuen Testament," *NTS* 15/4 (1969): 365-88.

1382   Jerome Kodell, "The Celibacy Logion in Matthew 19:12," *BTB* 8/1 (1978): 19-23.

1383   William A. Heth, "Another Look at the Erasmian View of Divorce and Remarriage," *JETS* 25/3 (1982): 263-72.

1384   Pierre-Rene Cote, "Les eunuques pour le Royaume (Mt. 19,12)," *EgT* 17/3 (1986): 321-34.

1385   William A. Heth, "Matthew's 'Eunuch Saying' (19:12) and Its Relationship to Paul's Teaching on Singleness in 1 Corinthians 7," doctoral dissertation, Dallas Theological Seminary, Dallas TX, 1986.

1386   William A. Heth, "Unmarried 'For the Sake of the Kingdom' (Matthew 19:12) in the Early Church," *GTJ* 8/1 (1987): 55-88.

19:13-15
1387   S. Légasse, "Jésus accueille les enfants: Marc, x,13-16 et paralleles," in *Jésus et l'enfant: 'Enfants', 'Petis' et 'simples' dans la tradition synoptique*. Paris: Gabalda, 1969. Pp. 36-43.

1388   Daniel Patte, "Jesus' Pronouncement about Entering the Kingdom Like a Child: A Structural Exegesis," *Semeia* 29 (1983): 3-42.

19:13-12
1389   A. Isaksson, *Marriage and Ministry in the New Temple. A Study with Special Reference to Mt. 19.13-12 and 1 Cor. 11.3-16*. Lund: Gleerup, 1965.

19:16-30
1390   A. F. J. Klijn, "The Question of the Rich Young Man in a Jewish-Christian Gospel," *NovT* 8 (1966): 149-15.

1391   J. M. R. Tillard, "Le Propos de Pauvrete et l'Exigence Evangelique," *NRT* 100/2 (1978): 207-32.

1392   Robert L. Thomas, "The Rich Young Man in Matthew," *GTJ* 3/2 (1982): 235-60.

19:16-22
1393   Gregory Murray, "The Rich Young Man," *DR* 103 (1985): 144-46.

1394   R. H. Fuller, "The Decalogue in the NT," *Int* 43/3 (1989): 243-55.

19:16
1395   J. W. Wenham, "Why Do You Ask Me About the Good? A Study of the Relation between Text and Source Criticism," *NTS* 28/1 (1982): 116-25.

19:17-18
1396   E. Yarnold, "*Teleios* in St. Matthew's Gospel," in F. Cross, ed., *Studia Evangelica IV*: Papers Presented to the Third International Congress on New Testament Studies, Christ Church, Oxford, 1965 (Part I—The New Testament Scriptures). Berlin: Akademie-Verlag, 1968. Pp. 269-73.

19:17
1397   Eric F. Osborn, "Origen and Justification: The Good Is One," *ABR* 24/1 (1976): 18-29.

19:23-30
1398   C. M. Martini. *Women in the Gospels*. New York: Crossroad, 1990.

19:24

1399　　José O'Callaghan, "Examen critico de Mt. 19,24," *Bib* 69/3 (1988): 401-05.

19:28

1400　　Fred W. Burnett, "Παλιγγενεσία in Matt. 19:28: A Window on the Matthean Community?" *JSNT* 17 (1983): 60-72.

1401　　J. D. M. Derrett, "Παλιγγενεσία (Matthew 19.28)," *JSNT* 20 (1984): 51-58.

19:30

1402　　José O'Callaghan, "Nota crítica sobre Mt. 19,30," *EB* 48 (1990): 271-73.

20:1-16

1403　　W. A. Curtis, "The Parable of the Labourers (Matt. 20, 1-16)," in *Adolf Jülicher zum achtzigjährigen Geburtstag*. Uppsala: Das neutestamentliche Seminar zu Uppsala, 1936. Pp. 61-69.

1404　　W. T. Williams, "The Parable of the Labourers in the Vineyard (Mt. 20,1-16)," *ET* 50 (1938-1939): 526.

1405　　E. Fuchs, "Das Wunder der Güte. Predigt über Matth 20,1-16," in *Glaube und Erfahrung: Zum christologie Problem im Neuen Testament*. Tübingen: Mohr, 1965. Pp. 471-74.

1406　　C. L. Mitton, "Expounding the Parables: The Workers in the Vineyard," *ET* 77 (1965-1966): 307-11.

1407　　L. J. Crampton, "St. Gregory's Homily XIX and the Institution of Septuagesima Sunday," *DR* 86 (1968): 162-66.

1408　　Jacques Dupont, "Les derniers appelés," in *Les Béatitudes*. Tome II: La bonne nouvelle. Paris: Gabalda, 1969. 2:251-76.

1409　　G. Eichholz, "Von den Arbeitern im Weinberg (Matth. 20,1-16a)," in *Gleichnisse der Evangelien: Form,*

Überlieferung, Auslegung. Neukirchen-Vluyn: Neukircher Verlag, 1971. Pp. 85-108.

1410   A. Orbe, "San Ireneo y la parábola de los obreros de la viñ: Mt. 20,1-16," *EE* 46 (1971): 35-62, 183-206.

1411   S. Meurer, "Zur Beziehung der Gerechtigkeit Gottes zum Recht. Dazu Auslegung von Mt. 20,1-16," in *Das Recht im Dienst der Versöhnung und des Friedens: Studie zur Frage des Rechts nach dem Neuen Testament.* Zürich: Theologischer Verlag, 1972. Pp. 29-44.

1412   Erhardt Guttgemanns, "Narrative Analyse Synoptischer Texte," *LB* 25 (1973): 50-73.

1413   D. A. Nelson, "An Exposition of Matthew 20:1-16," *Int* 29/3 (1975): 288-92.

1414   Frederic Manns, "L'Arriere-Plan Socio-Economique de la Parabole des Ouvries de la Onzieme Heure et ses Limites," *Ant* 55/1 (1980): 258-68.

1415   Franz Schnider, "Von der Gerechtigkeit Gottes: Beobachtungen zum Gleichnis von den Arbeitern im Weinberg (Matt. 20:1-16)," *K* 23/1 (1981): 88-95.

1416   Philip Culbertson, "Reclaiming the Matthean Vineyard Parables," *Enc* 49/4 (1988): 257-83.

1417   I. R. Cóbreces, " 'Los obreros de la viña.' Elementos midráshicos en la parábola de Mt. 20,1-16," *Stud* 30 (1990): 485-505.

1418   Robert T. Fortna, "You Have Made Them Equal to Us!" *JTSA* 72 (1990): 66-72.

20:1-15

1419   Rudolf Bultmann, "Matthäus 20,1-15," in *Marburger Predigten.* Tübingen: Mohr, 1956. Pp. 159-68.

1420   Rudolf Hoppe, "Gleichnis und Situation," *BZ* 28/1 (1984): 1-21.

1421   A. A. Bucher, *Gleichnisse verstehen lernen: Strukturgenetische Untersuchungen zur Rezeption synoptischer Parabeln.* Fribourg: Universitäts-Verlag, 1990.

<u>20:1-6</u>

1422   John G. Strelan, "Sermon Study: Matthew 20:1-6," *LTJ* 20/1 (1986): 19-21.

<u>20:1ff.</u>

1423   Gerhard Sellen, "Gleichnisstrukturen," *LB* 31 (1974): 89-115.

<u>20:4</u>

1424   F. C. Glover, "Workers for the Vineyard, Mt. 20,4," *ET* 86 (1975): 310-11.

<u>20:13</u>

1425   Albert Wifstrand, "Ett nytestamentligt ordföljdsproblem," in *Professor Johannes Lindblom: på hans 65-årsdag den 7 juni 1947.* Uppsala: Wretmans, 1948. Pp. 311-25.

<u>20:16</u>

1426   E. F. Sutcliffe, "Many Are Called But Few Are Chosen," *ITQ* 28 (1961): 126-31.

<u>20:21</u>

1427   J. O'Callaghan, "Fluctuación textual en Mt. 20, 21.26.27," *Bib* 71/4 (1990): 553-58.

<u>20:26</u>

1428   J. O'Callaghan, "Fluctuación textual en Mt. 20, 21.26.27," *Bib* 71/4 (1990): 553-58.

<u>20:27</u>

1429   J. O'Callaghan, "Fluctuación textual en Mt. 20, 21.26.27," *Bib* 71/4 (1990): 553-58.

<u>20:28</u>

1430   Roderic Dunkerley, "The Etiquette of the Kingdom," *LQHR* (1964): 151-53.

1431   Mogens Muller, "Mattaeusevangeliets Messiasbillede: et forsg pa at bestemme Mattaeusevangeliets forstaelse af Jesu messianitet," *SEÅ* (1986-1987): 51/52 168-79.

20:29-34
1432   C. Burger, "Der Davidssohn bei Matthäus," in *Jesus als Davidssohn: Eine traditionsgeschichteliche Untersuchung.* Göttingen: Vanderhoeck & Ruprecht, 1970. Pp. 72-106.

21-25
1433   E. Schweizer, "Matthäus 21-25," in *Orientierung an Jesus: Zur Theolohie der Synoptiker* (festschrift for Josef Schmid). Freiburg: Herder, 1973. Pp. 364-71.

21:1-17
1434   Renate Brandscheidt, "Messias und Tempel: Die alttestamentlichen Zitate in Mt. 21,1-17," *TTZ* 99 (1990): 36-48.

21:1-11
1435   Roman Bartnicki, "Das Zitat von Zach IX, 9-10 und die Tiere im Berichte von Matthaus über dem Einzug Jesu in Jerusalem (Mt. XXI,1-11)," *NovT* 18/3 (1976): 161-66.

21:1
1436   D. Durken, "Mountains and Matthew," *BibTo* 28 (1990): 304-307.

21:4
1437   James W. Scott, "Matthew's Intention to Write History," *WTJ* 47/1 (1985): 68-82.

21:5-7
1438   A. Frenz, "Mt. XXI.5.7," *NovT* 13 (1971): 259-60.

21:5
1439   Victor J. Eldridge, "Typology: The Key to Understanding Matthew's Formula Quotations?" *Coll* 15 (1982): 43-51.

21:9
1440   Sebastin Brock, "The Thrice-Holy Hymn in the Liturgy," *Sobor* 7/2 (1985): 24-34.

21:11
1441   Paul W. Meyer, "Matthew 21:11," *Int* 40/2 (1986): 180-85.

21:12-27
1442   F. Schnider and W. Stenger, "Die Tempelreinigung," in *Johannes und die Synoptiker: Verleich ihrer Parallelen.* Munich: Kösel, 1971. Pp. 26-53.

21:14-17
1443   E. Schweizer, "Matthäus 21,14-17," in *Matthäus und seine Gemeinde.* Stuttgart: KBW, 1974. Pp. 132-37.

21:15
1444   Savas Agourides, " 'Little Ones' in Matthew," *BT* 35/3 (1984): 329-34.

21:17
1445   George Howard, "A Note on Codex Sinaiticus and Shem-Tob's Hebrew Matthew," *NTS* 38 (1992): 187-204.

21:18-19
1446   H.-W. Bartsch, "Die 'Verfluchung' des Feigenbaums," *ZNW* 53 (1962): 256-60.

21:27-31
1447   Piet DeVries and Friedrich Wulf, "Gleichnisse von Vater und Seinen Sohnen," *GeistL* 44/1 (1971): 74-75.

21:28-22:14
1448   A. Ogawa, "Paraboles de l'Israel Veritable? Reconsideration Critique de Mt. XXI.28-XXII.14," *NovT* 21/2 (1979): 121-49.

21:28-32
1449   J. Ramsey Michaels, "The Parable of the Regretful Son," *HTR* 61 (1968): 15-26.

1450   J. Schmid, "Das textgeschichtliche Problem der Parabel von den zwei Söhnen," in *Evangelienforschung: Ausgewählte Aufsätze deutscher Exegeten.* Graz: Styria, 1968. Pp. 199-220.

1451   J. D. M. Derrett, "The Parable of the Two Sons," *ScanJT* 25 (1971): 109-16.

1452   H. Merkel, "Das Gleichnis von den 'ungleichen Söhnen' (Matth. xxi.28-32)," *NTS* 20 (1974): 254-61.

1453   W. L. Richards, "Another Look at the Parable of the Two Sons," *BR* 23 (1978): 5-14.

1454   Philip Culbertson, "Reclaiming the Matthean Vineyard Parables," *Enc* 49/4 (1988): 257-83.

21:28-31

1455   Gerhard Sellen, "Gleichnisstrukturen," *LB* 31 (1974): 89-115.

1456   Jean Doignon, "L'exegese latine de la parabole des deux fils (Matth. 21:28-31): Hilaire de Poitiers devant le probleme de l'obeisance a Dieu," *RHPR* 65/1 (1985): 53-59.

21:31

1457   Henry Osborn, "A Quadruple Quote in the Triumphal Entry Account in Warao," *BT* 18/1 (1967): 301-21.

21:33-48

1458   J. C. O'Neill, "The Source of the Parables of the Bridegroom and the Wicked Husbandmen," *JTS* 39 (1988): 485-89.

21:33-46

1459   Dominic Crossan, "The Parable of the Wicked Husbandmen," *JBL* 90/4 (1971): 451-65.

1460   Jack Dean Kingsbury, "The Parable of the Wicked Husbandmen and the Secret of Jesus' Divine Sonship in Matthew: Some Literary-Critical Observations," *JBL* 105 (1986): 643-55.

1461   C. Wrembek, "Das Gleichnis vom königlichen Hochzeitsmahl und vom Mann ohne hochzeitliches Gewand. Eine geistliche-theologische Erwägung zu Mt. 22,1-14," *GeistL* 64/1 (1991): 17-40.

21:33-45

1462   B. M. F. van Iersel, "Das Gleichnis von den bösen
            Winzern," in *"Der Sohn" in der synoptischen Jesusworten*.
            Leiden: Brill, 1961. Pp. 124-45.

1463   W. Trilling, "Das Winzergleichnis: 21,33-45," in *Das
            wahre Israel: Studien zur Theologie des Matthäus-
            Evangeliums*. Munich: Kösel, 1964. Pp. 55-65.

1464   X. Léon-Dufour, "La parabole des vignerons homicides,"
            in *Études d'évangile*. Paris: Seuil, 1965. Pp. 303-44.

1465   W. Trilling, "Gericht über das falsche Israel (Mt. 21,
            33-46)," in *Christusverkündigung in den synoptischen
            Evangelien*. Munich: Kösel, 1969. Pp. 165-90.

1466   J. D. M. Derrett, "The Parable of the Wicked
            Vinedressers," in *Law in the New Testament*. London:
            Longman & Todd, 1970. Pp. 286-312.

21:33-43

1467   Fred B. Craddock, "Homiletical Studies: Exegesis and
            Exposition of Gospel Lections for the Season after
            Pentecost," *QR* 1/4 (1981): 5-42.

21:33-41

1468   Jane E. Newell and Raymond R. Newell, "The Parable of
            the Wicked Tenants," *NovT* 14/3 (1972): 226-37.

21:38-42

1469   Edwin K. Broadhead, "An Example of Gender Bias in
            UBS3," *BT* 40/3 (1989): 336-38.

21:41

1470   K. H. Kuhn, "Kakie Kakos in the Sahidic Version of
            Matthew 21:41," *JTS* 36/2 (1985): 390-93.

21:43

1471   R. Swaeles, "L'Arrière-fond scripturaire de Matt. xxi. 43 et
            son lien avec Matt. xxi. 44," *NTS* 6 (1959-1960): 310-13.

1472   W. H. Gispen, "Het Oude Testament over de Toekomst van
            Israel," *GTT* 60 (1960): 50-63.

22:1-14

1473   Joseph Sickenberger, "Die Zusammenarbeitung verschiedener Parabeln im Matthäusevangelium," in Franz Dölger, ed., *Festgabe A. Heisenberg zum 60. Geburtstag.* Leipzig: Teubner, 1929. Pp. 253-61.

1474   H. Schlier, "Der Ruf Gottes (Mt. 22,1-14)," *GeistL* 28 (1955): 241-47.

1475   Edward F. Hanahoe, "The Mystery of Unity," *Unitas* 12 (1960): 93-98.

1476   Eta Linneman, "Überlegungen zur Parabel vom grossen Abendmahl, Lc 14,15-24 Mt,22 1-14," *ZNW* 51 (1960): 246-55.

1477   Otto Glombitza, "Das Grosse Abendmahl: Luk. 14:12-24," *NovT* 5 (1962): 10-16.

1478   V. Hasler, "Die königliche Hochzeit, Matth. 22,1-14," *TZ* 18 (1962): 25-35.

1479   F. Hahn, "Das Gleichnis von der Einladung zum Festmahl," in O. Böcher and K. Haacker, eds., *Verborum Veritas* (festschrift for Gustav Stählin). Wuppertal: Brockhaus, 1970. Pp. 51-82.

1480   G. Eichholz, "Von grossen Abendmahl (Luk. 14,12-24) und von der königlichen Hochzeit (Matth. 22,1-14)," in *Gleichnisse der Evangelien: Form, Überlieferung, Auslegung.* Neukirchen-Vluyn: Neukircher Verlag, 1971. Pp. 126-47.

1481   Dan O. Via, "The Relationship of Form to Content in the Parable: The Wedding Feast," *Int* 25 (1971): 171-84.

1482   A. Vögtle, "Die Einladung zum grossen Gastmahl und zum königlichen Hochzeitsmahl. Ein Paradigma für den Wandel des geschichtlichen Verständnishorizonts," in *Das Evangelium und die Evangelien.* Düsseldorf: Patmos, 1971. Pp. 171-218.

1483   Chan-Hie Kim, "The Papyrus Invitation," *JBL* 94/3 (1975): 391-402.

1484   Fred B. Craddock, "Homiletical Studies: Exegesis and
                    Exposition of Gospel Lections for the Season after
                    Pentecost," *QR* 1/4 (1981): 5-42.

1485   W. Bindemann, "Das Mahl des Königs. Gründe und
                    Hinrergründe der Redaktion von Mt. 22,1-14," *TV* 15
                    (1985): 21-29.

1486   C. Wrembek, "Das Gleichnis vom königlichen
                    Hochzeitsmahl und vom Mann ohne hochzeitliches Gewand.
                    Eine geistliche-theologische Erwägung zu Mt. 22,1-14,"
                    GeistL 64/1 (1991): 17-40.

22:1-10
1487   Erhardt Guttgemanns, "Narrative Analyse Synoptischer
                    Texte," *LB* 25 (1973): 50-73.

1488   Gerhard Sellen, "Gleichnisstrukturen," *LB* 31 (1974):
                    89-115.

1489   E. E. Lemcio, "The Parables of the Great Supper and the
                    Wedding Feast. History, Redaction and Canon," *HBT* 8/1
                    (1986): 1-26.

1490   Elaine Wainwright, "God Wills to Invite All to the
                    Banquet," *IRM* 77 (1988): 185-93.

1491   Peter Dschulnigg, "Positionen des Gleichnisverständnisses
                    im 20. Jahrhundert," *TZ* 45/4 (1989): 335-51.

22:1-4
1492   W. Trilling, "Zur Überlieferungsgeschichte des Glechnisses
                    vom Hochzeitsmahl," *BZ* 4 (1960): 251-65.

22:1ff.
1493   Paul H. Ballard, "Reasons for Refusing the Great Supper,"
                    JTS 23/2 (1972): 341-50.

22:2-10
1494   R. W. Resenhofft, "Jesu Gleichnis von den Talenten,
                    Erganzt durch die Lukas-Fassung," *NTS* 26/3 (1979-1980):
                    318-31.

22:7

1495 K. H. Rengstorf, "Die Stadt der Mörder (Mt. 22,7)," in Walther Eltester, ed. *Judentum, Urchristentum, Kirche* (festschrift for Joachim Jeremias). Berlin: Töpelmann, 1964. Pp. 106-29.

1496 Bo Reicke, "Synoptic Prophecies on the Destruction of Jerusalem," in D. E. Aune, ed., *Studies in New Testament and Early Christian Literature*. Leiden: Brill, 1972. Pp. 121-34.

22:11-14

1497 Erhardt Guttgemanns, "Narrative Analyse Synoptischer Texte," *LB* 25 (1973): 50-73.

22:11-13

1498 Johannes B. Bauer, "De Veste Nuptiali (Mt. 22,11-13)," *VD* 43 (1965): 15-18.

1499 G. Wainwright, "Mt. 22,11-13: une controverse primitive sur l'admission à la Sainte Cène," in E. A. Livingston, ed., *Studia Evangelica VI*: Papers Presented to the Fourth International Congress on New Testament Studies, Christ Church, Oxford, 1969. Berlin: Akademie-Verlag, 1973. Pp. 595-98.

1500 David C. Sim, "The Man without the Wedding Garment (Matthew 22:11-13)," *HeyJ* 31 (1990): 165-78.

22:12

1501 K. R. Cripps, "A Note on Matthew xxii.12," *ET* 69 (1957-1958): 30.

22:13

1502 C. Jaeger, "Remarques philologiques sur quelques passages des Synoptiques," *RHPR* 16 (1936): 246-49.

22:14

1503 E. F. Sutcliffe, "Many Are Called But Few Are Chosen," *ITQ* 28 (1961): 126-31.

1504 Ben F. Meyer, "Many (=All) Are Called, But Few (=Not All) Are Chosen," *NTS* 36/1 (1990): 89-97.

22:15-22

1505   J. D. M. Derrett, " 'Render to Caesar. . .'," in *Law in the New Testament*. London: Longman & Todd, 1970. Pp. 313-38.

1506   Fred B. Craddock, "Homiletical Studies: Exegesis and Exposition of Gospel Lections for the Season after Pentecost," *QR* 1/4 (1981): 5-42.

22:21

1507   Charles H. Giblin, " 'The Things of God' in the Questions Concerning Tribute to Caesar," *CBQ* 33/4 (1971): 510-27.

1508   P. C. Bori, "Date a Cesare quel che è di Cesare . . ." (Mt. 22,21). Linee di storia dell'interpretazione antica," *CrNSt* 7 (1986): 451-64.

22:30

1509   Thaddee Matura, "Le Celibat dans le Nouveau Testament," *NRT* 97/6 (1975): 481-500.

1510   Robert C. Newman, "The Ancient Exegesis of Genesis 6:2,4," *GTJ* 5/1 (1984): 13-36.

22:31-32

1511   D. M. Cohn-Sherbok, "Jesus' Defence of the Resurrection of the Dead," *JSNT* 11 (1981): 64-73.

22:32

1512   E. Manns, "La technique du 'Al Tiqra' dans les évangiles," *RevSR* 64 (1990): 1-7.

22:34-46

1513   J. Blank, "Siebzehnter Sonntag nach Pfingsten," in *Schriftauslegung in Theorie und Praxis*. Munich: Kösel, 1969. Pp. 221-36.

22:34-40

1514   Carl A. Clark, "The Neglected Commandment I (Matthew 22:34-40)," *SouJT* 3 (1960): 61-73.

1515   Robert Douglas, "The Neglected Commandment II (Matthew 22:34-40)," *SouJT* 3 (1960): 74-77.

1516   K. Berger, "Die Schriftauslegung in Mt. 22,34-40," in *Die Gesetzesauslegung Jesu: Ihr historischer Hintergrund im Judentum und im Alten Testament (Teil I: Markus und Parallelen)*. Neukirchen: Neukirchener Verlag, 1972. 1:202-208.

1517   Arland J. Hultgren, "The Double Commandment of Love in Mt. 22:34-40," *CBQ* 36 (1974): 373-78.

1518   E. E. Lemcio, "Pirke 'Abot 12(3) and the Synoptic Redactions of the Commands to Love God and Neighbor," *ATJ* 43 (1988): 43-53.

22:34-36
1519   Stanley Hauerwas, "The August Partiality of God's Love," *RJ* 39/5 (1989): 10-12.

22:34
1520   S. Clive Thexton, "Jesus' Use of the Scriptures," *LQHR* 179 (1954): 102-108.

22:40
1521   T. L. Donaldson, "The Law that 'Hangs' (Mt. 22:40): Rabbinic Formulation and Matthean Social World," *SBLSP* (1990): 14-33.

22:41-46
1522   Joseph A. Fitzmyer, "The Son of David Tradition and Mt. 22:41-46 and Parallels," in *Essays on the Semitic Background of the New Testament*. London: Chapman, 1971. Pp. 113-26.

23:1-12, 34
1523   B. T. Viviano, "Social World and Community Leadership: The Case of Matthew 23:1-12, 34," *JSNT* 39 (1990): 3-21.

23:2
1524   José O'Callaghan, "La variante neotestamentaria levadura de los panes," *Bib* 67 (1986): 98-100.

1525   Kenneth G. C. Newport, "A Note on the 'Seat of Moses'," *AUSS* 28 (1990): 53-58.

23:4

1526   George Howard, "A Note on Codex Sinaiticus and Shem-Tob's Hebrew Matthew," *NTS* 38 (1992): 187-204.

23:5-6

1527   Hyam Maccoby, "The Washing of Cups," *JSNT* 14 (1982): 3-15.

23:5

1528   J. Bowman, "Phylacteries," in Kurt Aland, et al., eds., *Studia Evangelica*: Papers Presented to the International Congress on the Four Gospels, Christ Church, Oxford, 1957. Berlin: Akademie-Verlag, 1959. Pp. 523-38.

23:8-10

1529   J. D. M. Derrett, "Mt. 23,8-10: A Midrash on Is. 54,13 and Jer. 31,33-34," *Bib* 62/3 (1981): 372-86.

23:8-9

1530   R. S. Barbour, "Uncomfortable Words. VIII: Status and Titles," *ET* 82/5 (1971): 137-42.

23:9

1531   J. T. Townsend, "Matthew 23:9," *JTS* 12 (1961): 56-59.

1532   David L. Holmes, "Fathers and Brethren," *ChH* 37/3 (1968): 298-318.

1533   W. C. Robinson, "The Virgin Birth: A Broader Base," *CT* 17/5 (1972): 238-40.

23:10

1534   Ceslaus Spicq, "Une allusion au docteur de justice dans Matthieu 23:10?" *RB* 66 (1959): 387-96.

1535   Bruce W. Winter, "The Messiah as the Tutor: The Meaning of Kathegetes in Matthew 23:10," *TynB* 42 (1991): 152-57.

23:15

1536   H. J. Flowers, "Matthew 23:15," *ET* 73 (1961): 67-69.

1537   John Hoad, "On Matthew 23:15: A Rejoinder," *ET* 73 (1962): 211-12.

1538 Paul S. Minear, "Yes or No: The Demand for Honesty in the Early Church," *NovT* 13 (1971): 1-13.

1539 John Nolland, "Proselytism or Politics in Horace Satires 1, 4, 138-143?" *VC* 33/4 (1979): 347-55.

23:23

1540 Dietrich Correns, "Die Verzehntung der Raute. Luk XI 42 und M Schebi IX I," *MeliT* 6/2 (1963): 110-12.

1541 Peter Harvey, "Vision and Obligation," *DR* 85 (1967): 62-70.

1542 Robert A. Wild, "The Encounter between Pharisaic and Christian Judaism: Some Early Gospel Evidence," *NovT* 27/2 (1985): 105-24.

23:24-30

1543 J. D. M. Derrett, "Receptacles and Tombs (Mt. 23,24-30)," *ZNW* 77 (1986): 255-66.

23:24-26

1544 Fred B. Craddock, "Homiletical Studies: Exegesis and Exposition of Gospel Lections for the Season after Pentecost," *QR* 1/4 (1981): 5-42.

23:25-35

1545 Robert J. Miller, "The Rejection of the Prophet in Q," *JBL* 107 (1988): 225-40.

23:25-26

1546 Robert A. Wild, "The Encounter between Pharisaic and Christian Judaism: Some Early Gospel Evidence," *NovT* 27/2 (1985): 105-24.

23:25

1547 J. M. Ross, "Which Zachariah?" *IBS* 9 (1987): 70-73.

23:27-28

1548 Samuel Tobias Lachs, "On Matthew 23:27-28," *HTR* 68/3 (1975): 385-88.

23:27
>   1549   G. Schwarz, " 'Unkenntliche Graber'? (Lukas XI. 44),"
>   NTS 23/2 (1977): 345-46.

23:29-24:2
>   1550   Ross E. Winkle, "The Jeremiah Model for Jesus in the
>   Temple," AUSS 24/2 (1986): 155-72.

23:29-36
>   1551   H. Pernot, "Matthieu XXIII,29-36. Luc XI,47-51," RHPR
>   13 (1933): 262-67.

23:29-31
>   1552   J. D. M. Derrett, "You Build the Tombs of the Prophet
>   (Lk. 11,47-51, Mt.23,29-31)," in F. Cross, ed., Studia
>   Evangelica IV: Papers Presented to the Third International
>   Congress on New Testament Studies, Christ Church,
>   Oxford, 1965. (Part I—The New Testament Scriptures).
>   Berlin: Akademie-Verlag, 1968. Pp. 187-93.

23:29
>   1553   J. Jeremias, Heiligengräberin Jesu Umwelt (Mt. 23:29; Lk.
>   11, 47): Eine Untersuchung zur Volksreligion der Zeit Jesu.
>   Göttingen: Vandenhoeck & Ruprecht, 1958.

23:34-40
>   1554   Robert Douglas, "The Neglected Commandment II
>   (Matthew 22:34-40)," SouJT 3 (1960): 74-77.

23:34-39
>   1555   C. Deutsch, "Wisdom in Matthew: Transformation of a
>   Symbol," NovT 32 (1990): 13-47.

23:34-36
>   1556   F. Christ, "Das Weisheitswort," in Jesus Sophia: Die
>   Sophia-Christologie bei den Synoptikern. Zürich: Zwingli,
>   1970. Pp. 120-35.

23:34
>   1557   O. J. F. Seitz, "The Commission of Prophets and
>   'Apostles': Re-examination of Matthew 23,34 with Luke
>   11,49," in F. Cross, ed., Studia Evangelica IV: Papers
>   Presented to the Third International Congress on New
>   Testament Studies, Christ Church, Oxford, 1965 (Part

I—The New Testament Scriptures). Berlin: Akademie-Verlag, 1968. Pp. 26-40.

23:35

1558 M. McNamara, "Zechariah the Son of Barachiah: Mt. 23,35 and Tg Lam 2,20," in *The New Testament and the Palestinian Targum to the Pentateuch*. Rome: Biblical Institute Press, 1966. Pp. 160-63.

1559 J. Barton Payne, " 'Zachariah Who Perished'," *GTJ* 8/3 (1967): 33-35.

23:37-39

1560 H. van der Kwaak, "Die Klage über Jerusalem (Matth. xxiii. 37-39)," *NovT* 8 (1966): 156-70.

1561 F. Christ, "Das Jerusalemwort," in *Jesus Sophia: Die Sophia-Christologie bei den Synoptikern*. Zürich: Zwingli, 1970. Pp. 136-52.

23:39

1562 Edouard Lohse, "Hosianna," *NovT* 6/2 (1963): 113-19.

1563 Dale C. Allison, "Matt. 23:39 = Luke 13:35b as a Conditional Prophecy," *JSNT* 18 (1983): 75-84.

24-25

1564 André Feuillet, "La synthèse eschatologique de saint Matthieu XXIV-XXV," *RB* 56 (1949): 340-64; 57 (1950): 62-91; 180-211.

1565 M. Miguens, "Anotaciones sobre Mateo cc. 24-25," *SBFLA* 6 (1955-1956): 125-95.

1566 Ray Summers, "Matthew 24-25: An Exposition," *REd* 59 (1962): 501-11.

1567 M. Laconi, "Il discorso escatologico," in *Il Messaggio della salvezza*. 5 vols. Torino: Leumann, 1966-1970. 4:421-32.

1568 P. Géoltrain, "Notes sur Matthieu 24-25," *FV* 5 (1967): 26-35.

1569   Morris A. Inch, "Matthew and the House-Churches," *EQ* 43/4 (1971): 196-202.

1570   John F. Walvoord, "Christ's Olivet Discourse on the End of the Age," *BSac* 128 (1971): 109-16.

1571   Jan Lambrecht, "The Parousia Discourse. Composition and Content in Mt., XXIV-XXV," in *L'Évangile selon Matthieu.* Gembloux: Duculot, 1972. Pp. 309-42.

1572   John F. Walvoord, "Christ's Olivet Discourse on the Time of the End," *BSac* 129 (1972): 20-32.

1573   Henry G. Waterman, "The Sources of Paul's Teaching on the Second Coming of Christ in 1 and 2 Thessalonians," *JETS* 18/2 (1975): 105-13.

1574   Bruce A. Ware, "Is the Church in View in Matthew 24-25?" *BSac* 138 (1981): 158-72.

24:1-2:15
1575   John F. Walvoord, "Will Israel Build a Temple in Jerusalem?" *BSac* 125 (1968): 99-106.

24:1-44
1576   F. W. Beare, "The Synoptic Apocalypse: Matthean Version," in J. Reumann, ed., *Understanding the Sacred Text* (festschrift for Morton S. Enslin). Valley Forge: Judson Press, 1972. Pp. 115-33.

1577   John F. Hart, "A Chronology of Matthew 24:1-44," doctoral dissertation, Grace Theological Seminary, Winona Lake IN, 1986.

24:1-41
1578   D. L. Turner, "The Structure and Sequence of Matthew 24:1-41: Interaction with Evangelical Treatments," *GTJ* 10 (1989): 3-27.

24:1-36
1579   Hugo Lattanzi, "Eschatologici Sermonis Domini Logica Interpretatio," *Div* 11/1 (1967): 71-92.

24:1-25
  1580   Bo Reicke, "Synoptic Prophecies on the Destruction of Jerusalem," in D. E. Aune, ed., *Studies in New Testament and Early Christian Literature*. Leiden: Brill, 1972. Pp. 121-34.

24:1-14
  1581   J. L. Ch. Abineno, "The Return of Christ and the End of the World," *RW* 34/1 (1976): 28-31.

24:3-28
  1582   W. S. Vorster, "A Reader-Response Approach to Matthew 24:3-28," *HTS* 47 (1991): 1099-1108.

24:3
  1583   Raymond E. Gingrich, "Adumbrations of Our Lord's Return: Political Alignments," *GTJ* 9/1 (1968): 3-14.

  1584   D. Durken, "Mountains and Matthew," *BibTo* 28 (1990): 304-307.

24:4-14
  1585   John F. Walvoord, "Christ's Olivet Discourse on the Time of the End: Prophecies Fulfilled in the Present Age," *BSac* 128 (1971): 206-14.

24:9-13
  1586   Justin Taylor, " 'The Love of Many Will Grow Cold': Matt. 24:9-13 and the Neronian Persecution," *RB* 96/3 (1989): 352-57.

24:10-12
  1587   David Wenham, "A Note on Matthew 24:10-12," *TynB* 31 (1980): 150-62.

24:12
  1588   Raymond E. Gingrich, "Adumbrations of Our Lord's Return: Global Iniquity," *GTJ* 8/3 (1967): 17-32.

  1589   Domingo Munoz Leon, "Jesus y la apocaliptica pesimista (a proposito de Lc 18:8b y Mt. 24:12)," *EB* 46/4 (1988): 457-95.

24:14
> **1590**   Raymond E. Gingrich, "Adumbrations of Our Lord's Return: Political Alignments," *GTJ* 9/1 (1968): 3-14.

24:15-22
> **1591**   John F. Walvoord, "Posttribulationism Today. Part IV: Posttribulational Denial of Imminency and Wrath," *BSac* 133 (1976): 108-18.

24:15-20
> **1592**   Gordon D. Fee, "A Text-Critical Look at the Synoptic Problem," *NovT* 22/1 (1980): 12-28.

24:15-16
> **1593**   Thomas S. McCall, "How Soon the Tribulation Temple?" *BSac* 128 (1971): 341-51.

24:15
> **1594**   B. Rigaux, "Bdelugma tès erêmôseôs (Mc 13,14; Mt. 24,15)," in *Studia Biblica et Orientalia*. 3 vols. Rome: Pontifical Institute, 1959. 2:107-15.

> **1595**   G. Ch. Aalders, "De 'Gruwel der Verwoesting'," *GTT* 60 (1960): 1-5.

24:20
> **1596**   Graham N. Stanton, " 'Pray That Your Flight May Not Be in Winter or on a Sabbath'," *JSNT* 37 (1989): 17-30.

> **1597**   E. K.-C. Wong, "The Matthean Understanding of the Sabbath: A Response to G. N. Stanton," *JSNT* 44 (1991): 3-18.

24:26-29
> **1598**   Bonnie B. Thurston, " 'Do This': A Study on the Institution of the Lord's Supper," *RQ* 30/4 (1988): 207-17.

24:26-28
> **1599**   Hjerl-Hansen Borge, "Did Christ Know the Qumran Sect? Jesus and the Messiah of the Desert: An Observation Based on Matthew 24:26-28," *RevQ* 1 (1959): 495-508.

24:27-30
>   **1600**   John F. Walvoord, "Christ's Coming to Reign," *BSac* 123 (1966): 195-203.

24:29-34
>   **1601**   John F. Walvoord, "The Parable of the Talents," *BSac* 129 (1972): 206-10.

24:29-31
>   **1602**   John S. Kloppenborg, "Didache 16:6-8 and Special Matthaean Tradition," *ZNW* 70/1 (1979): 54-67.

24:29
>   **1603**   George C. Fuller, "The Olivet Discourse: An Apocalyptic Time-Table," *WTJ* 28/2 (1966): 157-63.

24:30
>   **1604**   A. J. B. Higgins, "The Sign of the Son of Man (Matt. 24:30)," *NTS* 9 (1962-1963): 380-82.

>   **1605**   T. F. Glasson, "The Ensign of the Son of Man (Matt. 24:30)," *JTS* 15 (1964): 299-300.

>   **1606**   Donald V. Etz, "Comets in the Bible," *CT* 18/6 (1973): 338-40.

24:34
>   **1607**   S. Joseph Kidder, " 'This Generation' in Matthew 24:34," *AUSS* 21/3 (1983): 203-209.

24:35
>   **1608**   George Howard, "A Note on Codex Sinaiticus and Shem-Tob's Hebrew Matthew," *NTS* 38 (1992): 187-204.

24:37-39
>   **1609**   Edgar V. McKnight and Charles H. Talbert, "Can the Griesbach Hypothesis Be Falsified?" *JBL* 91/3 (1972): 338-68.

24:42
>   **1610**   Nunzio Conte, " 'Il Signore Vostre Viene' (Mt. 24,42) l'Aspetto Escatologico della Liturgia. Domenica Idiavento A," *Sale* 47/3 (1985): 511-27.

24:43-44

1611   A. Strobel, "Das Gleichnis vom nächtlichen Einbrecher," in *Untersuchungen zum eschatologischen Verzögerungsproblem auf Grund der spätjüdischurchristlichen Geschichte von Habakuk 2,2 ff.* Leiden: Brill, 1961. Pp. 207-15.

24:45-51

1612   E. Lövestam, "Das Gleichnis vom heimkehrenden Hausherrn und seinem Knecht (Mt. 24,45-51)," in *Spiritual Wakefulness in the New Testament.* Lund: Gleerup, 1963. Pp. 215-22.

1613   A. Weiser, "Das Gleichnis vom treuen und untreuen Knecht Mt. 24,45-51 par. Lk. 12,42-46.47f.," in *Die Knechtsgleichnisse der synoptischen Evangelien.* Munich: Kösel, 1971. Pp. 178-225.

24:51

1614   Otto Betz, "The Dichotomized Servant and the End of Judas Iscariot," *RevQ* 5/17 (1964): 43-58.

25:1-13

1615   G. Bornkamm, "Die Verzögerung des Parusie. Exegetische Bemerkung zu zwei synoptischen Texten," in W. Schmauch, ed., *In Memoriam Ernst Lohmeyer.* Stuttgart: Evangelisches Verlagswerk, 1951. Pp. 116-26.

1616   A. Strobel, "Das Gleichnis von den zehn Jungfrauen (Mt. 25,1-13)," in *Untersuchungen zum eschatologischen Verzögerungsproblem auf Grund der spätjüdischurchristlichen Geschichte von Habakuk 2,2 ff.* Leiden: Brill, 1961. Pp. 233-54.

1617   E. Lövestam, "The Parable of the Ten Virgins," in *Spiritual Wakefulness in the New Testament.* Lund: Gleerup, 1963. Pp. 108-22.

1618   J. M. Ford, "The Parable of the Foolish Scholars (Matt. 25:1-13)," *NovT* 9 (1967): 107-23.

1619   J. Jeremias, "Lampades in Matthew 25:1-13," in J. M. Richards, ed., *Soli Deo Gloria* (festschrift for William Childs Robinson). Richmond: John Knox Press, 1968. Pp. 83-87.

1620   G. Bornkamm, "Die Verzögerung der Parusie. Exegetische Bemerkungen zu zwei synoptischen Texten," in *Geschichte und Glaube*: Band III. Munich: Kaiser, 1968; Band IV. Munich: Kaiser, 1971. 1:46-55.

1621   L. Deiss, "La parabole des dix vierges (Mt. 25,1-13)," *AsSeign* N.S. 63 (1971): 20-32.

1622   K. P. Donfried, "The Allegory of the Ten Virgins (Matt. 25:1-13) as a Summary of Matthean Theology," *JBL* 93 (1974): 415-28.

1623   Gerhard Sellen, "Gleichnisstrukturen," *LB* 31 (1974): 89-115.

1624   K. P. Donfried, "The Ten Virgins (Mt. 25:1-13)," *TD* 23 (1975): 106-10.

1625   W. Schrenk, "Auferweckung der Toten oder Gericht nach den Werken. Tradition und Redaktion in Mattäus XXV: 1-13," *NovT* 20/4 (1978): 278-99.

1626   Nancy J. Duff, "Wise and Foolish Maidens, Matthew 25:1-13," *USQR* 40/3 (1985): 55-58.

25:1-12

1627   Patrick P. Saydon, "Some Biblioco-Liturgical Passages Reconsidered," *MeliT* 18/1 (1966): 10-17.

1628   Martino Conti, "La Sacra Scrittura nella Predicazione di San Bernardino," *Ant* 55/4 (1980): 549-72.

25:1-3

1629   Walter Magass, " 'Er aber Schlief' (Mt. 8,24)," *LB* 29/30 (1973): 55-59.

25:1

1630   J. Jeremias, "*Lampdes*. Mt. 25,1.3f," *ZAW* 56 (1965): 196-201.

25:14-30

1631   E. Kamlah, "Kritik und Interpretation der Parabel von den anvertrauten Geldern," *KD* 14 (1968): 28-38.

1632   A. Weiser, "Das Gleichnis von den anvertrauten Geldern Mt. 25,14-30 par. Lk. 19 12-27," in *Die Knechtsgleichnisse der synoptischen Evangelien.* Munich: Kösel, 1971. Pp. 226-72.

1633   Erhardt Guttgemanns, "Narrative Analyse Synoptischer Texte," *LB* 25 (1973): 50-73.

1634   Gerhard Sellen, "Gleichnisstrukturen," *LB* 31 (1974): 89-115.

1635   L. C. McGauchy, "The Fear of Yahweh and the Mission of Judaism: A Postexilic Maxim and Its Early Christian Expansion in the Parable of the Talents," *JBL* 94 (1975): 235-45.

1636   David C. Steinmetz, "Matthew 25:14-30," *Int* 34/2 (1980): 172-76.

1637   A. Puig i Tárrech, "La parabole des talents (Mt. 25,14-30) ou des mines (Lc. 19,11-28)," *RCT* 10 (1985): 269-317.

1638   Christian Dietzfelbinger, "Das Gleichnis von der anvertrauten Geldern," *BTZ* 6 (1989): 222-33.

1639   Daniel Lys, "Contre le salut par les oeuvres dans la prédiction des talents," *ÉTR* 64 (1989): 331-40.

1640   A. A. Bucher, *Gleichnisse verstehen lernen: Struktur-genetische Untersuchungen zur Rezeption synoptischer Parabeln.* Fribourg: Universitäts-Verlag, 1990.

25:21-23
1641   J. Vara, "Dos conjeturas textuales sobre Mateo 25,21.23 y Mateo 26,32/17,22 y par.," *Salm* 33 (1986): 81-86.

25:26
1642   J. Mutch, "The Man with the One Talent," *ET* 41 (1930-1931): 332-34.

1643   H. K. Nielsen, "Er den 'dovne' tjener doven? Om oversaettelsen af ὀκνηρός i Matth 25,26," *DTT* 53 (1990): 106-15.

25:30

1644   A. Marcus Ward, "Uncomfortable Words: IV. Unprofitable Servants," *ET* 81/7 (1970): 200-203.

25:31-46

1645   C. F. Burney, "St. Matthew 25:31-46 as a Hebrew Poem," *JTS* (1912-1913): 414-24.

1646   A. T. Cadoux, "The Parable of the Sheep and the Goats," *ET* 41 (1929-1930): 559-62.

1647   J. A. T. Robinson, "The 'Parable' of the Sheep and the Goats," *NTS* 2 (1955-1956): 225-37.

1648   J. Ramsey Michaels, "Apostolic Hardships and Righteous Gentiles," *JBL* 84 (1965): 27-37.

1649   H. E. W. Turner, "Expounding the Parables: The Parable of the Sheep and the Goats," *ET* 77 (1965-1966): 243-46.

1650   John F. Walvoord, "Christ's Coming to Reign," *BSac* 123 (1966): 195-203.

1651   Norman K. Bakken, "The New Humanity: Christ and the Modern Age: A Study in the Christ-Hymn: Philippians 2:6-11," *Int* 22/1 (1968): 71-82.

1652   Lamar Cope, "Matthew 25:31-46: 'The Sheep and the Goats' Reinterpreted," *NovT* 11 (1969): 32-44.

1653   S. Légasse, "La parabole du jugement dernier (Mt. xxv,31-46)," in *Jésus et l'enfant: 'Enfants', 'Petis' et 'simples' dans la tradition synoptique.* Paris: Gabalda, 1969. Pp. 85-100.

1654   J.-C. Ingelaere, "La 'parabole' du Jugement Dernier (Matthieu 25,31-46)," *RHPR* 50 (1970): 23-60.

1655   Dietfried Gewalt, "Matthaus 25,31-46 im Erwartungshorizont Heutiger Exgese," *LB* 25/26 (1973): 9-21.

1656   Erhardt Guttgemanns, "Narrative Analyse Synoptischer Texte," *LB* 25 (1973): 50-73.

1657   J. Manek, "Mit wem identifiziert sich Jesus (Matt.
            25:31-46)?" in B. Lindars and S. S. Smalley, eds. *Christ
            and Spirit in the New Testament* (festschrift for C. F. D.
            Moule). Cambridge: Cambridge University Press, 1973. Pp.
            15-25.

1658   Richard C. Oudersluys, "The Parable of the Sheep and
            Goats (Matthew 25:31-46): Eschatology and Mission, Then
            and Now," *RR* 26/3 (1973): 151-61.

1659   M. A. Chevallier, "Note à propos de l'exégète de Mt.
            25:31-46," *RevSR* 48 (1974): 398-400.

1660   Tibor Horvath, "3 Jn 11: An Early Ecumenical Creed?" *ET*
            85/11 (1974): 339-40.

1661   A. J. Mattill, Jr., "Matthew 25:31-46 Relocated," *RQ* 17/2
            (1974): 107-14.

1662   David L. Bartlett, "An Exegesis of Matthew 25:31-46,"
            Found 19/3 (1976): 211-13.

1663   Charles E. Booth, "An Exegesis of Matthew 25:31-46,"
            Found 19/3 (1976): 214-15.

1664   Paul M. Nagano, "An Exegesis of Matthew 25:31-46,"
            Found 19/3 (1976): 216-22.

1665   T. C. Smith, "An Exegesis of Matthew 25:31-46," *Found*
            19/3 (1976): 206-10.

1666   P. Bonnard, "Matt. 25:31-46: Questions de lecture et
            d'interprétation," *FV* 76 (1977): 81-87.

1667   Rudolf Brändle, "Jean Chrysostome—l'importance de
            Matth 25,31-46 pour son Éthique," *VC* 31/1 (1977): 47-52.

1668   J. Friedrich, *Gott im Brüder? Eine methodenkritische Unter
            suchung von Redaktion, Überlieferung und Traditionen in
            Mt. 25:31-46.* Calwer Theologische Monographien 7.
            Stuttgart: Calwer, 1977.

1669   Walter Altmann, "Libertação e justificação: Mateus
            25,31-46," *PerT* 11 (1979): 5-15.

1670   David R. Catchpole, "The Poor on Earth and the Son of Man in Heaven: A Reappraisal of Matthew 25:31-46," *BJRL* 61/2 (1979): 355-97.

1671   Rudolf Brändle, "Zur Interpretation von Mt. 25:31-46 im Matthäuskommentar des Origenes," *TZ* 36 (1980): 17-25.

1672   André Feuillet, "Le Caractere universel: Du Judgment et la Charite sans Frontieres en Mt. 25,31-46," *NRT* 102/2 (1980): 179-96.

1673   Lauree H. Meyer, "Understanding Ministry," *BLT* 25/1 (1980): 28-31.

1674   Martin Tripole, "A Church for the Poor and the World: At Issue with Moltmann's Ecclesiology," *TS* 42/4 (1981): 645-59.

1675   X. Pikaza, "La estructura de Mateo y su influencia en 25:31-46," *Salm* 30 (1983): 11-40.

1676   John M. Court, "Right and Left: The Implications for Matthew 25.31-46," *NTS* 31/2 (1985): 223-33.

1677   W. Weren, "Mt. 25,31-46: een analyse," *Schrift* 105 (1986): 114-20.

1678   L. J. Frahier, "L'interpretation du récit du jugement dernier (Mt. 25,31-46) dans l'oeuvre d'Augustin," *REA* 33 (1987): 70-84.

1679   Werner Fuchs, "Meditacao sobre Mateus 25:31-46," *EstT* 27/2 (1987): 81-186.

1680   Dan O. Via, "Ethical Responsibility and Human Wholeness in Matthew 25:31-46," *HTR* 80/1 (1987): 79-100.

1681   Sherman W. Gray, *The Least of My Brothers: Matthew 25:31-46—A History of Interpretation*. Atlanta: Scholars Press, 1989.

1682   J. J. Lapoorta, "Exegesis and Proclamation: 'Whatever You Did for One of the Least of These . . . You Did for Me' (Matt. 25:31-46)," *JTSA* 68 (1989): 103-109.

1683   Schuyler Brown, "Faith, the Poor and the Gentiles: A
                Tradition-Historical Reflection on Matthew 25:31-46," *TJT*
                6/2 (1990): 171-81.

1684   E. Farahian, "Relire Matthieu 25,31-46," *Greg* 72 (1991):
                437-57.

1685   Manfred Hutter, "Mt. 25:31-46 in der Deutung Manis,"
                NovT 33 (1991) 276-82.

1686   J. Sayer, " 'Ich hatte Durst, und ihr gabt mir zu trinken'.
                Zum Ansatz einer Theologie der menschlichen
                Grundbedürfnisse nach Mt. 25,31ff. im Rahmen der Pastoral
                der Befreiung," *MTZ* 42 (1991): 151-67.

25:31-33
1687   Wilfred Tooley, "The Shepherd and Sheep Image in the
                Teaching of Jesus," *NovT* 7/1 (1964): 15-25.

25:31
1688   James H. Smylie, "Uncle Tom's Cabin Revisited: The
                Bible, the Romantic Imagination and the Sympathies of
                Christ," *Int* 27/1 (1973): 67-85.

25:32
1689   François Martin, "The Image of Shepherd in the Gospel of
                St. Matthew," *ScE* 27 (1975): 261-301.

25:35ff
1690   J. A. Grassi, " 'I Was Hungry and You Gave Me
                Something to Eat'," *BTB* 11/3 (1981): 81-84.

25:37-26:3
1691   W. D. McHardy, "Matthew 25:37-26:3 in 074," *JTS* 46
                (1945): 190-91.

25:40
1692   G. Gross, "Die 'geringsten Brüder' Jesu im Mt. 25:40 in
                Auseinandersetzung mit der neueren Exegese," *BibL* 5
                (1964): 172-80.

1693   Michael Wilson, "Violence and Nonviolence in the Cure of
                Disease and the Healing of Patients," *CC* 87 (1970):
                756-58.

25:41-46
>
> **1694**   P. H. Bligh, "Eternal Fire, Eternal Punishment, Eternal Life (Mt. 25,41.46)," *ET* 83 (1971-72): 9-11.

25:46
>
> **1695**   Simone Frutiger, "Les lectures d'Evangile ou les textes disjoints: Matthieu 16:13 à 25:46," *FV* 82 (1983): 59-75.

26-28
>
> **1696**   K. G. Kuhn, "Jesus in Gethsemane," *EvT* 12 (1952-1953): 260-85.
>
> **1697**   S. J. Rieckert, "The Narrative Coherence in Matthew 26-28," *Neo* 16 (1982): 53-74.
>
> **1698**   François Martin, "Mourir: Matthieu 26-28," *SBib* 53 (1989): 18-47.
>
> **1699**   J. P. Heil, *The Death and Resurrection of Jesus: A Narrative-Critical Reading of Matthew 26-28*. Minneapolis: Fortress, 1991.

26-27
>
> **1700**   N. A. Dahl, "Die Passionsgeschichte bei Matthäus," *NTS* 2 (1955): 17-32.
>
> **1701**   A.-L. Descamps, "Rédaction et christologie dans le récit matthéen de la Passion," in *L'Évangile selon Matthieu*. Gembloux: Duculot, 1972. Pp. 359-415.
>
> **1702**   Donald Senior, "The Passion Narrative in the Gospel of Matthew," in *L'Évangile selon Matthieu*. Gembloux: Duculot, 1972. Pp. 343-57.

26:1-75
>
> **1703**   Frank J. Matera, "The Passion According to Matthew. Part One: Jesus Unleashes the Passion, 26:1-75," *ClerR* 62 (1987): 93-97.

26:1
>
> **1704**   David Hellholm, "En textgrammatisk konstruktion I Matteusevangeliet," *SEÅ* 51 (1986-1987): 80-89.

26:6-13

1705   J. D. M. Derrett, "The Anointing at Bethany," in F. Cross, ed., *Studia Evangelica II*: Papers Presented to the Second International Congress on New Testament Studies, Christ Church, Oxford, 1961 (Part I—The New Testament Scriptures). Berlin: Akademie-Verlag, 1964. Pp. 174-82.

1706   J. D. M. Derrett, "The Anointing at Bethany and the Story of Zacchaeus," in *Law in the New Testament*. London: Longman & Todd, 1970. Pp. 266-85.

1707   Ronald F. Thiemann, "The Unnamed Woman at Bethany," *TT* 44/2 (1987): 179-88.

1708   J. F. Coakley, "The Anointing at Bethany and the Priority of John," *JBL* 107/2 (1988): 241-56.

26:13

1709   A. Strobel, "Zum Verständnis von Mat. 26:13," *NTS* 2 (1957-1958): 199-227.

1710   J. H. Greenlee, "For Her Memorial: Mt. 26:13, Mk. 14:9," *ET* 71 (1959-1960): 245.

26:15

1711   E. Reiner, "Thirty Pieces of Silver," in W. W. Hallo, ed., *Essays in Memory of E. A. Speiser*. New Haven: American Oriental Society, 1968. Pp. 186-90.

1712   P. Colella, "Trenta denari," *RBib* 21 (1973): 325-27.

26:26-28

1713   D. B. Carmichael, "David Daube on the Eucharist and the Passover Seder," *JSNT* 42 (1991): 45-67.

26:27

1714   Phillip Sigal, "Another Note to 1 Corinthians 10.16," *NTS* 29/1 (1983): 134-39.

26:28

1715   J. M. R. Tillard, "L'Eucharistie, Purification de l'Eglise Peregrinante," *NRT* 84 (1962): 449-74, 579-97.

26:29-40
1716 H. A. Sanders, "A Third Century Papyrus of Matthew and Acts," in R. P. Casey, et al. eds., *Quantulacumque* (festschrift for Kirsopp Lake). London: Christophers, 1937. Pp. 151-61.

26:29-31
1717 E. Bammel, "P⁶⁴ (⁶⁷) and the Last Supper." *JTS* 24/1 (1973): 189.

26:31
1718 François Martin, "The Image of Shepherd in the Gospel of St. Matthew," *ScE* 27 (1975): 261-301.

26:32
1719 J. Vara, "Dos conjeturas textuales sobre Mateo 25,21.23 y Mateo 26,32/17,22 y par.," *Salm* 33 (1986): 81-86.

1720 D. Muñoz León, " 'Iré delante de vosotros a Galilea' (Mt. 26,32 y par.). Sentido mesiánico y posible sustrato arameo del logion," *EB* 48 (1990): 215-41.

26:34
1721 G. Zuntz, "A Note on Matthew 26:34 and 26:75," *JTS* 50 (1949): 182-83.

1722 Herbert Dennett, "The Need for a Neutral Idiom," *BT* 17 (1966): 39-41.

26:36-28:20
1723 T. Kayalaparampil, "Passion and Resurrection in the Gospel of Matthew," *BB* 16 (1990): 41-51.

26:36-46
1724 M. Galizzi, *Gesu nel Getsemani*. Zürich: Pas, 1972.

1725 Anna Maria Aagaard, "Doing God's Will: Matthew 26:36-46," *IRM* 77 (1988): 221-28.

26:50
1726 J. P. Wilson, "Matthew 26,50," *ET* 41 (1929-1930): 334.

1727 F. Rehkopf, "Mt. 26:50: Ἑταῖρε, ἐφ᾽ ὃ πάρει," *ZNW* 52 (1961): 109-15.

1728   W. Eltester, "Freund, wozu du gekommen bist (Mt. 26:50)," in *Neotestamentica et Patristica* (festschrift for Oscar Cullmann). Leiden: Brill, 1962. Pp. 70-91.

1729   G. M. Lee, "Matthew 26:50," *ET* 81 (1969-1970): 55.

1730   James L. Boyer, "Relative Clauses in the Greek New Testament: A Statistical Study," *GTJ* 9/2 (1988): 233-56.

26:52
1731   H. Kosmala, "Matthew 26:52. A Quotation from the Targum ," *NovT* 4 (1960-61): 3-5.

26:56
1732   James W. Scott, "Matthew's Intention to Write History," *WTJ* 47/1 (1985): 68-82.

26:57-27:2
1733   Birger Gerhardsson, "Confession and Denial before Men: Observation on Matt. 26:57-27:2," *JSNT* 13 (1981): 46-66.

26:59-66
1734   David R. Catchpole, "The Problem of the Historicity of the Sanhedrin Trial," in E. Bammel, ed., *The Trial of Jesus* (festschrift for C. F. D. Moule). London: SCM Press, 1970. Pp. 47-65.

1735   J. C. O'Neill, "The Charge of Blasphemy at Jesus' Trial before the Sanhedrin," in E. Bammel, ed., *The Trial of Jesus* (festschrift for C. F. D. Moule). London: SCM Press, 1970. Pp. 72-77.

26:63
1736   R. L. Mowery, "Subtle Differences: The Matthean 'Son of God' References," *NovT* 32 (1990): 193-200.

26:64
1737   F. Segarra, "Algunas observaciones sobre los principales textos escatológicos de Nuestro Señor: S. Mateo, XXVI,64," *EE* 15 (1936): 47-66.

1738   David R. Catchpole, "The Answer of Jesus to Caiaphas (Matthew 26:64)," *NTS* 17/2 (1971): 213-26.

1739   Renatus Kempthorne, "The Marcan Text of Jesus' Answer to the High Priest (Mark 14:62)," *NovT* 19/3 (1977): 197-208.

26:68
    1740   F. Neirynck, "Tis estin o paisas se." *ETL* 63/1 (1987): 5-47.

26:69-75
    1741   N. J. McEleney, "Peter's Denials—How Many? To Whom?" *CBQ* 52 (1990): 467-72.

26:69-72
    1742   Dietfried Gewalt, "Die Verlegnung des Petrus," *LB* 43 (1978): 113-44.

26:75
    1743   G. Zuntz, "A Note on Matthew 26:34 and 26:75," *JTS* 50 (1949): 182-83.

27:1-66
    1744   Frank J. Matera, "The Passion According to Matthew. Part Two: Jesus Suffers the Passion, 27:1-66," *P&P* 1 (1987): 13-17.

27:1-26
    1745   J. Escande, "Judas et Pilate prisonniers d'une même Structure (Mt. 27,1-26)," *FV* 18 (1979): 92-100.

27:2-66
    1746   G. M. Lee, "The Guard at the Tomb," *Theology* 72 (1969): 169-75.

27:3-10
    1747   G. Strecker, "Die Judasperikope (Mt. 27,3-10)," in *Der Weg der Gerechtigkeit: Untersuchung zur Theologie des Matthäus*. Göttingen: Vandenhoeck & Ruprecht, 1962. Pp. 76-82.

    1748   Donald Senior, "A Case Study in Matthean Creativity: Matthew 27:3-10," *BR* 19 (1974): 23-36.

    1749   L. Desautels, "La mort de Judas (Mt. 27,3-10; Ac 1,15-26)," *ScE* 38 (1986): 221-39.

1750   A. Conrad, "The Fate of Judas: Matthew 27:3-10," *TJT* 7 (1991): 158-68.

27:9-10
1751   M. Quesnel, "Les citations de Jérémie dans l'évangile selon saint Matthieu," *EB* 47 (1989): 513-27.

27:9
1752   E. F. Sutcliffe, "Matthew 27,9," *JTS* 3 (1952): 227-28.

1753   M. J. J. Menken, "The References of Jeremiah in the Gospel According to Matthew (Mt. 2,17; 16,14; 27,9)," *ETL* 60/1 (1984): 5-24.

1754   James W. Scott, "Matthew's Intention to Write History," *WTJ* 47/1 (1985): 68-82.

27:11-31
1755   L. Marin, "Jesus devant Pilate," *Études sémiologiques*. Paris: Klincksieck, 1971. Pp. 233-63.

27:11-26
1756   C. Rene Padilla, "Bible Studies," *Miss* 10/3 (1982): 319-38.

27:15-26
1757   W. Trilling, "Der Prozess vor Pilatus: 27,15-26," in *Das wahre Israel: Studien zur Theologie des Matthäus-Evangeliums*. Munich: Kösel, 1964. Pp. 66-74.

27:19
1758   E. Fascher, "Das Weib des Pilatus," in *Festheft Walter Bauer zum 70. Geburtstag gewidmet*. Leipzig: Hoppe, 1947. Pp. 201-203.

1759   A. Oepke, "Noch einmal das Weib des Pilatus," *TLZ* 73 (1948): 743-46.

1760   J. D. M. Derrett, "Haggadah and the Account of the Passion," *DR* 97 (1979): 308-15.

1761   F. M. Gilmann, "The Wife of Pilate (Matthew 27:19)," *LouvS* 17 (1992): 152-65.

27:24-25

1762 Frank J. Matera, "His Blood Be on Us and Our Children," *BibTo* 27 (1989): 345-50.

1763 T. B. Cargal, " 'His Blood Be Upon Us and Upon Our Children': A Matthean Double Entendre?" *NTS* 37/1 (1991): 102-12.

27:25

1764 H. Kosmala, "His Blood on Us and Our Children ," *ASTI* 7 (1970): 94-126.

1765 Klaus Haacker, " 'Sein Blut über uns'. Erwägungen zu Matthäus 27,25," *KIsr* 1 (1986): 47-50.

1766 R. H. Smith, "Matthew 27:25: The Hardest Verse in Matthew's Gospel," *CThM* 17 (1990): 421-28.

27:27

1767 Tomas Arvedson, "Jesus som narrkonung," in *Professor Johannes Lindblom: på hans 65-,35 årsdag den 7 juni 1947.* Uppsala: Wretmans, 1948. Pp. 9-19.

1768 Wallace M. Alston, "Christ and the Military Mind," *Int* 30/1 (1976): 26-35.

27:28

1769 J. M. Bover, "Un caso típico de crítica textual, Mt. 27,28," in *En torno al problema de la escatología individual del Antiguo Testamento.* Madrid: Científica Medinaceli, 1955. Pp. 221-26.

27:35

1770 Jospeh A. Fitzmyer, "Crucifixion in Ancient Palestine, Qumran Literature, and the New Testament," *CBQ* 40/4 (1978): 493-513.

27:37-44

1771 Terence L. Donaldson, "The Mockers and the Son of God (Matthew 27:37-44): Two Characters in Matthew's Story of Jesus," *JSNT* 41 (1991): 3-18.

27:44-54

1772 Hartmut Gese, "Psalm 22 und das Neue Testament," *ZTK* 65/1 (1968): 1-22.

27:46-47

1773   William C. Jordan, "The Last Tormentor of Christ: An Image of the Jew in Ancient and Medieval Exegesis, Art, and Drama," *JQR* 78/1 (1987): 21-47.

27:46

1774   F. Smith, "The Strangest 'Word' of Jesus," *ET* 44 (1932-1933): 259-61.

1775   D. H. C. Read, "The Cry of Dereliction," *ET* 68 (1956-1957): 260-62.

1776   S. Lewis Johnson, "The Death of Christ," *BSac* 125 (1968): 10-19.

27:49b

1777   Stephen Pennells, "The Spear Thrust," *JSNT* 19 (1983): 99-115.

27:51-54

1778   W. G. Essame, "Matthew 27:51-54 and John 5:25-29," *ET* 76 (1964-1965): 103.

1779   Frank J. Matera, "Matthew 27:51-54," *Int* 38 (1984): 55-59.

1780   R. D. Witherup, "The Death of Jesus and the Raising of the Saints: Matthew 27:51-54," *SBLSP* (1987): 574-85.

27:51-53

1781   Paul K. Jewett, "Can We Learn from Mariology?" *CC* 84/32 (1967): 1019-21.

1782   Donald Senior, "The Death of Jesus and the Resurrection of the Holy Ones (Mt. 27:51-53)," *CBQ* 38 (1976): 312-29.

1783   Rafael Aquirre, "Cross and Kingdom in Matthew's Theology," *TD* 29/2 (1981): 149-52.

1784   J. W. Wenham, "When Were the Saints Raised?" *JTS* 32/1 (1981): 150-52.

1785   David Hill, "Matthew 27:51-53 in the Theology of the Evangelist," *IBS* 7 (1985): 76-87.

27:51b-53
> **1786**   J. Blinzler, "Zur Erklarung von Mt. 27,51b-53," *TGl* 34 (1943): 91-93.

> **1787**   R. Aguirre, "El Reino de Dios y la muerte de Jesús en el evangelio de Mateo," *EE* 54 (1979): 363-82.

27:51
> **1788**   M. de Jonge, "Matthew 27:51 in Early Christian Exegesis," *HTR* 79/1 (1986): 67-79.

27:55
> **1789**   G. Schwarz, "ἀπὸ μακρόθεν/ἐπὶ τῆς ὁδοῦ," *BibN* 20 (1983): 56-57.

27:57-28:20
> **1790**   P. H. Lai, "Production du sens par la foi. Autorités religieuses contestées/fondées. Analyse structurale de Matthieu 27,57-28,20," *RechSR* 61 (1973): 65-96.

> **1791**   L. Pham, "Sinn-Erzeugung durch den Glauben-Widerlegte: Begrundete Religiose Authoritaten: Strukturale Analyse von Matth 27,57-28,20," *LB* 32 (1974): 1-37.

> **1792**   Charles H. Giblin, "Structural and Thematic Correlation in the Matthaean Burial-Resurrection Narrative (Matt. 27:57-28:20)," *NTS* 21 (1974-1975): 406-20.

27:57-28:15
> **1793**   C. Turiot, "Sémiotique et lisibilité du texte évangélique," *RechSR* 73 (1985): 161-75.

27:57-60
> **1794**   W. Boyd Barrick, "The Rich Man from Arimathea (Matt. 27:57-60) and 1QIsa," *JBL* 96/2 (1977): 235-39.

27:59
> **1795**   D. Moody Smith, "Mark 15:46: The Shroud of Turin as a Problem of History and Faith," *BA* 46/4 (1983): 251-54.

> **1796**   Jacques Winandy, "Les vestiges laisses dans le tombeau et la foi du disciple (Jn 20,1-9)," *NRT* 110/2 (1988) 212-19.

27:62-28:20

1797   Raymond E. Brown, *A Risen Christ in Eastertime: Essays on the Gospel Narratives of the Resurrection*. Collegeville, MN: Liturgical Press, 1991.

27:62-28:15

1798   B. Kratz, *Auferweckung als Befreiung: Eine Studie zur Passions- und Auferstehungstheologie des Matthaus (besonders Mt. 27,62-28,15)*. Stuttgart: KBW Verlag, 1973.

27:62-66

1799   I. Broer, "Mt. 27,62-66," in *Die Urgemeinde und das Grab Jesu: Eine Analyse der Grablegungsgeschichte im Neuen Testament*. Munich: Kösel, 1972. Pp. 69-78.

1800   Nikolaus Walter, "Eine Vormatthaische Schilderung derr Auferstehung Jesus," *NTS* 19/4 (1973): 415-29.

27:66

1801   A. Malamat, " 'Door-Sealings in the Mari Palace—A Textual-Archaeological Correlation'," *E-I* 18 (1985): 325-30.

28:1-18

1802   Edgar V. McKnight and Charles H. Talbert, "Can the Griesbach Hypothesis Be Falsified?" *JBL* 91/3 (1972): 338-68.

28:1-10

1803   E. L. Bode, "The Gospel of Matthew," in *The First Easter Morning: The Gospel Accounts of the Women's Visit to the Tomb of Jesus*. Rome: Biblical Institute Press, 1970. Pp. 50-58.

1804   Paul S. Minear, "Matthew 28:1-10," *Int* 38/1 (1984): 59-63.

1805   Cynthia A. Jarvis, "Matthew 28:1-10," *Int* 42/1 (1988): 63-68.

1806   Dorothy J. Weaver, "Matthew 28:1-10," *Int* 46 (1992): 399-402.

28:1-8

1807   W. Trilling, "Die Auferstehung Jesu, Anfang der neuen Weltzeit (Mt. 28,1-8)," in *Christusverkündigung in den synoptischen Evangelien.* Munich: Kösel, 1969. Pp. 212-43.

1808   X. Léon-Dufour, "Le message pascal selon saint Matthieu," in *Résurrection de Jésus et message pascal.* Paris: Seuil, 1971. Pp. 187-98.

1809   L. Marin, "Les femmes au tombeau," *Études sémiologiques.* Paris: Klincksieck, 1971. Pp. 221-31.

1810   B. Rigaux, "Mt. 28,1-8," in *Dieu l'a rcssuscité.* Gembloux: Duculot, 1973. Pp. 200-204.

1811   Nikolaus Walter, "Eine Vormatthaische Schilderung derr Auferstehung Jesus," *NTS* 19/4 (1973): 415-29.

28:1-7

1812   W. Trilling, "Das leere Grab bei Matthäus (Mt. 28,1-7)," in *Christusverkündigung in den synoptischen Evangelien.* Munich: Kösel, 1969. Pp. 112-24.

28:1-3

1813   C. A. Webster, "St. Matthew 28,1.3," *ET* 42 (1930-1931): 381-82.

28:1

1814   G. R. Driver, "Two Problems in the New Testament," *JTS* 16 (1965): 327-37.

28:2

1815   A. Krücke, "Der Engel am Grabe Christi," *ZNW* 33 (1934): 313-17.

28:2-4

1816   Nikolaus Walter, "Eine Vormatthaische Schilderung derr Auferstehung Jesus," *NTS* 19/4 (1973): 415-29.

28:4

1817   G. M. Lee, "The Guard at the Tomb," *Theology* 72 (1969): 169-75.

28:7

1818   A. G. van Aarde, "Ἠγέρθη ἀπὸ τῶν νεκρῶν (Mt. 28:7):
                A Textual Evidence on the Separation of Judaism and
                Christianity," *Neo* 23 (1989): 219-33.

28:9-10

1819   F. Neirynck, "John and the Synoptics: The Empty Tomb
                Stories," *NTS* 30/2 (1984): 161-87.

28:11-15

1820   Nikolaus Walter, "Eine Vormatthaische Schilderung derr
                Auferstehung Jesus," *NTS* 19/4 (1973): 415-29.

28:11-5

1821   G. M. Lee, "The Guard at the Tomb," *Theology* 72 (1969):
                169-75.

28:16-20

1822   H. M. Parker, "The Great Commission," *Int* 2 (1948):
                74-75.

1823   E. Lohmeyer, "Mir ist gegeben alle Gewalt! Eine Exegese
                von Mt. 28,16-20," in W. Schmauch, ed., *In Memoriam
                Ernst Lohmeyer*. Stuttgart: Evangelisches Verlagswerk,
                1951. Pp. 22-52.

1824   G. Strecker, "Die Grundlegung (Mt. 28,16-20)," in *Der
                Weg der Gerechtigkeit: Untersuchung zur Theologie des
                Matthäus*. Göttingen: Vandenhoeck & Ruprecht, 1962. Pp.
                208-14.

1825   G. Bornkamm, "Der Auferstandene und der Irdische. Mt.
                28,16-20," in E. Dinkler, ed., *Zeit und Geschichte*
                (festschrift for Rudolf Bultmann). Tübingen: Mohr, 1964.
                Pp. 171-91.

1826   Russell C. Tuck, "The Lord Who Said Go: Some
                Reflections on Matthew 28:16-20," *ANQ* 7/2 (1966): 85-92.

1827   Robert D. Culver, "What Is the Church's Commission?
                Some Exegetical Issues in Matthew 28:16-20," *BETS* 10/2
                (1967): 115-26.

1828   U. Luck, "Herrenwort und Geschichte in Matth. 28,16-20,"
                EvT 27 (1967): 494-508.

1829   B. J. Malina, "The Literary Structure and Form of Matt. 28:16-20," *NTS* 17 (1970-1971): 87-103.

1830   X. Léon-Dufour, "À l'origine des récits d'apparition: le type Galilée," in *Résurrection de Jésus et message pascal.* Paris: Seuil, 1971. Pp. 137-44.

1831   J. Zumstein, "Matthieu 28:16-20," *RTP* 22 (1972): 14-33.

1832   B. J. Hubbard, *The Matthean Redaction of a Primitive Apostolic Commissioning: An Exegesis of Matthew 28:16-20*. SBLDS #19. Missoula, MT: Scholars Press, 1974.

1833   Jack Dean Kingsbury, "The Composition and Christology of Matthew 28:16-20," *JBL* 93/4 (1974): 573-84.

1834   James Tanis, "Reformed Pietism and Protestant Missions," *HTR* 67/1 (1974): 65-73.

1835   Charles H. Giblin, "A Note on Doubt and Reassurance in Mt. 28:16-20," *CBQ* 37 (1975): 68-75.

1836   Grant R. Osborne, "Redaction Criticism and the Great Commission: A Case Study Toward a Biblical Understanding of Inerrancy," *JETS* 19/2 (1976): 73-85.

1837   Luis M. Bermejo, "The Alleged Infallibility of Councils," *Bij* 38/2 (1977): 128-62.

1838   John P. Meier, "Two Disputed Questions in Matt. 28:16-20," *JBL* 96/3 (1977): 407-24.

1839   L. G. Parkhurst, Jr., "Matthew 28:16-20 Reconsidered," *ET* 90 (1979): 179-80.

1840   Jacques Matthey, "The Great Commission According to Matthew," *IRM* 69 (1980): 161-73.

1841   Oscar S. Brooks, "Matthew 28:16-20 and the Design of the First Gospel," *JSNT* 10 (1981): 2-18.

1842   Larry R. McGraw, "An Examination of the Literary Context of the Great Commission in Matthew 28:16-20,"

164

doctoral dissertation, Southwestern Baptist Theological Seminary, Fort Worth TX, 1983.

1843 B. T. Viviano, "Matthew, Master of Ecumenical Infighting," *CThM* 10/6 (1983): 325-32.

1844 L. Legrand, "The Missionary Command of the Risen Lord Mt. 28:16-20," *ITS* 24 (1987): 5-28.

1845 Pheme Perkins, "Christology and Mission: Matthew 28:16-20," *List* 24/3 (1989): 302-309.

1846 C. Manus, " 'King-Christology': The Result of a Critical Study of Matt. 28:16-20 as an Example of Contextual Exegesis in Africa," *ScrSA* 39 (1991): 25-42.

1847 D. P. Scaer, "The Relation of Matthew 28:16-20 to the Rest of the Gospel," *CTQ* 55 (1991): 245-66.

1848 Cynthia M. Campbell, "Matthew 28:16-20," *Int* 46 (1992): 402-405.

1849 W. D. Davies and Dale C. Allison, "Matt. 28:16-20: Texts Behind the Text," *RHPR* 72 (1992): 89-98.

28:16
1850 A. Strobel, "Der Berg der Offenbarung (Mt. 28,16; Apg 1,12)," in O. Böcher and K. Haacker, eds., *Verborum Veritas* (festschrift for Gustav Stählin). Wuppertal: Brockhaus, 1970. Pp. 133-46.

28:17
1851 J. Kwik, "Some Doubted," *ET* 77 (1965-1966): 181.

1852 I. P. Ellis, "But Some Doubted," *NTS* 14 (1967-1968): 574-80.

1853 E. Margaret Howe, " 'But Some Doubted' (Matt. 28:17). A Re-Appraisal of Factors Influencing the Easter Faith of the Early Christian Community," *JETS* 18/3 (1975): 173-80.

1854 K. Grayston, "The Translation of Matthew 28:17," *JSNT* 21 (1984): 105-109.

1855   K. L. McKay, "The Use of *Hoi De* in Matthew 28.17," *JSNT* 24 (1985): 71-72.

1856   P. W. van der Horst, "Once More: The Translation of *Hoi De* in Matthew 28.17," *JSNT* 27 (1986): 27-30.

28:18-29
1857   Johann B. Umberg, "Die Grundbedeutung der Taufformel," in *75 Jahre Stella Matutina, Festschrift Band I*. Feldkirch: Selbstverlag, 1931. Pp. 533-52.

28:18-20
1858   W. Trilling, "Der Inhalt des Manifests 28,18-20," in *Das wahre Israel: Studien zur Theologie des Matthäus-Evangeliums*. Munich: Kösel, 1964. Pp. 21-51.

1859   A. Vögtle, "Das christologische und ekklesiologische Anliegen von Mt. 28,18-20," in F. Cross, ed., *Studia Evangelica II*: Papers Presented to the Second International Congress on New Testament Studies, Christ Church, Oxford, 1961 (Part I—The New Testament Scriptures). Berlin: Akademie-Verlag, 1964. Pp. 266-94.

1860   H. B. Green, "The Command to Baptize and Other Matthaean Interpolations," in F. Cross, ed., *Studia Evangelica IV*: Papers Presented to the Third International Congress on New Testament Studies, Christ Church, Oxford, 1965 (Part I—The New Testament Scriptures). Berlin: Akademie-Verlag, 1968. Pp. 60-63.

1861   W. Trilling, "Das Kirchenverständnis nach Matthäus (Mt. 28,18-20)," in *Vielfalt und Einheit im Neuen Testament: Zur Exegese und Verkündigung des Neuen Testaments*. Einsiedeln: Benziger, 1968. Pp. 125-39.

1862   J. Czerski, "Christozentrische Ekklesiologie im Matthäusevangelium," *BibL* 12 (1971): 55-66.

1863   Everett F. Harrison, "Did Christ Command World Evangelism?" *CT* 18/4 (1973): 210-14.

1864   P. T. O'Brien, "The Great Commission of Matthew 28:18-20," *RTR* 35/3 (1976): 66-78.

1865   Schuyler Brown, "The Matthean Community and the Gentile Mission," *NovT* 22/3 (1980): 193-221.

1866   Gerhard Friedrich, "Die Formale Struktur von Mt. 28,18-20," *ZTK* 80/2 (1983): 137-83.

28:18-19
1867   Dale Cowling, "Being the Church Today," *SouJT* 17/2 (1975): 65-72.

28:18
1868   Kair A. Syreeni, "Between Heaven and Earth: On the Structure of Matthew's Symbolic Universe," *JSNT* 40 (1990): 9-13.

28:19-20
1869   E. Luther Copeland, "The Great Commission and Missions," *SouJT* 9/2 (1967): 79-89.

1870   Robert D. Culver, "What Is the Church's Commission?" *BSac* 125 (1968): 239-53.

1871   Luther L. Grubb, "The Church Reaching Tomorrow's World," *GTJ* 12/3 (1971): 13-22.

28:19
1872   Joe Belcastro, "Jesus and Baptism," *Enc* 21 (1960): 269-78.

1873   D. R. A. Hare and D. J. Harrington, "Make Disciples of All the Gentiles (Matthew 28:19)," *CBQ* 37 (1975): 359-69.

1874   John P. Meier, "Nations or Gentiles in Matthew 28:19," *CBQ* 39/1 (1977): 94-102.

1875   Luise Abramowski, "Die Entstehung der Dreigliedrigen Taufformel-ein Versuch-mit einem exkurs: Jesus der Naziraer," *ZTK* 81/4 (1984): 417-46.

1876   David R. Plaster, "Baptism by Triune Immersion," *GTJ* 6/2 (1985): 383-90.

1877   S. H. Kio, "Understanding and Translating 'Nations' in Mt. 28:19," *BT* 41 (1990): 230-38.

28:23-34

1878   J. D. M. Derrett, "The Parable of the Unmerciful Servant," in *Law in the New Testament*. London: Longman & Todd, 1970. Pp. 132-47.

PART TWO

Citations by Subjects

anthropology

1879   Robert H. Taylor, "Jesus' Conception of Man in the Synoptics," doctoral dissertation, Southwestern Baptist Theological Seminary, Fort Worth TX, 1961.

1880   Heinrich Scheffer, "The Concept of Man in the Gospel of Matthew," doctoral dissertation, Union Theological Seminary in Virginia, Richmond VA, 1973.

apocalypse

1881   William J. Crowder, "Jesus' Use of Apocalyptic Language in the Synoptic Gospels," doctoral dissertation, Southern Baptist Theological Seminary, Louisville KY, 1937.

1882   H.-J. Schoeps, "Ebionitische Apokalyptic in Neuen Testament," *ZNW* 51 (1960): 101-11.

1883   J. S. Sibinga, "The Structure of the Apocalyptic Discourse, Matthew 24 and 25," *ScanJT* 29 (1975): 71-79.

1884   Schuyler Brown, "The Matthean Apocalypse," *JSNT* 4 (1979): 2-27.

1885   Donald A. Hagner, "Apocalyptic Motifs in the Gospel of Matthew: Continuity and Discontinuity," *BT* 7/2 (1985): 53-82.

1886   John J. Pilch, "Reading Matthew Anthropologically: Healing in Cultural Perspective," *List* 24/3 (1989): 278-89.

Aramaic

1887   J. Jeremias, "Die Muttersprache des Evangelisten Matthäus," *ZNW* 50 (1959): 270-74.

1888   Luis Diez Merino, "Testimonios judios sobre la existencia de un evangelio arameo," *EB* 41/1 (1983): 157-63.

1889   R. Buth, "Matthew's Aramaic Glue," *JeruP* 3 (1990): 10-12.

baptism

1890   Randall D. Sledge, "The Relation of Water Baptism to Spirit Baptism in the New Testament," doctoral dissertation, New Orleans Baptist Theological Seminary, New Orleans LA, 1954.

1891   Placide Roulin and Giles Carton, "Le Bapteme du Christ,"
               BVC 25 (1959): 39-48.

1892   G. H. P. Thompson, "Called-Proved-Obedient: A Study in
               the Baptism and Temptation Narratives of Matthew and
               Luke," *JTS* 10 (1960): 1-12.

1893   A. Strobel, "Die Täuferanfrage (Mt. 11,3/Luk 7,19)," in
               Untersuchungen zum eschatologischen Verzögerungs-
               problem auf Grund der spätjüdischurchristlichen Geschichte
               von Habakuk 2,2ff. Leiden: Brill, 1961. Pp. 265-77.

1894   James D. G. Dunn, "Spirit and Fire Baptism," *NovT* 14/2
               (1972): 81-92.

1895   Michael Moreton, "The Emergence and the Forms of a Rite
               of Initiation in the Church," *Theology* 75 (1972): 301-10.

1896   S. Légasse, "Baptême juif des prosélytes et baptême
               Chrétin," *BLE* 77 (1976): 3-40.

1897   David R. Plaster, "Baptism by Triune Immersion," *GTJ*
               6/2 (1985): 383-90.

beatitudes
1898   Klaus Krieger, "Fordert Mt. 5:39b das passive Erdulden
               von Gewalt? Ein kleiner Beitrag zur Redaktionskritik der 5
               Antithese," *BibN* 54 (1990): 28-32.

1899   Jacques Dupont, *Les beátitudes; le problème littéraire, le*
               message doctrinal. Bruges: Abbaye de Saint-André, 1954;
               vol. II: *La Bonne Nouvelle.* Paris: Gabalda, 1969; vol. III:
               Les évangélistes. Paris: Gabalda, 1973.

1900   R. W. Funk, "The Beatitudes and Turn the Other Cheek.
               Recommendations and Polling," *Forum* 2/3 (1986): 103-28.

1901   A. M. Ambrozic, "Reflections on the First Beatitude,"
               CICR 17 (1990): 95-104.

bibliography
1902   Raymond B. Brown, "The Gospel of Matthew in Recent
               Research," *REd* 59 (1962): 445-56.

1903   Ralph P. Martin, "St. Matthew's Gospel in Recent Study," *ET* 80 (1968-1969): 132-36.

1904   F. van Segbroeck, "Les citations d'accomplissement l'Évangile selon Matthieu d'après trois ouvrages récents," in *L'Évangile selon Matthieu*. Gembloux: Duculot, 1972. Pp. 107-30.

1905   H. Frankemölle, "Neue Literatur zur Bergpredigt," *TR* 79 (1983): 177-98.

1906   John A. Ziesler, "What is the Best Commentary? I. The Gospel According to St Matthew," *ET* 97/3 (1985): 67-71.

1907   R. T. France, "Matthew's Gospel in Recent Study," *Themelios* 14 (1988): 41-46.

birth stories
1908   E. Nestle, "Zu Mt. 2" *ZNW* 8 (1907): 73-74.

1909   Gonzague Ryckmans, "De l'or, de l'encens et de la myrrhe," *RB* 58 (1951): 372-76.

1910   H. J. Richards, "The Three Kings (Mt. 2:1-12)," *Scr* 8 (1956): 23-28.

1911   H. E. W. Turner, "Expository Problems: The Virgin Birth," *ET* 68 (1956): 12-17.

1912   G. W. van Beek, "Frankincense and Myrrh," *BA* 23 (1960): 70-95.

1913   Albert Denis, "L'Adoration des Mages Vue par S. Matthieu," *NRT* 82 (1960): 32-39.

1914   William H. Cook, "A Comparative Evaluation of the Place of the Virgin Birth in Twentieth-Century Literature," doctoral dissertation, Southwestern Baptist Theological Seminary, Fort Worth TX, 1960.

1915   D. Squillaci, "I Magi," *PalCl* 39/1 (1960): 16-20.

1916   A. R. C. Leaney, "The Birth Narratives in St. Luke and St. Matthew," *NTS* 8 (1962): 158-66.

1917   M. Strange, "King Herod the Great in a Representative Role," *BibTo* 1/3 (1962): 188-93.

1918   C. H. Cave, "St. Matthew's Infancy Narrative," *NTS* 9 (1962-1963): 382-90.

1919   A. Vögtle, "Die Genealogie Mt. 1, 2-16 und die matthaische Kindheitsgeschichte (I. Teil)," *BZ* 8/1 (1964): 45-58.

1920   S. Lewis Johnson, "The Genesis of Jesus," *BSac* 122 (1965): 331-42.

1921   X. Léon-Dufour, "Libro della Genesi di Gesu Cristo," *RBib* 13/3 (1965): 223-37.

1922   W. C. Robinson, "A Re-study of the Virgin Birth of Christ. God's Son Was Born of a Woman: Mary's Son Prayed 'Abba Father'," *EQ* 37/4 (1965): 198-211.

1923   A. Vögtle, "Die Genealogie und die matthaische Kindheitsgeschichte (II. Teil)" *BZ* 9 (1965): 32-49.

1924   A. Henry, "La visite des Mages," *TerreS* 1 (1966): 2-4.

1925   A. Pelletier, "L'Annonce à Joseph," *RechSR* 54/1 (1966): 67-68.

1926   J. N. M. Wifngaards, "The Episode of the Magi and Christian Kerygma," *IJT* 61/1 (1967): 30-41.

1927   A. Paul, *L'Evangile de l'enfance selon saint Matthieu.* Paris: Cerf, 1968.

1928   H. Schöllig, "Die Zahlung der Generationen im matthaischen Stammbaum," *ZNW* 59/3 (1968): 261-68.

1929   L. Soubigou, "A Narracao da Epifania segundo Sao Mateus," *RCB* 5/10 (1968): 8-14.

1930   J. Heer, "Der Bethlehemspruch Michas und die Geburt Jesu (Mich 5,1-3)," *BK* 25/4 (1970): 106-109.

1931 Antonio Charbel, "Mt. 2,1.7: Os Reis Magos eram Nabateus?" *RCB* 8/1 (1971): 96-103.

1932 Antonio Charbel, "Mt. 2,1.7: I Magi erano Nabatei?" *RBib* 20 (1972): 571-83.

1933 Paula Seethaler, "Eine Kleine Bemerkung zu den Stammbaumen Jesu nach Matthäus und Lukas," *BZ* 16/2 (1972): 256-57.

1934 J. O. Tuni, "La Tipología Israel-Jesús en Mt. 1-2," *EE* 47 (1972): 361-76.

1935 L. Zani, "Influsso del genere letterario midrashico su Mt. 2,1-12," *StPa* 19/2 (1972): 257-320.

1936 R. Laurentin, "Les évangiles de l'enfance," *LV* 119 (1974): 84-105.

1937 Raymond E. Brown, "The Meaning of the Magi: The Significance of the Star," *Worship* 49 (1975): 574-82.

1938 P. L. Maier, "The Infant Massacre—History or Myth?" *CT* 20 (1975): 299-302.

1939 D. E. Nineham, "The Genealogy in St. Matthew's Gospel and its Significance for the Study of the Gospels" *BJRL* 58 (1976): 421-44.

1940 Herman C. Waetjen, "The Genealogy as the Key to the Gospel According to Matthew," *JBL* 95/2 (1976): 205-30.

1941 C. H. Gordon, "Paternity at Two Levels" *JBL* 96 (1977): 101.

1942 W. Barnes Tatum, " 'The Origin of Jesus Messiah' (Mt. 1:1, 18a): Matthew's Use of the Infancy Traditions," *JBL* 96 (1977): 523-35.

1943 M. J. Down, "The Matthaean Birth Narratives: Matthew 1:18-2:23" *ET* 90 (1978): 51-52.

1944 C. H. Gordon, "The Double Paternity of Jesus," *BAR* 4 (1978): 26-27.

1945   Raymond E. Brown, *The Birth of the Messiah*. New York: Doubleday, 1979.

1946   R. T. France, "Herod and the Children of Bethlehem," *NovT* 21 (1979): 98-120.

1947   Robert K. Gnuse, "The Dream Theophany of Samuel: Its Structure in Relation to Ancient Near Eastern Dreams and Its Theological Significance," doctoral dissertation, Vanderbilt University, Nashville TN, 1980.

1948   M. R. Mulholland, Jr., "The Infancy Narratives in Matthew and Luke: Of History, Theology, and Literature," *BAR* 7/2 (1981): 46-59.

1949   Antonio Charbel, "Mateo 2:1-12: los Magos en el ambiente del Reino Nabateo," *RevB* 46/1 (1984): 147-58.

1950   Kent R. Hughes, "The Magi's Worship," *CT* 29/18 (1985): 26-28.

1951   Kathleen M. Irwin, "The Liturgical and Theological Correlations in the Associations of Representations of the Three Hebrews and the Magi in the Christian Art of Late Antiquity," doctoral dissertation, Graduate Theological Union, Berkeley CA, 1985.

1952   G. Segalla, "Matteo 1-2: dalla narrazione teologica della tradizione alla teologia kerygmatica della redazione," *Teologia* 11 (1986): 197-225.

1953   Walter Kasper, "Brief zum Thema 'Jungfrauengeburt'," *IKaZ* 16 (1987): 531-35.

1954   J. Cosslett Quin, "The Infancy Narratives with Special Reference to Matthew 1 and 2," *IBS* 9 (1987): 63-69.

1955   François Martin, "Naitre entre juifs et paiens," *FilN* 1/1 (1988): 77-93.

1956   Michal Wojciechowski, "Herod and Antipater? A Supplementary Clue to Dating the Birth of Jesus," *BibN* 44 (1988): 61-62.

1957 Carol Mork, "Revelation and Response: Matthean Texts for Christmas and Epiphany," *WW* 9 (1989): 394-99.

1958 Michael Oberweis, "Beobachtungen zum AT-Gebrauch in der matthaeischen Kindheitsgeschichte," *NTS* 35/1 (1989): 131-49.

1959 Robert L. Brawley, "Joseph in Matthew's Birth Narrative and the Irony of Good Intentions," *CumSem* 28 (1990): 69-76.

1960 André Feuillet, "Le Sauveur messianique et sa mere dans les recits de l'enfance de Saint Matthieu et de Saint Luc," *Div* 34/1 (1990): 17-52.

1961 R. H. Fuller, *He That Cometh: The Birth of Jesus in the New Testament.* Harrisburg, PA: Morehouse, 1990.

Christology

1962 Tomas Arvedson, *Das Mysterium Christi: Eine Studie zu Mt. 11,25-30.* Uppsala: Wretmans, 1937.

1963 R. Gutzwiller, *Jesus der Messias: Christus im Matthäusevangelium.* Einsiedeln: Benziger, 1949.

1964 Paul S. Minear, "The Coming of the Son of Man," *TT* 9 (1953): 489-93.

1965 T. De Kruijf, *Der Sohn des lebendigen Gottes: Ein Beitrag zur Christologie des Matthäusevangeliums.* Rome: Pontifical Biblical Institute, 1962.

1966 Frank Stagg, "The Christology of Matthew," *REd* 59 (1962): 457-68.

1967 G. Strecker, "Der Titel 'Davidssohn'," in *Der Weg der Gerechtigkeit: Untersuchung zur Theologie des Matthäus.* Göttingen: Vandenhoeck & Ruprecht, 1962. Pp. 118-20.

1968 I. Giordani, *Christ, Hope of the World.* Boston: St. Paul Editions, 1964.

1969 Birger Gerhardsson, "Jésus livré et abandonne d'après la Passion selon saint Matthieu," *RB* 76 (1969): 206-27.

1970   M. J. Suggs, *Wisdom, Christology, and Law in Matthew's Gospel*. Cambridge: Harvard University Press, 1970.

1971   K. Gutbrod, *Die 'Weihnachtsgeschichten' des Neuen Teshments*. Stuttgart: Calwer, 1971.

1972   A. Vögtle, *Messias und Gottessohn: Herkunft und Sinn der matthäischen Geburts- und Kindheitsgeschichte*. Dusseldorf: Patmos, 1971.

1973   F. Wulf, "Die ungleichen Söhne," *GeistL* 44 (1971): 75-77.

1974   Birger Gerhardsson, "Gottes Sohn als Diener Gottes," *ScanJT* 27 (1973): 73-106.

1975   B. Kratz, *Auferweckung als Befreiung: Eine Studie zur Passions- und Auferstehungstheologie des Matthaus (besonders Mt. 27,62-28,15)*. Stuttgart: KBW Verlag, 1973.

1976   Clyde G. Glazener, "An Investigation of Jesus' Usage of the Term 'Son of Man': A Possible Interpretive Key to the Gospel of Matthew," doctoral dissertation, Southwestern Baptist Theological Seminary, Fort Worth TX, 1974.

1977   M. D. Johnson, "Reflections on a Wisdom Approach to Matthew's Christology," *CBQ* 36 (1974): 44-64.

1978   Lloyd Gaston, "The Messiah of Israel As Teacher of the Gentiles: The Setting of Matthew's Christology," *Int* 29 (1975): 24-40.

1979   Jack Dean Kingsbury, *Matthew: Structure, Christology, Kingdom*. Philadelphia: Fortress, 1975.

1980   Jack Dean Kingsbury, "The Title 'Kyrios' in Matthew's Gospel," *JBL* 94 (1975): 246-55.

1981   Jack Dean Kingsbury, "Title 'Son of Man' in Matthew's Gospel," *CBQ* 37 (1975): 193-202.

1982   Jack Dean Kingsbury, "Title 'Son of David' in Matthew's Gospel," *JBL* 95 (1976): 591-602.

1983 Hugh M. Humphrey, "The Relationship of Structure and Christology in the Gospel of Matthew," doctoral dissertation, Fordham University, Bronx NY, 1977.

1984 George W. Nickelsburg, "Good News/Bad News: The Messiah and God's Fractured Community," *CThM* 4 (1977): 324-32.

1985 C. Blanc, "Qui est Jésus-Christ?" *BLE* 80 (1979): 241-56.

1986 John P. Meier, *The Vision of Matthew: Christ, Church, and Morality in the First Gospel*. New York: Paulist, 1979.

1987 David Hill, "Son and Servant: An Essay on Matthean Christology," *JSNT* 6 (1980); 2-16.

1988 Jose M. Casciaro Ramirez, "Universalidad de la Etica Cristiana," *ScripT* 14/1 (1982): 305-28.

1989 Geir Hellemo, "Transfigurasjonen og det kristologiske paradoks," *NTT* 86/2 (1985): 65-78.

1990 David Hill, "The Quest of Matthean Christology," *IBS* 8 (1986): 135-42.

1991 Dale C. Allison, "The Son of God in Israel: A Note on Matthaean Christology," *IBS* 9 (1987): 74-81.

1992 D. J. Verseput, "The Role and Meaning of 'the Son of God' Title in Matthew's Gospel," *NTS* 33 (1987): 532-56.

1993 Frances T. Gench, "Wisdom in the Christology of Matthew," doctoral dissertation, Union Theological Seminary in Vriginia, Richmond VA, 1988.

1994 R. D. Mattison, "God/Father: Translation and Interpretation," *RR* 42 (1989): 189-206.

1995 Chrys C. Caragounis, *Peter and the Rock*. New York: de Gruyter, 1990.

1996 W. L. Kynes, *A Christology of Solidarity: Jesus as the Representative of His People in Matthew*. Lanham: University Press of America, 1991.

church

1997   K. Barth, "Kirche gestern, heute, morgen," *EvT* 1 (1934-1935): 289-95.

1998   Dan O. Via, "The Doctrine of the Church in the Gospel of Matthew," doctoral dissertation, Duke University, Durham NC, 1956.

1999   A. M. Javierre, *La Sucesión primacial y apostólica enelevangelio de Mateo*. Torino: Societa Editrice Internazionale, 1958.

2000   Dan O. Via, "The Church as the Body of Christ in the Gospel of Matthew," *SJT* 11 (1958): 271-86.

2001   Dan O. Via, "Jesus and His Church in Matthew 16:17-19," *RevExp* 55 (1958): 22-39.

2002   B. Schultze, "Die ekklesioklogische Bedeutung des Gleichnisses vom Senfkorn," *OCP* 27 (1961): 362-86.

2003   A-M. Malo, "L'Évangile de saint Matthieu, évangile ecclésiastique," in *L'Église dans la Bible*. Bruges: Desclée de Brouwer, 1962. Pp. 19-34.

2004   B. M. Metzger, "The New Testament View of the Church," *TT* 19 (1962): 369-80.

2005   Jose M. Casciaro Ramirez, "Iglesia y pueblo de Dios en el Evangelio de san Mateo," in *Concepto de la Iglesia en el Nuevo Testamento*. Madrid: Científica Medinaceli, 1962. Pp. 19-99.

2006   R. Hummel, *Die Auseinandersetzung zwischen Kirche und Judentum im Matthäusevangelium*. München: Kaiser, 1963.

2007   C. W. F. Smith, "The Mixed State of the Church in Matthew's Gospel," *JBL* 82 (1963): 149-68.

2008   W. Trilling, "Zum Kirchenbild I. Kirche aus Juden und Heiden?" in *Das wahre Israel: Studien zur Theologie des Matthäus-Evangeliums*. Munich: Kösel, 1964. Pp. 124-42.

2009   W. Trilling, "Zum Kirchenbild II. Der theologische Ort der Ekklesia," in *Das wahre Israel: Studien zur Theologie des Matthäus-Evangeliums*. Munich: Kösel, 1964. Pp. 143-63.

2010   A. Vögtle, "Das christologische und ekklesiologische Anliegen von Mt. 28,18-20," in F. Cross, ed., *Studia Evangelica II*: Papers Presented to the Second International Congress on New Testament Studies, Christ Church, Oxford, 1961 (Part I—The New Testament Scriptures). Berlin: Akademie-Verlag, 1964. Pp. 266-94.

2011   Walter A. Ray, "The Relationship between Eschatology and Ecclesiology in the Gospel of Matthew: A Study in Redaktionsgeschichte," doctoral dissertation, Princeton Theological Seminary, Princeton NJ, 1967.

2012   Rudolf Schnackenburg, "Die Kirche in der Welt: Aspeke aus dem Neuen Testament," *BZ* 11/1 (1967): 1-20.

2013   Luther L. Grubb, "The Church Reaching Tomorrow's World," *GTJ* 12/3 (1971): 13-22.

2014   O. Knoch, " 'Machet alle Völker zu meinen Jüngern!' Die Botschaft des Evangeliums nach Mattäus," *BK* 26 (1971): 65-69.

2015   A. Kretzer, "Der 'ekklesiologische' Ort des mt Basileiaverständnisses," in *Der Herrschaft der Himmel und die Söhne des Reiches: Eine redaktionsgeschichte Untersuchung zum Base'eiabegriff und Basileiaverständnis im Matthäusevangelium*. Stuttgart: KBW, 1971. Pp. 225-60.

2016   J. W. Roberts, "The Meaning of Ekklesia in the New Testament," *RQ* 15/1 (1972): 27-36.

2017   H. Schlier, "Die Kirche nach Matthaus," in J. Feiner and M. Löhrer, *Mysterium Salutis: Grundriss heilsgeschichtlicher Dogmatik*. Einsiedeln: Benziger, 1972. Pp. 102-16.

2018   D. Broughton Knox, "De-Mythologising the Church," *RTR* 32/2 (1973): 48-55.

2019   H. Frankemölle, "Kollektiv-bildliche Begriffe in der mt Ekklesiologie," in *Jahwebund und Kirche Christi, Studien zur Form- und Traditionsgeschichte des 'Evangeliums' nach Mattäus*. Münster: Aschendorff, 1974. Pp. 191-256.

2020   E. Schweizer, "Die Kirche des Matthäus ," in *Matthäus und seine Gemeinde*. Stuttgart: KBW, 1974. Pp. 138-70.

2021   E. Schweizer, *Matthäus und seine Gemeinde*. Stuttgart: Katholisches Bibelwerk, 1974.

2022   Richard J. Dillon, "Law of Christ and the Church of Christ according to Saint Matthew," *CICR* 2 (1975): 32-53.

2023   James P. Martin, "The Church in Matthew," *Int* 29/1 (1975): 41-56.

2024   Edgar Krentz, "The Egalitarian Church of Matthew," *CThM* 4/6 (1977): 333-41.

2025   Georg Kuenzel, "Studien zum Gemeindeverstaendnis des Matthaeus-Evangeliums," *TLZ* 102 (1977): 851-53.

2026   J. G. F. Collison, "The Church in the Synoptics: The Gospel of Matthew," *IJT* 28/3 (1979): 158-68.

2027   Thomas F. McKenna, "Matthew on Church Authority," *BibTo* 102 (1979): 2035-41.

2028   John P. Meier, *The Vision of Matthew: Christ, Church, and Morality in the First Gospel*. New York: Paulist, 1979.

2029   Martin Tripole, "A Church for the Poor and the World: At Issue with Moltmann's Ecclesiology," *TS* 42/4 (1981): 645-59.

2030   R. Kühschelm, "Das Verhaltnis von Kirche und Israel bei Mätthaus," *BL* 59 (1986): 165-76.

2031   Edgar Krenz, "Community and Character: Matthew's Vision of the Church," *SBLSP* (1987): 565-73.

2032   Robert W. Wall, "Law and Gospel, Church and Canon," *WesTJ* 22 (1987): 38-70.

2033   Klaus Pantle-Schieber, "Anmerkungen zur Auseinander-setzung von Ekklesia und Judentum im Matthäus-evangelium," *ZNW* 80/3 (1989): 145-62.

2034   F. D. Bruner, *Matthew: A Commentary*. Vol. 2. *The Churchbook: Matthew 13-28*. Dallas: Word, 1990.

2035   M. A. Chevallier, "Jesus a-t-il voulu l'eglise?" *ÉTR* 65/4 (1990): 489-503.

2036   John P. Meier, *The Vision of Matthew. Christ, Church, and Morality in the First Gospel*. New York: Crossroad, 1991.

community
2037   B. C. Butler, "M. Vaganay and the 'Community Discourse'," *NTS* 1 (1954-1955): 283-90.

2038   Kenzo Tagawa, "People and Community in the Gospel of Matthew," *NTS* 16/2 (1970): 149-62.

2039   E. Schweizer, "Christus und Gemeinde im Matthäusevangelium," in *Matthäus und seine Gemeinde*. Stuttgart: KBW, 1974. Pp. 9-68.

2040   Eugene A. La Verdiere and William G. Thompson, "New Testament Communities in Transition: A Study of Matthew and Luke," *TS* 37 (1976): 567-97.

2041   Graham N. Stanton, "The Communities of Matthew," *Int* 46 (1992): 379-91.

composition
2042   C. M. Martini, "Composizione del vangelo di Matteo," in *Il Messaggio della salvezza*. 5 vols. Torino: Leumann, 1966-1970. 4:233-58.

2043   H. Philip West, Jr., "A Primitive Version of Luke in the Composition of Matthew," *NTS* 14/1 (1967): 75-95.

conflict/controversy
2044   Etan Levine, "The Sabbath Controversy According to Matthew," *NTS* 22/4 (1976): 480-83.

2045　　Matty Cohen, "La controverse de Jésus et des Pharisiens à propos de la cueillette des épis, selon l'Évangile de Saint Matthieu," *MSR* 34/1 (1977): 3-12.

2046　　Arland J. Hultgren, *Jesus and His Adversaries: The Form and Function of the Conflict Stories in the Synoptic Tradition*. Minneapolis: Augsburg, 1979.

2047　　Jack Dean Kingsbury, "The Developing Conflict between Jesus and the Jewish Leaders in Matthew's Gospel: A Literary-Critical Study," *CBQ* 49 (1987): 57-73.

disciples

2048　　M. Kiddle, "The Conflict between the Disciples, the Jews, and the Gentiles in St. Matthew's Gospel," *JTS* 36 (1935): 33-44.

2049　　Clarence B. Burke, "The Attitude of the Synoptic Writers Towards the Twelve," master's thesis, Southern Baptist Theological Seminary, Louisville KY, 1955.

2050　　S. Freyne, *The Twelve: Disciples and Apostles: A Study in the Theology of the First Three Gospels*. London: Sheed & Ward, 1968.

2051　　Ulrich Luz, "Die Jünger im Matthäusevangelium," *ZNW* 62 (1971): 141-71.

2052　　M. Sheridan, "Disciples and Discipleship in Matthew and Luke," *BTB* 3 (1973): 235-55.

2053　　Paul S. Minear, "The Disciples and the Crowds in the Gospel of Matthew," *ATR* Suppl. 3 (1974): 28-44.

2054　　Robert E. Morosco, "Matthew's Formation of a Commissioning-Type Scene Out of the Story of Jesus' Commissioning of the Twelve," *JBL* 104/4 (1984): 539-56.

discipleship

2055　　William T. Smith, "Cross-Bearing in the Synoptic Gospels," doctoral dissertation, Southern Baptist Theological Seminary, Louisville KY, 1953.

2056　　M. H. Franzmann, *Follow Me: Discipleship according to Saint Matthew*. St. Louis: Concordia, 1961.

2057   M. Sheridan, "Disciples and Discipleship in Matthew and Luke," *BTB* 3 (1973): 235-55.

2058   D. R. A. Hare and D. J. Harrington, "Make Disciples of All the Gentiles (Matthew 28:19)," *CBQ* 37 (1975): 359-69.

divorce/marriage
2059   A. Allgeier, "Die crux interpretum im neutestamentlichen Ehescheidungs-verbot. Eine philologische Untersuchung zu Mt. 5,32 und 19,9," in *Reverendissimo Patri Iacobo Mariae Vosté*. Roma: Salita del Grillo, 1943. Pp. 128-42.

2060   J. M. Gonzalez Ruiz, "El divorcio en Mt. 5,32 y 19,9," in *La enciclica Humani Generis*. Madrid: Científica Medinaceli, 1952. Pp. 511-28.

2061   Oral Collins, "Divorce in the New Testament," *GR* 7 (1964): 158-69.

2062   A. Isaksson, "The Origin of the Clause on Unchastity," in *Marriage and Ministry in the New Temple: A Study with Special Reference to Mt. 19,3-12 and 1 Cor. 11,3-16*. Lund: Gleerup, 1965. Pp. 75-92.

2063   A. Isaksson, "The Synoptic Logion on Divorce," in *Marriage and Ministry in the New Temple: A Study with Special Reference to Mt. 19,3-12 and 1 Cor. 11,3-16*. Lund: Gleerup, 1965. Pp. 66-74.

2064   H. G. Coiner, "Those 'Divorce and Remarriage' Passages," *CTM* 39/6 (1968): 367-84.

2065   D. Heinrich Greeven, "Ehe nach dem Neuen Testament," *NTS* 15/4 (1969): 365-88.

2066   Richard N. Soulen, "Marriage and Divorce: A Problem in New Testament Interpretation," *Int* 23/4 (1969): 439-50.

2067   T. van Eupen, "De Onverbreekbaarheid van de Huwelijksbandd Een Eenstemmige Traditie?" *TijT* 10/3 (1970): 291-303.

2068   Roger Balducelli, "The Decision for Celibacy," *TS* 36/2 (1975): 219-42.

2069   Thaddee Matura, "Le Celibat dans le Nouveau Testament," *NRT* 97/6 (1975): 481-500.

2070   Joseph A. Fitzmyer, "The Matthean Divorce Texts and Some New Palestine Evidence," *TS* 37/2 (1976): 197-226.

2071   Mark Geldard, "Jesus' Teaching on Divorce: Thoughts on the Meaning of Porneia in Matthew 5:32 and 19:9," *Ch* 92/2 (1978): 134-43.

2072   Augustine Stock, "Matthean Divorce Texts," *BTB* 8/1 (1978): 24-33.

2073   William A. Heth, "Another Look at the Erasmian View of Divorce and Remarriage," *JETS* 25/3 (1982): 263-72.

2074   Charles C. Ryrie, "Biblical Teaching on Divorce and Remarriage," *GTJ* 3/2 (1982): 177-92.

2075   B. N. Wambacq, "Matthieu 5,31-32: Possibilite de Divorce ou Obligation de Rompre une Union Illigitime," *NRT* 104/1 (1982): 34-49.

2076   Marc Christiaens, "Pastoral van de Echtscheiding Volgens Matteus," *TijT* 23/1 (1983): 3-23.

2077   M. J. Down, "The Sayings of Jesus about Marriage and Divorce," *ET* 95/11 (1984): 332-34.

2078   Ben Witherington, "Matthew 5.32 and 19.9—Exception or Exceptional Situation?" *NTS* 31/4 (1985): 571-76.

2079   E. de la Serna, "¿Divorico en Mateo?" *RevB* 51 (1989): 91-110.

2080   Don T. Smith, "The Matthean Exception Clauses in the Light of Matthew's Theology and Community," *SBT* 17/1 (1989): 55-82.

2081 Michael W. Holmes, "The Text of the Matthean Divorce Passages: A Comment on the Appeal to Harmonization in Textual Decisions," *JBL* 109 (1991): 651-54.

2082 M. J. Molldrem, "A Hermeneutic of Pastoral Care and the Law/Gospel Paradigm Applied to the Divorce Texts of Scripture," *Int* 45 (1991): 43-54.

eschatology

2083 F. Segarra, "Algunas observaciones sobre los principales textos escatológicos de Nuestro Señor," *EE* 10 (1931): 475-99; 12 (1933): 345-67.

2084 C. L. Mitton, "Expository Problems: Present Justification and Final Judgment: A Discussion of the Parable of the Sheep and the Goats," *ET* 68 (1956-1957): 46-50.

2085 G. E. Ladd, "Consistent or Realized Eschatology in Matthew," *SouJT* 5 (1962): 55-63.

2086 G. Strecker, "Das eschatologische Motiv," in *Der Weg der Gerechtigkeit: Untersuchung zur Theologie des Matthäus.* Göttingen: Vandenhoeck & Ruprecht, 1962. Pp. 123-84.

2087 Royce Clark, "Eschatology and Matthew 10:23," *RQ* 6 (1963): 73-81.

2088 A. Vögtle, "Das christologische und ekklesiologische Anliegen von Mt. 28,18-20," in F. Cross, ed., *Studia Evangelica* II: Papers Presented to the Second International Congress on New Testament Studies, Christ Church, Oxford, 1961 (Part I—The New Testament Scriptures). Berlin: Akademie-Verlag, 1964. Pp. 266-94.

2089 D. M. Roark, "The Great Eschatological Discourse," *NovT* 7 (1964-1965): 123-27.

2090 Royce Clark, "Matthew 10:23 and Eschatology (II)," *RQ* 8 (1965): 53-69.

2091 Walter A. Ray, "The Relationship between Eschatology and Ecclesiology in the Gospel of Matthew: A Study in Redaktionsgeschichte," doctoral dissertation, Princeton Theological Seminary, Princeton NJ, 1967.

2092   A. Vögtle, "Zwei Wendungen matthaischer Eschatologie," in *Das Neue Testament und die Zukunft des Kosmos*. Düsseldorf: Patmos, 1970. Pp. 151-66.

2093   Richard C. Oudersluys, "The Parable of the Sheep and Goats (Matthew 25:31-46): Eschatology and Mission, Then and Now," *RR* 26/3 (1973): 151-61.

2094   Sigfred Pedersen, "Die Proklamation Jesu als des Eschatologischen Offenbarungstragers," *NovT* 17/4 (1975): 241-64.

2095   John F. Walvoord, "Posttribulationism Today [8 parts]," *BSac* 132 (1975): 16-24; 114-22; 208-15;304-15; 133 (1976): 11-18; 108-118; 202-12; 299-311.

2096   Fred W. Burnett, "Prolegomenon to Reading Matthew's Eschatological Discourse: Redundancy and the Education of the Reader in Matthew," *Semeia* 31 (1985): 91-109.

2097   Timothy R. Carmody, "The Relationship of Eschatology to the Use of Exclusion in Qumran and New Testament Literature," doctoral dissertation, Catholic University of America, Washington DC, 1986.

2098   Gerhard L. Miller, "Purgatory," *TD* 33/4 (1986): 31-36.

2099   Charles E. Cole, "To the End of Time: Preaching from Matthew in Pentecost," *QR* 7/3 (1987): 54-73.

2100   Melvin R. Storm, "Excommunication in the Life and Theology of the Primitive Christian Ccommunities," doctoral dissertation, Baylor University, Waco TX, 1987.

2101   Chaim Milikowsky, "Which Gehenna: Retribution and Eschatology in the Synoptic Gospels and in Early Jewish Texts," *NTS* 34/2 (1988): 238-49.

2102   G. E. Okeke, "The After-Life in St. Matthew as an Aspect of Matthean Ethic," *MelJT* 4 (1988): 35-44.

2103   Nlenanya Onwu, "Righteousness and Eschatology in Matthew's Gospel: A Critical Reflection," *ITS* 25 (1988): 213-35.

2104   Paul Trudinger, "The 'Our Father' in Matthew as Apocalyptic Eschatology," *DR* 107 (1989): 49-54.

2105   A. Sand, "Die Gemeinde zwischen 'jenen Tagen Jesu' und 'dem Tag des Gerichts.' Zum Gedchichtssssverständnis des Matthäusevangeliums," *TTZ* 99 (1990): 49-71.

ethics
2106   Wilbur A. Holman, "Right and Wrong According to the Gospel of Matthew," master's thesis, Midwestern Baptist Theological Seminary, Kansas City KS, 1954.

2107   D. W. Shriver, "The Prayer That Spans the World. An Exposition: Social Ethics and the Lord's Prayer," *Int* 21 (1967): 274-88.

2108   John P. Meier, *The Vision of Matthew: Christ, Church, and Morality in the First Gospel*. New York: Paulist, 1979.

2109   Leander E. Keck, "Ethics in the Gospel according to Matthew," *IliffR* 41 (1984): 39-56.

2110   Paul W. Meyer, "The Parable of Responsibility," *PSB* 6/2 (1985): 131-34.

2111   John R. Donahue, "The 'Parable' of the Sheep and the Goats: A Challenge to Christian Ethics," *TS* 47 (1986): 3-31.

2112   John J. Pilch, "The Health Care System in Matthew: A Social Science Analysis," *BTB* 16/3 (1986): 102-106.

2113   Nlenanya Onwu, "Righteousness in Matthew's Gospel: Its Social Implications," *BB* 13 (1987): 151-78.

2114   Joseph A. Loya, " 'Not by Bread Alone . . .,': Reflections on the Spirit of Poverty in the Eastern Tradition," *Diakonia* 22/2 (1988-1989): 105-10.

2115   Frank J. Matera, "The Ethics of the Kingdom in the Gospel of Matthew," *List* 24/3 (1989): 241-50.

2116   John P. Meier, *The Vision of Matthew. Christ, Church, and Morality in the First Gospel*. New York: Crossroad, 1991.

genre criticism

2117   Janice C. Anderson, "Matthew: Gender and Reading,"
                   Semeia 28 (1983): 3-27.

2118   Janice C. Anderson, "Double and Triple Stories: The
                   Implied Reader, and Redundancy in Matthew," *Semeia* 31
                   (1985): 71-89.

2119   David R. Bauer, *The Structure of Matthew's Gospel: A
                   Study in Literary Design*. Sheffield: Academic Press, 1988.

history

2120   G. Strecker, "Das Geschichtsverständnis des Matthäus,"
                   EvT 26 (1966): 57-74.

2121   Howard Clark Kee, "The Transformation of the Synagogue
                   after 70 CE: Its Import for Early Christianity," *NTS* 36
                   (1990): 1-24.

history of interpretation

2122   D. J. Harrington, "Matthean Studies since Joachim Rohde,"
                   HeyJ 16 (1975): 375-88.

2123   David R. Bauer, "The Interpretation of Matthew's Gospel
                   in the Twentieth Century," *ATLA* 42 (1988): 119-45.

Holy Spirit

2124   G. Earl Guinn, "The Holy Spirit in the Christology of the
                   Gospel," doctoral dissertation, New Orleans Baptist
                   Theological Seminary, New Orleans LA, 1944.

2125   Lester G. Philbin, "The Contemporary Understanding of the
                   Holy and Its Reflection in Matthew's Gospel," *RL* 42
                   (1973): 508-13.

2126   William W. Combs, "The Blasphemy against the Holy
                   Spirit," doctoral dissertation, Grace Theological Seminary,
                   Winona Lake IN, 1985.

introduction

2127   A. Dieterich, "Die Weisen aus dem Morgenlande," *ZNW*
                   (1902): 1-14.

2128   L. G. Broughton, *Blackboard Lectures on Matthew*. Nashville: Sunday School Board, 1919.

2129   K. L. Brooks, *Matthew's Gospel*. Los Angeles: Bible Institute, 1923.

2130   B. W. Bacon, *Studies in Matthew*. New York: Holt, 1930.

2131   J. Chapman, *Matthew, Mark and Luke*. London: Longmans, Green, 1937.

2132   J. N. Darby, "Matthew," *Synopsis of the Books of the Bible*. 5 vols. New York: Loizeaux, 1942. 3:29-209.

2133   M. E. Andrews, "The Historical Gospel," *JBL* 62 (1943): 45-57.

2134   F.-M. Catherinet, "Y a-t-il un ordre chronologique dans l'évangile de saint Matthieu?" in *Mélanges E. Podechard: Études de sciences religieuses*. Lyon: Facultés catholiques, 1945. Pp. 27-36.

2135   J. M. Bover, *El evangelio de san Mateo*. Barcelona: Balmes, 1946.

2136   K. W. Clark, "The Gentile Bias in Matthew," *JBL* 66 (1947): 165-72.

2137   H. A. Ironside, *Expository Notes on the Gospel of Matthew*. New York: Loizeaux, 1948.

2138   D. G. McKee, "The Gospel According to Matthew," *Int* 3 (1949): 194-205.

2139   G. Lindeskog, "Logia-Studien," *ScanJT* 4 (1950): 129-89.

2140   Robert E. Burks, "Some Primitive Elements in the Gospels—Chronology and Folklore," master's thesis, Southern Baptist Theological Seminary, Louisville KY, 1955.

2141   R. Lee Gallman, "The Purpose of the Gospel of Matthew," doctoral dissertation, New Orleans Baptist Theological Seminary, New Orleans LA, 1955.

2142   David M. Stanley, "Panel Discussion on the Methods of Teaching Scripture [pt 4: Teaching Matthew's Gospel]," *CBQ* 17 (1955): 44-49.

2143   G. Schille, "Bemerkungen zur Formgeschichte des Evangeliums. II. Das Evangelium des Matthäus als Katechismus," *NTS* 4 (1957-1958): 101-14.

2144   Gerard S. Sloyan, "The Gospel according to St. Matthew," *Worship* 32/6 (1958) 342-51.

2145   J. C. Fenton, "Inclusio and Chiasmus in Matthew," in Kurt Aland, et al., eds., *Studia Evangelica*: Papers Presented to the International Congress on the Four Gospels, Christ Church, Oxford, 1957. Berlin: Akademie-Verlag, 1959. Pp. 174-79.

2146   R. Gutzwiller, *Meditationen über Matthäus*. Einsiedeln: Benziger, 1959.

2147   W. Hamilton, *The Modern Reader's Guide to Matthew and Luke*. New York: Association, 1959.

2148   G. Hebert, "The Problem of the Gospel according to Matthew," *SJT* 14 (1961): 403-13.

2149   Douglas B. Maccorkle, "Interpretive Problems of the Gospel of Matthew," doctoral dissertation, Dallas Theological Seminary, Dallas TX, 1961.

2150   Paul L. Hammer, "Principles of Interpretation in Matthew," *TLife* 5 (1962): 25-36.

2151   W. H. Davies, *Davis' Notes on Matthew*. Nashville: Broadmann, 1962.

2152   William E. Hull, "A Teaching Outline of the Gospel of Matthew," *REd* 59 (1962): 433-44.

2153   T. W. Manson, "The Gospel according to St. Matthew," in Matthew Black, ed., *Studies in the Gospels and Epistles*. Manchester: University Press, 1962. Pp. 68-104.

2154   J. Munck, "Die Tradition über das Matthausevangelium bei Papias," in *Neotestamentica et Patristica* (festschrift for Oscar Cullmann). Leiden: Brill, 1962. Pp. 249-60.

2155   G. Strecker, "Das historische Motiv," in *Der Weg der Gerechtigkeit: Untersuchung zur Theologie des Matthäus.* Göttingen: Vandenhoeck & Ruprecht, 1962. Pp. 86-122.

2156   Ray Summers, "The Plan of Matthew," *SouJT* 5 (1962): 7-16.

2157   Thomas C. Urrey, "The Background of Matthew," *SouJT* 5 (1962): 17-28.

2158   S. Clark, "Matthew," in *A Survey of the Bible*. London: Robinson, 1963. Pp. 3-40.

2159   J. Kurzinger, "Irenaeus und sein Zeugnis zur Sprache des Matthaus-Evangelium," *NTS* 10 (1963): 108-15.

2160   P. Gaechter, *Das Matthäus Evangelium*. Innsbruck: Tyrolia, 1964.

2161   P. Gaechter, *Die literarische Kunst im Matthäus-Evangelium*. Stuttgart: KBW, 1965.

2162   H. Kosmala, "The Conclusion of Matthew," *ASTI* 4 (1965): 132-47.

2163   M. G. Gutzke, *Plain Talk on Matthew*. Grand Rapids: Zondervan, 1966.

2164   J. S. Sibinga, "Ignatius and Matthew," *NovT* 8 (1966): 263-83.

2165   D. R. A. Hare, *The Theme of Jewish Persecution of Christians in the Gospel According to St Matthew*. Cambridge: Cambridge University Press, 1967.

2166   Edward M. Panosian, et al., "Focus on Matthew," *BibView* 1/2 (1967): 75-149.

2167   G. Strecker, "The Concept of History in Matthew," *JAAR* 35 (1967): 219-30.

2168   C. S. Petrie, "The Authorship of 'The Gospel According to Matthew': A Reconsideration of the External Evidence," *NTS* 14 (1967-1968): 15-32.

2169   G. Braumann, "Die Zweizahl und Verdoppelungen im Matthäus-Evangelium," *TZ* 24 (1968): 255-266.

2170   H. Braun, *Jesus: Der Mann aus Nazareth und seine Zeit.* Stuttgart: Kreuz, 1969.

2171   Jack D. Kingsbury, *The Parables of Jesus in Matthew 13. A Study in Redaction Criticism.* London: S.P.C.K., 1969.

2172   E. L. Abel, "Who Wrote Matthew?" *NTS* 17/2 (1971): 138-52.

2173   A. Fuchs, *Sprachliche Untersuchungen zu Matthäus und Lukas.* Rome: Biblical Institute Press, 1971.

2174   Harold A. Guy, *The Gospel of Matthew.* London: Macmillan, 1971.

2175   L. Hartman, "Scriptural Exegesis in the Gospel of St. Matthew and the Problem of Communication," in *L'Évangile selon Matthieu.* Gembloux: Duculot, 1972. Pp. 131-52.

2176   J. S. Sibinga, "Eine literarische Technik im Matthäusevangelium," in *L'Évangile selon Matthieu.* Gembloux: Duculot, 1972. Pp. 99-105.

2177   G. Danieli, "Analisi strutturale ed esegesi di Matteo a proposito del recente libro di J. Radermakers," *RBib* 21 (1973): 433-39.

2178   H. Frankemölle, "Amtskritik im Matthäus-Evangelium?" *Bib* 54 (1973): 247-62.

2179   R. E. Osborne, "The Provenance of Matthew's Gospel," *SR* 3 (1973): 220-35.

2180   J. Rodhe, "Die Behandlung des Matthäus-Evangeliums," in E. A. Livingston, ed., *Studia Evangelica VI*: Papers Presented to the Fourth International Congress on New

Testament Studies, Christ Church, Oxford, 1969. Berlin: Akademie-Verlag, 1973. Pp. 44-97.

2181   Bruno De Solages, *Comment sont nés les évangiles: Marc-Luc-Matthieu*. Toulouse: Privat, 1973.

2182   H. Frankemölle, "Individuell-personale Begriffe in der mt Ekklesiologie," in *Jahwebund und Kirche Christi, Studien zur Form- und Traditionsgeschichte des 'Evangeliums' nach Mattäus*. Münster: Aschendorff, 1974. Pp. 84-190.

2183   H. Frankemölle, *Jahwebund und Kirche Christi: Studien zur Form- und Traditionsgeschichte des 'Evangeliums' nach Matthäus*. Münster: Aschendorff, 1974.

2184   H. Frankemölle, "Das Mt Ev als Geschichtsdeutung," in H. Frankemölle, *Jahwebund und Kirche Christi, Studien zur Form- und Traditionsgeschichte des 'Evangeliums' nach Mattäus*. Münster: Aschendorff, 1974. Pp. 308-400.

2185   William G. Thompson, "An Historical Perspective in the Gospel of Matthew," *JBL* 93 (1974): 243-62.

2186   William Barclay, *Introduction to the First Three Gospels*. Philadelphia: Westminster, 1975.

2187   C. E. Carlston, "Interpreting the Gospel of Matthew," *Int* 29 (1975): 3-12.

2188   Jack Dean Kingsbury, "Form and Message of Matthew," *Int* 29/1 (1975): 13-23.

2189   John P. Meier, "Salvation-History in Matthew: In Search of a Starting Point," *CBQ* 37/2 (1975): 203-15.

2190   William R. Farmer, "Matthew and the Bible: An Essay in Canonical Criticism," *LexTQ* 11/2 (1976): 57-66.

2191   William R. Farmer, "The Post-Sectarian Character of Matthew and Its Post-War Setting in Antioch of Syria," *PRS* 3/3 (1976): 235-47.

2192   William G. Thompson, "New Testament Communities in Transition: A Study of Matthew and Luke," *TS* 37/4 (1976): 567-97.

2193   G. Dambricourt, *Matthieu*. Toulouse: Privat, 1977.

2194   Graham N. Stanton, "5 Ezra and Matthean Christianity in the Second Century," *JTS* 28 (1977): 67-83.

2195   W. O. Walker, "A Method for Identifying Redactional Passages in Matthew on Functional Grounds," *CBQ* 39/1 (1977): 76-93.

2196   F. F. Bruce, *Matthew*. London: Scripture Union, 1978.

2197   W. L. Lipscomb, "A Tradition from the Book of Jubilees in Armenian," *JJS* 29/2 (1978): 149-64.

2198   Jean D. Dubois, ed., "L'Évangile de Matthieu en reconnaissance a Pierre Bonnard," *FV* 78 (1979): 3-129.

2199   Sean P. Kealy, "The Modern Approach to Matthew," *BTB* 9/4 (1979): 165-78.

2200   B. T. Viviano, "Where Was the Gospel According to Matthew Written?" *CBQ* 41/4 (1979): 533-46.

2201   F. W. Beare, *The Gospel According to Matthew*. San Francisco: Harper & Row, 1981.

2202   M. E. Glasswell, "St Matthew's Gospel: History or Book?" *CICR* 24/1 (1981): 41-45.

2203   E. E. Lemcio, "The Gospels and Canonical Criticism," *BTB* 11/4 (1981): 114-21.

2204   Donald Senior, "The Gospel of Matthew," *BibTo* 19/1 (1981): 7-15.

2205   Victor J. Eldridge, "Typology: The Key to Understanding Matthew's Formula Quotations?" *Coll* 15/1 (1982): 43-51.

2206   K. A. Smith, "Duress in Matthean Catechesis: Stress and the Growth of Faith," *REd* 78 (1983): 108-18.

2207.   Dennis G. Tevis, "An Analysis of Words and Phrases Characteristic of the Gospel of Matthew," doctoral dissertation, Southern Methodist University, Dallas TX, 1983.

2208   Christine Trevett, "Approaching Matthew from the Second Century: The Under-Used Ignation Correspondence," *JSNT* 20 (1984): 59-67.

2209   James E. Davison, "Anomia and the Question of an Antinomian Polemic in Matthew," *JBL* 104/4 (1985): 617-35.

2210   David L. Procter, "A Redaction-Critical Study of Synoptic Tendencies with Special Reference to Bultmann's Law of Increasing Distinctness," doctoral dissertation, Baylor University, Waco TX, 1985.

2211   Tjitze Baarda, "To the Roots of the Syriac Diatessaron Tradition (TA25:1-3)," *NovT* 28/1 (1986): 1-25.

2212   Paul D. Fueter, "The Therapeutic Language of the Bible," *BT* 37/3 (1986): 309-19.

2213   Frans Neirynck, "L'influence de l'évangile de Matthieu. À propos d'une réimpression," *ETL* 62 (1986): 399-404.

2214   H. Giesen, "Matthäus und seine Gemeinde. Neue Kommentare zum Mattäus-Evangelium," *TGl* 30 (1987): 257-66.

2215   Robert R. Hann, "Judaism and Jewish Christianity in Antioch: Charisma and Conflict in the First Century," *JRH* 14 (1987): 341-60.

2216   Jack Dean Kingsbury, "Reflections on 'the Reader of Matthew's Gospel'," *NTS* 34 (1988): 443-60.

2217   William R. Stegner, "Narrative Christology in Early Jewish Christianity," *SBLSP* 27 (1988): 249-62.

2218   Schuyler Brown, "Universalism and Particularism in Matthew's Gospel: A Jungian Approach." *SBLSP* 28 (1989): 388-99.

2219   R. T. France, *Matthew: Evangelist and Teacher*. Grand
            Rapids: Zondervan, 1989.

2220   Hans Klein, "Jüdenchristliche Frömmigkeit im Sondergut
            des Matthäus," *NTS* 35/3 (1989): 466-74.

2221   François Martin, "Sortir du livre," *SémBib* 54 (1989): 1-18.

2222   C. Richards, *According to Matthew*. Glasgow: Blackie,
            1989.

2223   W. Dicharry, *Human Authors of the New Testament*. Vol.
            1. *Mark, Matthew, and Luke*. Collegeville: Liturgical Press,
            1990.

2224   David B. Howell, *Matthew's Inclusive Story: A Study in the
            Narrative Rhetoric of the First Gospel*. Sheffield: JSOT
            Press, 1990.

2225   B. B. Scott, "The Birth of the Reader," *Semeia* 52 (1990):
            83-102.

2226   P. Stulmacher, *The Gospel and the Gospels*. Grand Rapids:
            Eerdmans, 1991.

2227   David R. Bauer, "The Major Characters of Matthew's
            Story: Their Function and Significance," *Int* 46 (1992):
            357-67.

2228   Jack Dean Kingsbury, "The Plot of Matthew's Story," *Int*
            46 (1992): 347-56.

2229   Mark A. Powell, "The Plot and Subplots of Matthew's
            Gospel," *NTS* 32 (1992): 187-204.

Jesus

2230   T. C. Hall, *The Message of Jesus according to the
            Synoptists*. The Messages of the Bible #9. New York:
            Scribner, 1901.

2231   J. A. Findlay, *Jesus in the First Gospel*. London: Hodder &
            Stoughton, 1925.

2232   W. E. Bundy, *Jesus and the First Three Gospels.* Cambridge: Harvard University Press, 1955.

2233   F. W. Beare, "Concerning Jesus of Nazareth," *JBL* 87 (1968): 125-35.

2234   William R. Farmer, "Jesus and the Gospels: A Form-Critical and Theological Essay," *PJ* 28 (1975): 1-62.

2235   J. Breech, *The Silence of Jesus.* Philadelphia: Fortress, 1983.

2236   R. A. Edwards, *Matthew's Story of Jesus.* Philadelphia: Fortress, 1985.

2237   Meinrad Limbeck, "Der kleine Weg der grösseren Gerechtigkeit: Die Inkarnation Gottes als Ausgangspunkt einer neuen Schöpfung," *BK* 44 (1989): 158-63.

2238   R. Knopp, *Finding Jesus in the Gospels: A Companion to Mark, Matthew, Luke and John.* Notre Dame: Ave Maria, 1989.

2239   Adela Yarbro Collins, "Jesus the Prophet," *BR* 36 (1991): 30-34.

Jesus and the Spirit
2240   Robert E. Burks, "Jesus and the Spirit in the Synoptic Gospels," doctoral dissertation, Southern Baptist Theological Seminary, Louisville KY, 1961.

Jesus and women
2241   Jane Kopas, "Jesus and Women in Matthew," *TT* 47/1 (1990): 13-21.

Jesus as teacher
2242   H. Shanks, "The Origins of the Title 'Rabbi'," *JQR* 59 (1968): 152-57.

2243   M. Trainor, "The Begetting of Wisdom: The Teacher and the Disciples in Matthew's Community," *Pacifica* 4 (1991): 148-64.

Jesus tradition
2244   J. F. O'Grady, *The Four Gospels and the Jesus Tradition.* New York: Paulist, 1989.

Jesus, attitude of
2245   Lemuel Hall, "The Growing Apprehension of Jesus in the Synoptics," doctoral dissertation, Southern Baptist Theological Seminary, Louisville KY, 1928.

2246   Roy D. Keller, "The Attitude of Jesus Toward Hypocrisy," doctoral dissertation, New Orleans Baptist Theological Seminary, New Orleans LA, 1942.

Jesus, authority of
2247   J. M. Reese, "How Matthew Portrays the Communication of Christ's Authority," *BTB* 7/3 (1977): 139-44.

Jesus, life of
2248   T. W. Manson, "The Life of Jesus: A Survey of the Available Material: (4) The Gospel According to St. Matthew," *BJRL* 29 (1945-1946): 392-428.

2249   Dominic Crossan, "Divine Immediacy and Human Immediacy: Towards a New First Principle in Historical Jesus Research," *Semeia* 44 (1988): 121-40.

2250   John L. White, "Jesus the Actant," *BR* 36 (1991): 19-29.

Jesus, ministry of
2251   Norman D. Price, "The Place of Galilee in the Ministry of Christ," doctoral dissertation, Southern Baptist Theological Seminary, Louisville KY, 1941.

2252   Theodore N. Swanson, "The Ministry of Jesus as Pictured in the Gospel of Mathew: A Bible Study," *BTF* 21 (1989): 65-75.

2253   G. Magnatt, "The Public Ministry of Jesus in the Gospel of Matthew," *BB* 16 (1990): 20-40.

Jesus, mission of
2254   Mark H. Richards, "The Mission of Jesus as Revealed in the Gospel of Matthew," doctoral dissertation, Midwestern Baptist Theological Seminary, Kansas City KS, 1951.

Jesus, teachings of

2255   A. Jülicher, *Die Gleichnisreden Jesu*. Tübingen: Mohr, 1910.

2256   W. A. Curtis, *Jesus Christ the Teacher*. London: Oxford University Press, 1945.

2257   G. Bornkamm, "Matthäus als Interpret der Herrenworte," *TLZ* 79 (1954): 341-46.

2258   J. Benjamin Bedenbaugh, "Ransom Saying of Our Lord," *LQ* 7 (1955): 26-31.

2259   Arthur L. Walker, "An Inquiry into the Inherent Universality of the Teaching of Jesus in the Gospel of Matthew,' dctoral dissertation, New Orleans Baptist Theological Seminary, New Orleans LA, 1956.

2260   F. W. Beare, "The Sayings of Jesus in the Gospel according to St. Matthew," in F. Cross, ed., *Studia Evangelica IV:* Papers Presented to the Third International Congress on New Testament Studies, Christ Church, Oxford, 1965 (Part I—The New Testament Scriptures). Berlin: Akademie-Verlag, 1968. Pp. 146-57.

2261   Sharon H. Ringe, "The Jubilee Proclamation in the Ministry and Teaching of Jesus: A Tradition-Critical Study in the Synoptic Gospels and Acts," doctoral dissertation, Union Theological Seminary, New York NY, 1982.

2262   Gary A. Phillips, "Parables Discourse," *Semeia* 31 (1985): 111-38.

2263   Hans Kvalbein, "Jesus and the Poor: Two Texts and a Tentative Conclusion," *Themelios* 12/3 (1987): 80-87.

2264   Clayton Jefford, "An Analysis of the Sayings of Jesus in the Teaching of the Twelve Apostles: The Role of the Matthean Community," doctoral dissertation, Claremont Graduate School, Claremont CA, 1988.

2265   Thomas D. Lea, "Understanding the Hard Sayings of Jesus," *SouJT* 35 (1992): 20-27.

Jesus, titles for

2266   John M. Gibbs, "Purpose and Pattern in Matthew's Use of the Title 'Son of David'," *NTS* 10 (1963-1964): 446-64.

2267   W. Grundmann, "Matth. xi. 27 und die Johanneischen 'Der Vater-Der Sohn'-Stellen," *NTS* 12 (1965-1966): 42-49.

2268   Jack Dean Kingsbury, "Title 'Son of God' in Matthew's Gospel," *BTB* 5 (1975): 3-31.

2269   A. G. van Aarde, "Immanuel as die geïnkarneerde tora: Funksionele Jesusbenaminge in die Matteusevangelie as vertelling," *HTS* 43 (1987): 242-77.

2270   Fred W. Burnett, "The Undecidability of the Proper Name 'Jesus' in Matthew," *Semeia* 54 (1991): 123-44.

Jewish leaders

2271   S. Van Tilborg, *The Jewish Leaders in Matthew*. Leiden: Brill, 1972.

2272   Matty Cohen, "La controverse de Jésus et des Pharisiens à propos de la cueillette des épis, selon l'Évangile de Saint Matthieu," *MSR* 34/1 (1977): 3-12.

2273   Arland J. Hultgren, *Jesus and His Adversaries: The Form and Function of the Conflict Stories in the Synoptic Tradition*. Minneapolis: Augsburg, 1979.

2274   D. A. Carson, "The Jewish Leaders in Matthew's Gospel: A Reappraisal," *JETS* 25 (1982): 161-74.

2275   Jack Dean Kingsbury, "The Developing Conflict between Jesus and the Jewish Leaders in Matthew's Gospel: A Literary-Critical Study," *CBQ* 49 (1987): 57-73.

John the Baptist

2276   James L. Jones, "References to John the Baptist in the Gospel According to St. Matthew," *ATR* 41 (1959): 298-302.

2277   Lamar Cope, "The Death of John the Baptist in the Gospel of Matthew; or, the Case of the Confusing Conjunction," *CBQ* 38/4 (1976): 515-19.

2278   John P. Meier, "John the Baptist in Matthew's Gospel," *JBL* 99 (1980): 383-405.

2279   Kent M. Nerburn, "John the Baptist according to Matthew: An Exercise in Visual Theology," doctoral dissertation, Graduate Theological Union, Berkeley CA, 1980.

2280   Edgar Krentz, "None Greater among Those Born from Women: John the Baptist in the Gospel of Matthew," *CThM* 10/6 (1983): 333-38.

2281   Michael Cleary, "The Baptist of History and Kerygma," *ITQ* 54 (1988): 211-27.

2282   Ben Witherington, "Jesus and the Baptist—Two of a Kind?" *SBLSP* 27 (1988): 225-44.

kingdom
2283   F. B. Harris, *The Kingdom of God*. Salem OR: Harris, 1913.

2284   William R. Bates, "The Relation of the Messianic Kingdom to the Kingdom of God in the Gospel of Matthew," doctoral dissertation, Southern Baptist Theological Seminary, Louisville KY, 1951.

2285   Leon B. Patterson, "A Comparative Study of the Johannine Concept of Eternal Life and the Synoptic Concept of the Kingdom," master's thesis, Southwestern Baptist Theological Seminary, Fort Worth TX, 1958.

2286   W. O. Walker, "The Kingdom of the Son of Man and the Kingdom of the Father in Matthew," *CBQ* 30/4 (1968): 573-79.

2287   Barclay M. Newman, "The Kingdom of God/ Heaven in the Gospel of Matthew," *BT* 27/4 (1976): 427-34.

2288   G. Todd Wilson, "Conditions for Entering the Kingdom According to St. Matthew," *PRS* 5/1 (1978): 42-53.

2289   Margaret Pamment, "The Kingdom of Heaven according to the First Gospel," *NTS* 27 (1981): 211-32.

2290   Barry S. Crawford, "Near Expectation in the Sayings of
             Jesus," *JBL* 101/2 (1982): 225-44.

2291   Robert H. Albers, "Perspectives on the Parables: Glimpses
             of the Kingdom of God," *WW* 4 (1984); 437-54.

2292   Caleb T. Huang, "Jesus' Teaching on 'Entering the
             Kingdom of Heaven' in the Gospel according to Matthew,"
             doctoral dissertation, Concordia Theological Seminary, St.
             Louis MO, 1986.

2293   Thomas R. Wolthuis, "Experiencing the Kingdom: Reading
             the Gospel of Matthew," doctoral dissertation, Duke
             University, Durham NC, 1987.

2294   David Peel, "Missing the Signs of the Kingdom," *ET* 99
             (1988): 114-15.

law

2295   E. Schweizer, "Gesetz und Enthusiasmus bei Matthaus," in
             G. Strecker, ed., *Der Weg der Gerechtigkeit: Untersuchung
             zur Theologie des Matthäus*. Göttingen: Vandenhoeck &
             Ruprecht, 1962. Pp. 49-70.

2296   J. D. M. Derrett, "Law in the New Testament: The Parable
             of the Talents and Two Logia," *ZNW* 56 (1965): 184-95.

2297   E. Schweizer, "Observance of the Law and Charismatic
             Activity in Matthew," *NTS* 16/3 (1970): 213-30.

2298   M. J. Suggs, *Wisdom, Christology, and Law in Matthew's
             Gospel*. Cambridge: Harvard University Press, 1970.

2299   John P. Meier, *Law and History in Matthew's Gospel*.
             Rome: Biblical Institute Press, 1976.

2300   Brice L. Martin, "Matthew on Christ and the Law," *Sale*
             44/1 (1983): 53-70.

2301   Klyne Snodgrass, "Matthew's Understanding of the Law,"
             Int 46 (1992): 368-78.

literary criticism

2302 F. Neirynck, "The Gospel of Matthew and Literary Criticism: Critical Analysis of A. Gaboury's Hypothesis," in *L'Évangile selon Matthieu*. Gembloux: Duculot, 1972. Pp. 37-69.

2303 Robert H. Gundry, *Matthew: A Commentary on His Literary and Theological Art*. Grand Rapids: Eerdmans, 1982.

2304 Stephen D. Moore, *Literary Criticism and the Gospels*. New Haven: Yale University Press, 1989.

2305 David B. Howell, *Matthew's Inclusive Story: A Study in the Narrative Rhetoric of the First Gospel*. Sheffield: Academic Press, 1990.

2306 Brigid C. Frein, "Fundamentalism and Narrative Approaches to the Gospels," *BTB* 22/1 (1992): 13-18.

literary style

2307 Harry Boonstra, "Satire in Matthew," *CT* 29/4 (1980): 32-45.

2308 J. Engelbrecht, "'n nuwe benadering tot die styl van Matteus," *ScrSA* 35 (1990): 26-34.

Lord's Prayer

2309 E. Lohmeyer, *Das Vater-unser*. Zürich: Zwingli Verlag, 1952.

2310 J. Jeremias, "The Lord's Prayer in Modern Research," *ET* 71 (1959-1960): 141-46.

2311 M. D. Goulder, "The Composition of the Lord's Prayer," *JTS* 14 (1963): 32-45.

2312 G. G. Willis, "The Lord's Prayer in Irish Gospel Manuscripts," in F. Cross, ed., *Studia Evangelica III*: Papers Presented to the Second International Congress on New Testament Studies, Christ Church, Oxford, 1961 (Part II—The New Testament Message). Berlin: Akademie-Verlag, 1964. Pp. 282-88.

2313   J. Jeremias, *Abba*. Göttingen: Vandenhoeck & Ruprecht, 1966.

2314   C. M. Laymon, *The Lord's Prayer in Its Biblical Setting*. Nashville: Abingdon Press, 1966.

2315   D. W. Shriver, "The Prayer That Spans the World. An Exposition: Social Ethics and the Lord's Prayer," *Int* 21 (1967): 274-88.

2316   C. F. D. Moule, "An Unsolved Problem in the Temptation Clause in the Lord's Prayer," *RTR* 33/3 (1974): 65-75.

2317   David J. Clark, "Our Father in Heaven," *BT* 30/2 (1979): 210-13.

2318   Krister Stendahl, et al. eds., "The Lord's Prayer," *IRM* 69 (1980); 265-351.

2319   Andrew Bandstra, "The Original Form of the Lord's Prayer," *CalTJ* 16/1 (1981): 15-37.

2320   Andrew Bandstra, "The Lord's Prayer and Textual Criticism: A Response," *CalTJ* 17/1 (1982): 88-97.

2321   Jacob van Bruggen, "The Lord's Prayer and Textual Criticism," *CalJT* 17/1 (1982): 78-87.

2322   W. O. Walker, "The Lord's Prayer in Matthew and in John," *NTS* 28/2 (1982): 237-56.

2323   D. Y. Hadidian, "The Lord's Prayer and the Sacraments of Baptism and of the Lord's Supper in the Early Church," *StL* 15/3 (1982-1983): 132-44.

2324   M. Dhavamony, "The Lord's Prayer in the Sanskrit Bible," *Greg* 68 (1987): 649-70.

2325   Hal Taussig, "The Lord's Prayer," *Forum* 4/4 (1988): 25-41.

2326   D. Templeton, "The Lord's Prayer as Eucharist in Daily Life," *IBS* 11 (1989): 133-40.

2327   David E. Garland, "The Lord's Prayer in the Gospel of Matthew," *RevExp* 89 (1992): 215-28.

Lord's Supper

2328   Fred David Howard, "An Interpretation of the Lord's Supper in the Teaching of the New Testament," doctoral dissertation, New Orleans Baptist Theological Seminary, New Orleans LA, 1957.

2329   E. Bammel, "P[64] (67) and the Last Supper." *JTS* 24/1 (1973): 189.

2330   Bonnie B. Thurston, " 'Do This': A Study on the Institution of the Lord's Supper," *RQ* 30/4 (1988): 207-17.

marriage/divorce

2331   A. Allgeier, "Die crux interpretum im neutestamentlichen Ehescheidungs-verbot. Eine philologische Untersuchung zu Mt. 5,32 und 19,9," in *Reverendissimo Patri Iacobo Mariae Vosté*. Roma: Salita del Grillo, 1943. Pp. 128-42.

2332   J. M. Gonzalez Ruiz, "El divorcio en Mt. 5,32 y 19,9," in *La enciclica Humani Generis*. Madrid: Científica Medinaceli, 1952. Pp. 511-28.

2333   Oral Collins, "Divorce in the New Testament," *GR* 7 (1964): 158-69.

2334   A. Isaksson, "The Origin of the Clause on Unchastity," in *Marriage and Ministry in the New Temple: A Study with Special Reference to Mt. 19,3-12 and 1 Cor. 11,3-16*. Lund: Gleerup, 1965. Pp. 75-92.

2335   A. Isaksson, "The Synoptic Logion on Divorce," in *Marriage and Ministry in the New Temple: A Study with Special Reference to Mt. 19,3-12 and 1 Cor. 11,3-16*. Lund: Gleerup, 1965. Pp. 66-74.

2336   H. G. Coiner, "Those 'Divorce and Remarriage' Passages," *CTM* 39/6 (1968): 367-84.

2337   D. Heinrich Greeven, "Ehe nach dem Neuen Testament," *NTS* 15/4 (1969): 365-88.

2338   Richard N. Soulen, "Marriage and Divorce: A Problem in
           New Testament Interpretation," *Int* 23/4 (1969): 439-50.

2339   T. van Eupen, "De Onverbreekbaarheid van de
           Huwelijksbandd Een Eenstemmige Traditie?" *TijT* 10/3
           (1970): 291-303.

2340   Roger Balducelli, "The Decision for Celibacy," *TS* 36/2
           (1975): 219-42.

2341   Thaddee Matura, "Le Celibat dans le Nouveau Testament,"
           NRT 97/6 (1975): 481-500.

2342   Joseph A. Fitzmyer, "The Matthean Divorce Texts and
           Some New Palestine Evidence," *TS* 37/2 (1976): 197-226.

2343   Mark Geldard, "Jesus' Teaching on Divorce: Thoughts on
           the Meaning of Porneia in Matthew 5:32 and 19:9," *Ch*
           92/2 (1978): 134-43.

2344   Augustine Stock, "Matthean Divorce Texts," *BTB* 8/1
           (1978): 24-33.

2345   William A. Heth, "Another Look at the Erasmian View of
           Divorce and Remarriage," *JETS* 25/3 (1982): 263-72.

2346   Charles C. Ryrie, "Biblical Teaching on Divorce and
           Remarriage," *GTJ* 3/2 (1982): 177-92.

2347   B. N. Wambacq, "Matthieu 5,31-32: Possibilite de Divorce
           ou Obligation de Rompre une Union Illigitime," *NRT* 104/1
           (1982): 34-49.

2348   Marc Christiaens, "Pastoral van de Echtscheiding Volgens
           Matteus," *TijT* 23/1 (1983): 3-23.

2349   M. J. Down, "The Sayings of Jesus about Marriage and
           Divorce," *ET* 95/11 (1984): 332-34.

2350   Ben Witherington, "Matthew 5.32 and 19.9—Exception or
           Exceptional Situation?" *NTS* 31/4 (1985): 571-76.

2351   E. de la Serna, "¿Divorico en Mateo?" *RevB* 51 (1989):
           91-110.

2352   Don T. Smith, "The Matthean Exception Clauses in the Light of Matthew's Theology and Community," *SBT* 17/1 (1989): 55-82.

2353   Michael W. Holmes, "The Text of the Matthean Divorce Passages: A Comment on the Appeal to Harmonization in Textual Decisions," *JBL* 109 (1991): 651-54.

2354   M. J. Molldrem, "A Hermeneutic of Pastoral Care and the Law/Gospel Paradigm Applied to the Divorce Texts of Scripture," *Int* 45 (1991): 43-54.

Mary

2355   G. G. Fournelle, "Our Lady's Marriage to Saint Joseph," *MarSt* 7 (1956): 122-29.

2356   A. Smitmans, *Maria im Neuen Testament*. Stuttgart: Katholisches Bibelwerk, 1970.

2357   J. M. Ford, "Mary's Virginitas, Post-Partum and Jewish Law" *Bib* 54 (1973): 269-72.

Matthew, as author/redactor

2358   Percival Hadfield, "Matthew the Apocalyptic Editor," *LQHR* 184 (1959): 128-32.

2359   H. J. Held, "Matthäus als Interpret der Wundergeschichten," in G. Bornkamm, G. Barth, H. J. Held, eds., *Überlieferung und Auslegung im Matthäusevangelium*. Neukirchen-Vluyn: Neukircher Verlag, 1961. Pp. 155-287.

2360   P. F. Ellis, *Matthew: His Mind and His Message*. Collegeville, MN: Liturgical Press, 1974.

2361   Lamar Cope, *Matthew: A Scribe Trained for the Kingdom of Heaven*. CBQMS 5. Washington: Catholic Biblical Association, 1976.

2362   J. E. Morgan-Wayne, "Matthew the Pastor," *BQ* 26/7 (1976): 294-302.

2363   H. Frankemölle, "Evangelist und Gemeinde. Eine Methodenkritische Besinnung (mit Beispielen aus dem Mattäus Evangelium)," *Bib* 60/2 (1979): 153-90.

2364   Stanley M. Rosenbaum, "St. Matthew and St. Kafka," *Enc* 43/4 (1982): 355-60.

Midrash

2365   M. D. Goulder, *Midrash and Lection in Matthew*. London: SPCK, 1974.

2366   J. D. M. Derrett, "Midrash in Matthew," *HeyJ* 16 (1975): 51-56.

2367   Douglas J. Moo, "Matthew and Midrash: An Evaluation of Robert H. Gundry's Approach," *JETS* 26/1 (1983): 31-86.

2368   Scott Cunningham and Darrell L. Bock, "Is Matthew Midrash? *BSac* 144 (1987): 157-180.

miracles

2369   Hershel H. Hobbs, "The Miraculous Element in Matthew," *SouJT* 5 (1962): 41-54.

2370   J. P. Heil, "Significant Aspects of the Healing Miracles in Matthew," *CBQ* 41/2 (1979) 274-87.

missions

2371   A. Ehrhardt, "The Gates of Hell," in Franz Hildebrandt, *And Other Pastors of Thy Flock: A German Tribute to the Bishop of Chichester*. Cambridge: Cambridge University Press, 1942. Pp. 19-24.

2372   Edgar S. Mizell, "The Missionary Idea in the Synoptic Gospels," doctoral dissertation, Midwestern Baptist Theological Seminary, Kansas City KS, 1946.

2373   G. Baumbach, "Die Mission im Matthäus-Evangelium," *TLZ* 92 (1967): 889-93.

2374   Yong K. Riew, "Biblical Principles Regarding the Missionary Role Found in the Gospel of Matthew," master's thesis, Fuller Theological Seminary, Pasadena CA, 1983.

money
> **2375** Eric E. May, "Translation of Monetary Terms in St. Matthew's Gospel," *CBQ* 18 (1956): 140-43.

> **2376** Werner G. Marx, "Money Matters in Matthew," *BSac* 136 (1979): 148-57.

narrative criticism
> **2377** H. J. B. Combrink, "The Structure of the Gospel of Matthew as Narrative," *TynB* 34 (1983): 61-90.

> **2378** R. A. Edwards, "Reading Matthew: The Gospel as Narrative," *List* 24/3 (1989): 251-61.

> **2379** J. A. Grassi, "Matthew's Gospel as Live Performance," *BT* 27 (1989): 225-32.

> **2380** Mark A. Powell, "Toward a Narrative-Critical Understanding of Matthew," *Int* 46 (1992): 341-46.

non-canonical writings
> **2381** J. A. Findlay, "The First Gospel and the Book of Testimonies," in H. G. Wood, ed., *Amicitiae Corolla: A Volume of Essays Presented to James Rendel Harris.* London: University of London, 1933. Pp. 57-71.

> **2382** William H. Crouch, "Jesus and the Teaching of the Elders in the Synoptic Gospels," master's thesis, Southern Baptist Theological Seminary, Louisville KY, 1954.

> **2383** Jesse Sell, "Johannine Traditions in Logion 61 of the Gospel of Thomas," *PRS* 7/1 (1980): 24-37.

> **2384** John M. Court, "The Didache and St. Matthew's Gospel," *SJT* 34/2 (1981): 109-20.

> **2385** Johannes B. Bauer, "Jesusüberlieferungen in der Apokryphen," *BK* 42 (1987): 158-61.

parables
> **2386** A. T. Cadoux, *The Parables of Jesus.* London: Clarke, 1930.

2387   James M. Bulman, "Parables of Revelation and Judgment,"
            RevExp 53 (1956): 314-25.

2388   A. M. Hunter, *Interpreting the Parables*. Philadelphia:
            Westminster, 1960.

2389   Harold Songer, "A Study of the Background of the
            Concepts of Parable in the Synoptic Gospels," doctoral
            dissertation, Southern Baptist Theological Seminary,
            Louisville KY, 1962.

2390   G. V. Jones, *The Art and Truth of the Parables*. London:
            SPCK, 1964.

2391   Jack D. Kingsbury, *The Parables of Jesus in Matthew 13.
            A Study in Redaction Criticism*. London: SPCK, 1969.

2392   R. L. Cargill, *All the Parables of Jesus*. Nashville:
            Broadman, 1970.

2393   A. M. Hunter, *The Parables Then and Now*. Philadelphia:
            Westminster, 1971.

2394   E. Schweizer, "Zur Sondertradition der Gleichnisse bei
            Matthäus," in G. Jeremias, et al., eds., *Tradition und
            Glaube: Das frühe Christentum in seiner Unwelt* (festschrift
            for Karl Georg Kuhn). Göttingen: Vandenhoeck &
            Ruprecht, 1971. Pp. 277-82.

2395   Dominic Crossan, "Parable as Religious and Poetic
            Experience," *JR* 53/3 (1973): 330-58.

2396   J. M. Henry, "The Parable of the Pounds: A Study in
            Parable Hermeneutics," doctoral dissertation, Southwestern
            Baptist Theological Seminary, Fort Worth TX, 1983.

2397   Robert H. Albers, "Perspectives on the Parables: Glimpses
            of the Kingdom of God," *WW* 4 (1984): 437-54.

2398   François Bovon, "Parabole d'Evangile, parabole du
            Royaume," *RTP* 122/1 (1990): 33-41.

2399   James D. Hester, "Socio-Rhetorical Criticism and the
            Parable of the Tenents," *JSNT* 45 (1992): 27-57.

passion

2400   J. Johnston, "The Words from the Cross: IV. The Cry of Desolation," *ET* 41 (1929-1930): 281-83.

2401   C. Schneider, "Der Hauptmann am Kreuz," *ZNW* 33 (1934): 1-17.

2402   Martin Dibelius, "Gethsemane," *CrozQ* 12 (1935): 254.

2403   C. B. Chavel, "The Releasing of a Prisoner on the Eve of Passover in Ancient Jerusalem," *JBL* 60 (1941): 273-78.

2404   F. Zimmermann, "The Last Words of Jesus," *JBL* 66 (1947): 465-66.

2405   Robert R. Darby, "A Study of the Variations of the Gethsemane sayings of Jesus Common to the Synoptics," doctoral dissertation, New Orleans Baptist Theological Seminary, New Orleans LA, 1953.

2406   Jan W. Doeve, "Purification du Temple et Dessèchement du Figuier," *NTS* 1 (1954-1955): 297-308.

2407   W. Blight, "The Cry of Dereliction," *ET* 68 (1956-1957): 285.

2408   Paul Winter, "Marginal Notes on the Trial of Jesus," *ZNW* 50 (1959): 14-33.

2409   Ivor Buse, "The Cleansing of the Temple in the Synoptics and in John," *ET* 70 (1959-1960): 22-24.

2410   Ivor Buse, "St. John and the Passion Narratives of St. Matthew and St. Luke," *NTS* 7 (1960): 65-76.

2411   H.-W. Bartsch, "Die Passions- und Ostergeschichten bei Matthäus. Ein Beitrag zur Redaktionsgeschichte des Evangeliums," *TF* 26 (1962): 80-92.

2412   Roderic Dunkerley, "Was Barabbas also Called Jesus?" *ET* 74 (1962-1963): 126-27.

2413   N. Q. Hamilton, "Temple Cleansing and Temple Bank," *JBL* 83 (1964): 365-72.

2414   F. Fensham, "Judas' Hand in the Bowl and Qumran,"
            RevQ 5 (1965): 259-61.

2415   W. Trilling, "Der Passionsbericht nach Matthäus,"
            TischWo 3 (1965): 33-44,

2416   William R. Stegner, "Wilderness and Testing in the Scrolls
            and in Matthew 4:1-11," *BR* 18 (1967): 18-27.

2417   Frans Neirynck, "Les Femmes au Tombeau: Étude de la
            rédaction Matthéenne," *NTS* 15 (1968-1969): 168-90.

2418   É. Trocmé, "L'expulsion des marchands du Temple," *NTS*
            15 (1968-1969): 1-22.

2419   J. Bligh, "Matching Passages, 2: St. Matthew's Passion
            Narrative," *Way* 9 (1969): 59-73 .

2420   B. A. Mastin, "The Date of the Triumphal Entry," *NTS* 16
            (1969-1970): 76-82.

2421   J. F. Quinn, "The Pilate Sequence in the Gospel of
            Matthew," *DunR* 10 (1970): 154-77.

2422   M. Herranz Marco, "Un problema de crítica histórica en el
            relato de la Pasión: la liberación de Barrabás," *EB* 30
            (1971): 137-60.

2423   B. Steinseifer, "Der Ort der Erscheinungen des
            Auferstandenen," *ZNW* 63/3 (1971): 232-65.

2424   K. P. G. Curtis, "Three Points of Contact between Matthew
            and John in the Burial and Resurrection Narratives," *JTS*
            23 (1972): 440-44.

2425   A.-L. Descamps, "Rédaction et christologie dans le récit
            matthéen de la Passion," *BETL* 29 (1972): 359-416.

2426   Donald Senior, "The Passion Narrative in the Gospel of
            Matthew," *BETL* 29 (1972): 343-57.

2427   R. Desjardins, "Les Vestiges du Seigneur au Mont des
            Oliviers," *BLE* 73 (1972): 51-72.

2428   E. Margaret Howe, " 'But Some Doubted' (Matt. 28:17). A Re-Appraisal of Factors Influencing the Easter Faith of the Early Christian Community," *JETS* 18/3 (1975): 173-80.

2429   Donald Senior, *The Passion Narrative According to Matthew: A Redactional Study*. Louvain Press, 1975.

2430   Kevin Smyth, "Matthew 28: Resurrection as Theophany," *ITQ* 42/4 (1975): 259-71.

2431   K. M. Fischer, "Redaktionsgeschichtliche Bermerkungen zur Passionsgeschichte des Matthäus," in Joachim Rogge, et al. eds., *Theologische Versuche*. Berlin: Evangelishce Verlagsanstalt, 1976. II, 109-29.

2432   Donald Senior, "The Death of Jesus and the Resurrection of the Holy Ones (Mt. 27:51-53)," *CBQ* 38 (1976): 312-29.

2433   G. Punnakottil, "The Passion Narrative According to Matthew. A Redaction Critical Study," *BB* 3 (1977): 20-47.

2434   J. D. M. Derrett, "Haggadah and the Account of the Passion," *DR* 97 (1979): 308-15.

2435   P. Hinnebusch, *Saint Matthew's Earthquake*. Ann Arbor, MI: Servant Books, 1980.

2436   R. H. Smith, "Celebrating Easter in the Matthean Mode," *CThM* 11 (1984): 79-82.

2437   Raymond E. Brown, "The Passion According to Matthew," *Worship* 58/2 (1984): 98-107.

2438   Jean Calloud, "Entres les écritures et la volence: La passion du témoin," *RSR* 73/1 (1985): 111-28.

2439   Jean Delorme, "Sémiotique du récit de la Passion," *RSR* 73/1 (1985): 85-110.

2440   Lynn A. Losie, "The Cleansing of the Temple: A History of a Gospel Tradition in Light of Its Background in the Old Testament and in Early Judaism," doctoral dissertation, Fuller Theological Seminary, Pasadena CA, 1985.

2441 Wolfgang Stegemann, "Die Versuchung Jesu im Matthaeusevangelium," *EvT* 45 (1985): 29-44.

2442 J. C. Lodge, "Matthew's Passion-Resurrection Narrative," *CS* 25 (1986): 3-20.

2443 Donald Senior, "Matthew's Special Material in the Passion Story: Implications for the Evangelist's Redactional Technique and Theological Perspective," *ETL* 63 (1987): 272-94.

2444 Eugene A. La Verdiere, "The Passion Story as Prophecy," *Emmanuel* 93 (1987): 85-90.

2445 J. P. Heil, "The Blood of Jesus in Matthew: A Narrative-Critical Perspective," *PRS* 18 (1991): 117-24.

2446 J. P. Heil, *The Death and Resurrection of Jesus: A Narrative-Critical Reading of Matthew 26-28*. Minneapolis: Fortress Press, 1991.

Peter

2447 C. F. D. Moule, "Some Reflections on the 'Stone' *Testimonia* in Relation to the Name Peter," *NTS* 2 (1955-1956): 56-58.

2448 Peter Milward, "Prophetic Perspective and the Primacy of Peter," *AmER* 144 (1961): 122-29.

2449 Jospeh A. Fitzmyer, "The Name Simon," *HTR* 56 (1963): 1-5.

2450 Jack Dean Kingsbury, "The Figure of Peter in Matthew's Gospel as a Theological Problem," *JBL* 98 (1979): 67-83.

2451 R. Aguirre, "Pedro en el Evangelio de Mateo," *EB* 47 (1989): 343-61.

2452 Peter Dschulnigg, "Gestalt and Funktion des Petrus im Matthäusevangelium," *SNTU-A* 14 (1989): 161-83.

prayer

2453 K. Emmerich, "Prayer in the Inner Chamber," in Franz Hildebrandt, ed., *And Other Pastors of Thy Flock: A*

German Tribute to the Bishop of Chichester. Cambridge: Cambridge University Press, 1942. Pp. 6-18.

2454   Robert M. Cooper, "Prayer: A Study in Matthew and James," *Enc* 3 (1968): 268-77.

2455   J. Harold Ellens, "Communication Theory and Petitionary Prayer," *JPT* 5/1 (1977): 48-54.

prophecy

2456   James C. Bunn, "The Element of Determinism in Prophecy as It Is Reflected in the Gospel of Matthew," doctoral dissertation, Southwestern Baptist Theological Seminary, Fort Worth TX, 1952.

2457   James C. Bunn, "The Element of Determinism in Prophecy as It Is Reflected in the Gospel of Matthew," doctoral dissertation, Southwestern Baptist Theological Seminary, Fort Worth TX, 1953.

Q

2458   B. H. Streeter, "On the Original Order of Q," in William Sanday, ed., *Studies in the Synoptic Problem by Members of the University of Oxford.* Oxford: Clarendon, 1911. Pp. 141-64.

2459   B. H. Streeter, "St. Mark's Knowledge and Use of Q," in William Sanday, ed., *Studies in the Synoptic Problem by Members of the University of Oxford.* Oxford: Clarendon, 1911. Pp. 165-208.

2460   M. Helm, "A History of the Q Hypothesis: Prolegomena to a Study of the Relation of the Gospel of Luke to the Gospel of Matthew," doctoral dissertation, Harvard University, Cambridge MA, 1932.

2461   R. A. Edwards, *The Sign of Jonah in the Theology of the Evangelists and Q.* London: SCM, 1971.

2462   G. Frizzi, "Carattere originale e rilevanza degli 'apostoli inviati' in Q," *RBib* 21 (1973): 401-12.

2463   Martin Cawley, "Health of the Eyes: Gift of the Father: In the Gospel Tradition 'Q'," *WS* 3 (1981): 41-70.

2464   Jirair S. Tashjian, "The Social Setting of the Mission Charge in Q," doctoral dissertation, Claremont Graduate School, Claremont CA, 1987.

2465   Eugene Boring, "The Historical-Critical Method's 'Criteria of Authenticity': The Beatitudes in Q and Thomas as a Test Case," *Semeia* 44 (1988): 9-44.

2466   Robert J. Miller, "The Rejection of the Prophet in Q," *JBL* 107 (1988): 225-40.

2467   Darla D. Turlington, "Views of the Spirit of God in Mark and 'Q': A Tradition-Historical Study," doctoral dissertation, Columbia University, New York NY, 1988.

2468   Hugh M. Humphrey, "Temptation and Authority: Sapiential Narratives in Q," *BTB* 21 (1991): 43-50.

2469   D. Kosch, "Q and Jesus," *BZ* 36/1 (1992): 30-38.

Qumran
2470   Bertil Gartner, "Habakkuk Commentary (DSH) and the Gospel of Matthew," *ScanJT* 8/1 (1954): 1-24.

2471   Berge A. Hoogasian, "The Dead Sea Scrolls and the Gospel of Matthew: A Structural Comparison," master's thesis, Southern Baptist Theological Seminary, Louisville KY, 1958.

2472   B. J. Roberts, "The Second Isaiah Scroll from Qumran (IQIsb)," *BJRL* 42 (1959): 132-44.

2473   D. Flusser, "Matthew 27:24-27 and the Dead Sea Sect," *Tarbiz* 31 (1961): 150-56.

2474   J. Gnilka, " 'Die Kirche des Matthäus und die Gemeinde von Qumran," *BZ* 7 (1963): 43-63.

2475   William R. Stegner, "Wilderness and Testing in the Scrolls and in Matthew 4:1-11," *BR* 18 (1967): 18-27.

2476   Benno Przybylski, "The Meaning and Significance of the Concept of Righteousness in the Gospel of Matthew with Special Reference to the Use of this Concept in the Dead

Sea Scrolls and the Tannaitic Literature," doctoral dissertation, McMaster University, Hamilton, Ontario, Canada, 1975.

2477 Emanuel Tov, "A Modern Textual Outlook Based on the Qumran Scrolls," *HUCA* 53 (1982): 1-27.

2478 Craig A. Evans, "1Q Isaiah and the Absence of Prophetic Critique at Qumran," *RevQ* 11/4 (1984): 537-42.

relation to John
2479 Percival Gardner-Smith, "St. John's Knowledge of Matthew," *JTS* 4 (1953): 31-35.

2480 Edwin D. Johnston, "A Re-Examination of the Relation of the Fourth Gospel to the Synoptics," doctoral dissertation, Southern Baptist Theological Seminary, Louisville KY, 1954.

2481 John Muddiman, "John's Use of Matthew: A British Exponent of the Theory," *ETL* 59/4 (1983): 333-37.

relation to OT
2482 W. Caspari, "Hebräische Spruchquelle des Matthäus und hellenistisch-phönikischer Schauplatz Jesu," *ZNW* 31 (1932): 209-33.

2483 S. E. Johnson, "The Biblical Quotations in Matthew," *HTR* 36 (1943): 135-53.

2484 H. Scheops, "Restitutio Principii as the Basis of the *Nova Lex Jesu*," *JBL* 66 (1947): 453-64.

2485 H. F. D. Sparks, "St. Matthew's References to Jeremiah," *JTS* 1 (1950): 155-56.

2486 I. Daumoser, *Berufung und Erwählung bei den Synoptikern*. Stuttgart: KBW, 1954.

2487 Krister Stendahl, *The School of St. Matthew and Its Use of the Old Testament*. Uppsala: Gleerup, 1954.

2488   S. Clive Thexton, "Jesus' Use of the Scriptures," *LQHR* 179 (1954): 102-108.

2489   A. Baumstark, "Die Zitate des Mt. Evangeliums aus dem Zwölf propheten buch," *Bib* 37 (1956): 296-313.

2490   George L. Balentine, "The Concept of the New Exodus in the Gospels," doctoral dissertation, Southern Baptist Theological Seminary, Louisville KY, 1961.

2491   S. V. McCasland, "Matthew Twists the Scriptures," *JBL* 80 (1961): 143-48.

2492   K. H. Rengstorf, "Old and New Testament Traces of a Formula of the Judean Royal Ritual," *NovT* 5 (1962): 229-44.

2493   G. Strecker, "Israel," in *Der Weg der Gerechtigkeit: Untersuchung zur Theologie des Matthäus*. Göttingen: Vandenhoeck & Ruprecht, 1962. Pp. 99-118.

2494   G. Strecker, "Das Verhältnis zum alttestamentlichen Gesetz," in *Der Weg der Gerechtigkeit: Untersuchung zur Theologie des Matthäus*. Göttingen: Vandenhoeck & Ruprecht, 1962. Pp. 143-48.

2495   W. Trilling, "Gericht über Israel," in *Das wahre Israel: Studien zur Theologie des Matthäus-Evangeliums*. Münich: Kösel, 1964. Pp. 75-96.

2496   Robert H. Gundry, *The Use of the Old Testament in St. Matthew's Gospel*. Leiden: Brill, 1967.

2497   John M. Gibbs, "The Son of God as the Torah Incarnate in Matthew," in F. Cross, ed., *Studia Evangelica IV*: Papers Presented to the Third International Congress on New Testament Studies, Christ Church, Oxford, 1965 (Part I—The New Testament Scriptures). Berlin: Akademie-Verlag, 1968. Pp. 38-46.

2498   C. F. D. Moule, "Fulfillment Words in the New Testament: Use and Abuse," *NTS* 14/3 (1968): 293-320.

2499   W. Rothfuchs, *Die Erfüllungszitate des Matthäus-Evangeliums*. Stuttgart: Kohlhammer, 1969.

2500   S. Légasse, " 'L'anti-judaïsme' l'Évangile selon Matthieu," in *L'Évangile selon Matthieu*. Gembloux: Duculot, 1972. Pp. 417-28.

2501   L. L. Collins, "The Significance of the Use of Isaiah in the Gospel of Matthew," doctoral dissertation, Southwestern Baptist Theological Seminary, Fort Worth TX, 1973.

2502   David Hill, "On the Use and Meaning of Hosea 6:6 in Matthew's Gospel," *NTS* 24 (1977): 107-19.

2503   Samuel Tobias Lachs, "Studies in the Semitic Background to the Gospel of Matthew," *JQR* 67/4 (1977): 195-217.

2504   L. Sabourin, "Matthieu 5,17-20 et le rôle prophétique de la Loi," *SE* 30 (1978): 303-11.

2505   Phillip Sigal, "The Halakhah of Jesus of Nazareth according to the Gospel of Matthew," doctoral dissertation, University of Pittsburgh, Pittsburg PA, 1979.

2506   Samuel Tobias Lachs, "Hebrew Elements in the Gospels and Acts," *JQR* 71/1 (1980): 31-43.

2507   W. R. G. Loader, "Son of David, Blindness, Possession, and Duality in Matthew," *CBQ* 44/4 (1982): 560-85.

2508   Michael J. Cook, "Interpreting 'Pro-Jewish' Passages in Matthew," *HUCA* 54 (1983): 135-46.

2509   John Goldingay, "The Old Testament and Christian Faith: Jesus and the Old Testament in Matthew 1-5, Part 2," *Themelios* 8/2 (1983): 5-12.

2510   Yoshito Anno, "The Mission to Israel in Matthew: The Intention of Matthew 10:5b-6 Considered in the Light of the Religio-Political Background," doctoral dissertation, Lutheran School of Theology, Chicago IL, 1984.

2511   William H. Marty, "The New Moses," doctoral dissertation, Dallas Theological Seminary, Dallas TX, 1984.

2512   M. J. J. Menken, "The References of Jeremiah in the Gospel According to Matthew (Mt. 2,17; 16,14; 27,9)," *ETL* 60/1 (1984): 5-24.

2513   Graham N. Stanton, "The Gospel of Matthew and Judaism," *BJRL* 66/2 (1984): 264-84.

2514   Edgar A. Johnson, "Aspects of the Remnant Concept in the Gospel of Matthew," doctoral dissertation, Andrews University, Berrien Springs MI, 1985.

2515   A. Hunter, "Rite of Passage: The Implications of Matthew 4:11 for an Understanding of the Jewishness of Jesus," *ChJR* 19 (1986): 7-22.

2516   R. E. Menninger, "The Concept of Remnant in the Gospel of Matthew," *SBT* 14 (1986): 5-35.

2517   M. Hengel, "Zur matthäischen Bergpredigt und ürem jüdishen Hintergrund," *TR* 52 (1987): 327-400.

2518   Paul Beauchamp, "L'evangile de Matthieu et l'heritage d'Israel," *RechSR* 76 (1988): 5-38.

2519   S. Freyne, "Oppression from the Jews: Matthew's Gospel as an Early Christian Response," *Conci* 200 (1988): 47-54.

2520   E. Elizabeth Johnson, "Jews and Christians in the New Testament: John, Matthew and Paul," *RR* 42/2 (1988): 113-28.

2521   F. H. Gorman, "When the Law Becomes Gospel: Matthew's Transformed Torah," *List* 24 (1989): 227-40.

2522   D. J. Harrington, "A Dangerous Text: Matthew on Jerusalem and Judaism," *CanaCR* 7 (1989): 135-42.

2523   Frederick A. Niedner, "Rereading Matthew on Jerusalem and Judaism," *BTB* 19/2 (1989): 43-47.

2524   J. T. Pawlikowski, "Christian-Jewish Dialogue and Matthew," *BibTo* 27 (1989): 356-62.

2525   Donald Senior, "The Gospel of Matthew and Our Jewish Heritage," *BibTo* 27 (1989): 325-31.

2526   A. Chouraqui, *Les Evangiles. Matthieu - Marc - Luc - Jean.* Turmhout: Brepols, 1990.

2527   David J. Zucker, "Jesus and Jeremiah in the Matthean Tradition," *JES* 27 (1990): 288-305.

2528   V. Mora, *La symbolique de la création dans l'évangile de Matthieu.* Paris: Cerf, 1991.

2529   Harold Songer, "The Sermon on the Mount and Its Jewish Foreground," *RevExp* 89 (1992): 165-77.

relation to Paul

2530   Dwight M. Beck, "The Influence of Pauline Theology in the Gospel of Matthew," doctoral dissertation, Boston University Graduate School, Boston MA, 1928.

2531   J. W. Bailey, "Light from Paul on Gospel Origins," *ATR*, 28 (1946): 217-26.

2532   C. H. Dodd, "Matthew and Paul," *ET* 58 (1946-1947): 293-98.

2533   A. W. Argyle, "M and the Pauline Epistles," *ET* 81 (1969): 340-42.

2534   P. Richardson, "Post-Pauline Developments: Matthew," in *Israel in the Apostolic Church.* Cambridge: University Press, 1969. Pp. 188-94.

resurrection

2535   James L. Hall, "A Study of the Significance of the Appearances of Christ after the Resurrection," master's thesis, Southern Baptist Theological Seminary, Louisville KY, 1949.

2536   Charles W. Hedrick, "Resurrection: Radical Theology in the Gospel of Matthew," *LexTQ* 14/3 (1979): 40-45.

righteousness

2537   Manfred Ossege, "Einige Aspekte zur Gliederung des neutestamentlichen Wortschatzes (am Beispiel von δικαιοσύνη bei Matthäus)," *LB* 34 (1975): 37-101.

2538   Benno Przybylski, *Righteousness in Matthew and His World of Thought*. SNTS #41. Cambridge: University Press, 1980.

2539   Robert G. Bratcher, " 'Righteousness' in Matthew," *BT* 40/2 (1989): 228-35.

2540   Wiard Popkes, "Die Gerechtigkeitstradition im Matthäus-Evangelium," *ZNW* 80/1 (1989): 1-23.

sermon on mount

2541   J. H. Farmer, "An Analysis of the Sermon on the Mount," *RevExp* 1 (1904): 71-80.

2542   Paul Fiebig, *Jesu Bergpredigt: Rabbinische Texte zum Verständnis der Bergpredigt, ins Deutsche übersetzt, in ihren Ursprachen dargeboten und mit Erlauterungen und Lesanen versehen*. Göttingen: Vandenhoeck & Ruprecht, 1924.

2543   F. C. Grant, "The Sermon on the Mount," *ATR* 24 (1942): 131-44.

2544   Ernest R. Pinson, "Some Revolutionary Teachings of Jesus in the Sermon on the Mount," doctoral dissertation, New Orleans Baptist Theological Seminary, New Orleans LA, 1945.

2545   A. M. Hunter, "The Meaning of the Sermon on the Mount," *ET* 63 (1952): 176-79.

2546   Karlmann Beyschlag, "Die Bergpredigt bei Franz von Assisi und Luther," *TLZ* 11 (1953): 688-89.

2547   C. Kopp, "Die Stäte der Bergpredigt und Brotvermehrung," *BK* 8/3 (1953): 10-16.

2548   A. M. Hunter, *Design for Life: An Exposition of the Sermon on the Mount, Its Making, Its Exegesis and Its Meaning*. London: SCM Press, 1954.

2549   Karlmann Beyschlag, *Die Bergpredigt und Franz von Assisi*. Gütersloh: C. Bertelsmann, 1955.

2550   Henlee Barnette, "The Ethic of the Sermon on the Mount," *RevExp* 53 (1956): 23-33.

2551   Jacob J. Rabinowitz, "The Sermon of the Mount and the School of Shammai," *HTR* 49 (1956): 79.

2552   J. Staudinger, *Die Bergpredict*. Vienna: Herder, 1957.

2553   D. Heinrich Greeven, "Diskussion zur Auslegung der Bergpredigt," *ZEE* 2 (1958): 116-17.

2554   I. W. Batdorf, "How Shall We Interpret the Sermon on the Mount?" *JBR* 27 (1959): 211-17.

2555   J. Jeremias, *The Sermon on the Mount*. London: Athlone Press, 1961.

2556   H. K. McArthur, *Understanding the Sermon on the Mount*. London: Epworth Press, 1961.

2557   J. Héring, "Le Sermon sur la Montagne dans la nouvelle traduction anglaise de la Bible," *RHPR* 42 (1962): 122-12.

2558   W. D. Davies, *The Setting of the Sermon on the Mount*. Cambridge: University Press, 1964.

2559   J. Schmid, "Ich aber sage euch: Der Anruf der Bergpredigt," *BK* 19 (1964): 75-79.

2560   K. R. Cripps, "Love Your Neighbour as Yourself," *ET* 76 (1964-1965): 26.

2561   G. Eichholz, *Auslegung der Bergpredigt*. Neukirchen: Verlag des Erziehungsvereins, 1965.

2562   W. D. Davies, *The Sermon on the Mount*. Cambridge: University Press, 1966.

2563   Tal D. Bonham, *The Demands of Discipleship: The Relevance of the Sermon on the Mount*. Pine Bluff, AR: Discipleship Book Company, 1967.

2564   C. F. D. Moule, "Fulfillment Words in the New Testament:
            Use and Abuse," *NTS* 14/3 (1968): 293-320.

2565   C. Daniel, " 'Faux Prophete': Surnom des Esseniens dans
            le Sermon sur la Montagne," *RevQ* 7/25 (1969): 45-79.

2566   P. Hoffman, "Die Stellung der Bergpredigt im
            Mattäusevangelium. Auslegung der Bergpredigt," *BibL* 10
            (1969): 57-65, 111-12, 175-89, 264-75.

2567   P. Bonnard, *L'Évangile selon saint Matthieu*. 2d ed. CNT
            1. Paris: Delachaux & Niestlé, 1970.

2568   P. Hoffman, "Die Stellung der Bergpredigt im
            Mattäusevangelium. Auslegung der Bergpredigt," *BibL* 11
            (1970): 89-104.

2569   G. Smith, "Matthaean 'Additions' to Lord's Prayer," *ET*
            82 (1970-1971): 54-55.

2570   G. Schmahl, "Gültigkeit und Verbindlichkeit der
            Bergpredigt," *BibL* 14 (1973): 180-87.

2571   J. Coppens, "Les Béatitudes," *ETL* 50 (1974): 256-60.

2572   J. Bligh, *The Sermon on the Mount*. Slough: St. Paul
            Publications, 1975.

2573   I. Broer, "Die Antithesen und der Evangelist Mättaus," *BZ*
            19 (1975): 50-63.

2574   Warren S. Kissinger, *The Sermon on the Mount: A History
            of Interpretation and Bibliography*. Metuchen: Scarecrow
            Press, 1975.

2575   Barclay M. Newman, "Some Translational Notes on the
            Beatitudes," *BT* 26/1 (1975): 106-20.

2576   A. Paul, "Béatitudes," *Chr* 22 (1975): 326-29.

2577   Harald Lang, "Verschrankung von Narrativer Syntax und
            Kommunikativen Einheiten und Ihre Abhangigkeit vom
            Sozio-Kulturellen Kontext Dargestellt am Beispiel der
            Bergpredigt," *LB* 37 (1976): 16-30.

2578   G. Menestrina, "Matteo 5-7 e Luca 6,20-49 nell'Evangelo di Tommaso," *BibO* 18 (1976) 65-67.

2579   Karlmann Beyschlag, "Zur Geschichte der Bergpredigt in der Alten Kirche," *ZTK* 74/3 (1977): 291-322.

2580   G. Bornkamm, "Der Aufbau der Bergpredigt," *NTS* 24 (1978): 419-32.

2581   Christoph Burchard, "The Theme of the Sermon on the Mount," in Lusie Schottroff, ed., *Essays on the Love Commandment*. Philadelphia: Fortress Press, 1978.

2582   D. A. Carson, "Reflections on Critical Approaches to the Sermon on the Mount," in *The Sermon on the Mount: An Evangelical Exposition of Matthew 5-7*. Grand Rapids: Baker Book House, 1978. Pp. 139-49.

2583   D. A. Carson, "Reflections on Theological Interpretation to the Sermon on the Mount," in *The Sermon on the Mount: An Evangelical Exposition of Matthew 5-7*. Grand Rapids: Baker Book House, 1978. Pp. 151-57.

2584   Jacques Dupont, "Le message des Béatitudes," *CE* 24 (1978): 215-31.

2585   R. M. Grant, "The Sermon on the Mount in Early Christianity," *Semeia* 12 (1978): 215-31.

2586   Samuel Tobias Lachs, "Some Textual Observations on the Sermon on the Mount," *JQR* 69/2 (1978): 98-111.

2587   G. Strecker, "Die Antitheses der Gergpredigt," *ZNW* 69/1 (1978): 36-72.

2588   M. Bouttier, "Hesiode et le sermon sur la montagne," *NTS* 25 (1978-1979): 129-30.

2589   Hans Dieter Betz, "The Sermon on the Mount: Its Literary Genre and Function," *JR* 59 (1979): 285-97.

2590   Christian Dietzfelbinger, "Die Antithesen der Bergpredigt im Verständnis des Matthaus," *ZNW* 70/1 (1979): 1-15.

2591   N. J. McEleney, "The Principles of the Sermon on the
        Mount," *CBQ* 41/4 (1979): 552-70.

2592   C. Heubüly, "Mt. 5:17-20: Ein Beitrag zur Theologie des
        Evangelisten Matthäus," *ZNW* 71 (1980): 143-49.

2593   J.-M. Carrière, "La loi: Matthieu 5-7," *Chr* 28 (1981):
        422-30.

2594   A.-L. Descamps, "Le Discours sur la montagne: Esquisse
        de théologie biblique," *RTL* 12 (1981): 5-39.

2595   W. Egger, "I titoli delle pericope bibliche come chiave di
        lettura," *RBib* 29 (1981): 33-43.

2596   J. Moltmann, *Nachfolge und Bergpredigt*. Munich: Kaiser,
        1981.

2597   G. Strecker, "Compliance-Love of One's Enemy—The
        Golden Rule," *ABR* 29 (1981): 38-46.

2598   R. A. Guelich, *The Sermon on the Mount: A Foundation for
        Understanding*. Waco: Word Books, 1982.

2599   C. J. A. Hickling, "Conflicting Motives in the Redaction of
        Matthew: Some Considerations on the Sermon on the
        Mount and Matthew 18:15-20," in E. A. Livingstone, ed.,
        Studia Evangelica VII: Papers Presented to the Fifth
        International Congress on New Testament Studies, Oxford,
        1973. Sheffield: JSOT Press, 1982. Pp. 247-60.

2600   Robert M. Johnston, " 'The Least of the Commandments':
        Deuteronomy 22:6-7 in Rabbinic Judasim and Early
        Christianity," *AUSS* 20/3 (1982): 200-15.

2601   E. Bader, "Bergpredigt, sozialphilosophische Aspekte," *BL*
        56 (1983): 144-49.

2602   H. Frankemölle, "Neue Literatur zur Bergpredigt," *TR* 79
        (1983): 177-98.

2603   Perry V. Kea, "Discipleship in the Great Sermon: A
        Literary-Critical   Approach,"   doctoral   dissertation,
        University of Virginia, Charlottesville VA, 1983.

2604   F. Montagnini, "Echi del discorso del monte nella Didaché," *BibO* 25 (1983): 137-43.

2605   C. M. Tuckett, "The Beatitudes: A Source-Critical Study: With a Reply by M. D. Goulder," *NovT* 25/3 (1983): 193-216.

2606   David Wenham, "Guelich on the Sermon on the Mount: A Critical Review," *TriJ* 4/2 (1983): 92-108.

2607   Daniel T. W. Chow, "A Study of the Sermon on the Mount: With Special Reference to Matthew 5:21-48," *EAJT* 2/2 (1984): 312-14.

2608   Leander E. Keck, "Ethics in the Gospel according to Matthew," *IliffR* 41 (1984): 39-56.

2609   Harvey H. Potthoff, "The Sermon as Theological Event: Interpretations of Parables," *QR* 4 (1984): 76-102.

2610   Clarence Bauman, *The Sermon on the Mount: The Modern Quest for Its Meaning*. Macon GA: Mercer University Press, 1985.

2611   Gary T. Meadors, "The 'Poor' in the Beatitudes of Matthew and Luke," *GTJ* 6/2 (1985): 305-14.

2612   J. Nagórny, "Kazanie na górze (Mt. 5-7) jako moralne oredize nowego przymierza," *RoczTK* 32 (1985): 5-21.

2613   Perry V. Kea, "The Sermon on the Mount: Ethics and Eschatological Time," *SBLSP* 25 (1986): 88-98.

2614   John Martin, "Dispensational Approaches to the Sermon on the Mount," in S. Toussaint and C. Dyer, eds., *Essays in Honor of J. Dwight Pentecost*. N.p., 1986.

2615   Yves Simoens, "The Sermon On The Mount: Light for the Christian Conscience," *LV* 41/2 (1986): 127-43.

2616   L. J. White, "Grid and Group in Matthew's Community: The Righteousness/Honor Code in the Sermon on the Mount," *Semeia* 35 (1986): 61-90.

2617   C. Burchard, "Le thème du Sermon sur la Montogne," *ÉTR* 62 (1987): 1-17.

2618   S. L. Cahill, "The Ethical Implications of the Sermon on the Mount," *Int* 41 (1987): 144-56.

2619   R. A. Guelich, "Interpreting the Sermon on the Mount," *Int* 41 (1987): 131-40.

2620   C.-H. Kang, "The Literary Affinities of the Sermon on the Mount with Special Reference to Deuteronomic Features," doctoral dissertation, Fuller Theological Seminary, Pasadena CA, 1987.

2621   Jack Dean Kingsbury, "The Place, Structure and Meaning of the Sermon on the Mount within Matthew," *Int* 41/2 (1987): 131-43.

2622   Kari A. Syreeni, "The Making of the Sermon on the Mount: A Procedural Analysis of Matthew's Redactoral Activity," doctoral dissertation, Helsingin Yliopisto, Finland, 1987.

2623   Dale C. Allison, "A New Approach to the Sermon on the Mount," *ETL* 64 (1988): 405-14.

2624   P. W. van Boxel, "You Have Heard That It Was Said," *Bij* 49/4 (1988): 362-77.

2625   C. E. Carlston, "Betz on the Sermon on the Mount: A Critique," *CBQ* 50 (1988): 47-57.

2626   Stanley Hauerwas, "The Sermon on the Mount, Just War and the Quest for Peace," *Conci* 195 (1988): 36-43.

2627   Émile Puech, "Un Hymne Essenien en Partie Retrouve et les Beatitudes: 1QH V 12-VI 18 (= Col. XIII-XIV 7) et 4QBeat," *RevQ* 13/1 (1988): 59-88.

2628   J. D. M. Derrett, *The Ascetic Discourse: An Explanation of the Sermon on the Mount.* Eilsbrunn: Ko'amar, 1989.

2629   R. J. Miller, "The Lord's Prayer and Other Items from the Sermon on the Mount," *Forum* 5 (1989): 177-86.

2630   R. E. Strelan, "The Gospel in the Sermon on the Mount," *LTJ* 23 (1989): 19-26.

2631   A. Wright, "The Gospel in the Sermon on the Mount: A Jewish View," *NBlack* 70 (1989): 182-89.

2632   M. D. Hamm, *The Beatitudes in Context. What Luke and Matthew Meant.* Willimington, DE: Glazier, 1990.

2633   S. Hellestam, "Mysteriet med saltet," *SEÅ* 55 (1990): 59-63.

2634   J. G. Williams, "Paraenesis, Excess, and Ethics: Matthew's Rhetoric in the Sermon on the Mount," *Semeia* 50 (1990): 163-87.

2635   Dennis C. Duling, " 'Do Not Swear . . . by Jerusalem Because It Is the City of the Great King," *JBL* 110 (1991): 291-309.

2636   Adrian M. Leske, "The Beatitudes, Salt and Light in Matthew and Luke," *SBLSP* 30 (1991): 816-39.

2637   I. A. Massey, *Interpreting the Sermon on the Mount in the Light of Jewish Tradition as Evidenced in the Palestinian Targums of the Penteteuch.* Lewiston, NY: Mellen, 1991.

2638   Ernest W. Saunders, "A Response to H. D. Betz on the Sermon on the Mount," *BR* 36 (1991): 81-87.

2639   J. M. Talbot, *Blessings: Reflections on the Beatitudes.* New York: Crossroad, 1991.

2640   Loyd Allen, "The Sermon on the Mount in the History of the Church," *RevExp* 89 (1992): 245-62.

2641   Lorin L. Cranford, "Bibliography for the Sermon on the Mount," *SouJT* 35 (1992): 34-38.

2642   Guy Greenfield, "The Ethics of the Sermon on the Mount," *SouJT* 35 (1992): 13-19.

2643   Harold Songer, "The Sermon on the Mount and Its Jewish Foreground," *RevExp* 89 (1992): 165-77.

2644   Glen H. Stassen, "Grace and Deliverance in the Sermon on the Mount," *RevExp* 89 (1992): 229-44.

2645   William B. Tolar, "The Sermon on the Mount from an Exegetical Perspective," *SouJT* 35 (1992): 4-12.

sin
2646   G. Danieli, "A proposito della origini della tradizione sinottica sulla concezione verginale," *DivT* 72/3 (1969): 312-31.

2647   Miguel A. Tibet, "La Distinzione Dei Peccati Secondo La Loro Gravita Nell'Insegnamento Di Gesu," *AnnT* 2/1 (1988): 3-33.

2648   T. W. Buckley, *Seventy Times Seven: Sin, Judgment, and Forgivess in Matthew.* Collegeville, MN: Liturgical Press, 1991.

sociology
2649   R. H. Smith, "Were the Early Christians Middle-Class: A Sociological Analysis of the New Testament," *CThM* 7 (1980); 260-76.

2650   John K. Riches, "The Sociology of Matthew: Some Basic Questions Concerning Its Relation to the Theology of the New Testament," *SBLSP* 22 (1983): 259-71.

2651   J. Andrew Overman, *"Matthew's Gospel and Formative Judaism: The Social World of the Matthean Community.* Philadelphia: Fortress Press, 1990.

source criticism
2652   A. E. Breen, *A Harmonized Exposition of the Four Gospels.* 4 vols. Rochester, NY: Smith, 1908.

2653   G. D. Kilpatrick, *The Origins of the Gospel according to St. Matthew.* Oxford: Clarendon Press, 1946.

2654   E. P. Blair, "Recent Study of the Sources of Matthew," *JBR* 27 (1959): 206-10.

2655   A. Farrer, *St. Matthew and St. Mark.* 2nd ed. Westminster: Dacre Press, 1966.

2656   P. Benoit, and M.-É. Boismard, *Synopse des quatre Évangiles avec parallèles des apocryphes et des Pères.* Paris: Cerf, 1972.

2657   J. W. Wenham, "Why Do You Ask Me About the Good? A Study of the Relation between Text and Source Criticism," *NTS* 28/1 (1982): 116-25.

2658   William R. Farmer, "Source Criticism: Some Comments on the Present Situation," *USQR* 42/1 (1988): 49-58.

2659   J. Engelbrecht, "The Language of the Gospel of Matthew," *Neo* 24 (1990): 199-213.

2660   Hugh M. Humphrey, "Temptation and Authority: Sapiential Narratives in Q," *BTB* 21 (1991): 43-50.

2661   D. Kosch, "Q and Jesus," *BZ* 36/1 (1992): 30-38.

structure

2662   T. L. Aborn, *The Lectures of St. Matthew.* Milwaukee: Morehouse, 1932.

2663   O. Michel, "Der Abschluss des Matthausevangeliums," *EvT* 10 (1950-1951): 16-26.

2664   F. V. Filson, "Broken Patterns in the Gospel of Matthew," *JBL* 75 (1956): 227-31.

2665   David Daube, "The Earliest Structure of the Gospels," *NTS* 5 (1958-1959): 184ff.

2666   Edgar Krentz, "The Extent of Matthew's Prologue," *JBL* 83 (1964): 409-14.

2667   D. Flusser, "The Conclusion of Matthew in a New Jewish Christian Source," *ASTI* 5 (1967): 110-20.

2668   H. B. Green, "The Structure of St. Matthew's Gospel," in F. Cross, ed., *Studia Evangelica IV*: Papers Presented to the Third International Congress on New Testament Studies, Christ Church, Oxford, 1965 (Part I—The New Testament Scriptures). Berlin: Akademie-Verlag, 1968. Pp. 47-59.

2669   Philippe Rolland, "From the Genesis to the End of the World: The Plan of Matthew's Gospel," *BTB* 2 (1972): 155-76.

2670   Jack Dean Kingsbury, "The Structure of Matthew's Gospel and His Concept of Salvation-History," *CBQ* 35 (1973): 451-74.

2671   L. Ramaroson, "La structure du premier Évangile," *SE* 26 (1974): 69-112.

2672   Tommy B. Slater, "Notes on Matthew's Structure," *JBL* 99 (1980): 436.

2673   David J. Clark and Jan de Waard, "Discourse Structure in Matthew's Gospel," *ScrSA* 1 (1982): 1-97.

2674   Terence J. Keegan, "Introductory Formulae for Matthean Discourses," *CBQ* 44 (1982): 415-30.

2675   Janice C. Anderson, "Over and Over and Over Again: Repetition in the Gospel of Matthew," doctoral dissertationa, University of Chicago, Chicago IL, 1985.

2676   David R. Bauer, "The Structure of Matthew's Gospel: A Literary-Critical Examination," doctoral dissertation, Union Theological Seminary in Virginia, Richmond VA, 1985.

2677   David Hill, "The Conclusion of Matthew's Gospel. Some Literary-Critical Observations," *IBS* 8 (1986): 54-63.

2678   David W. Gooding, "Structure litteraire de Matthieu 13:53-18:35," *RB* 85 (1987): 227-52.

2679   Frank J. Matera, "The Plot of Matthew's Gospel," *CBQ* 49 (1987): 233-53.

2680   R. Doyle, "Matthew's Intention as Discerned by His Structure," *RB* 95 (1988): 34-54.

2681   J. A. Grassi, "Matthew as a Second Testament Deuteronomy," *BTB* 19/1 (1989): 23-29.

2682 M. Trimaille, "Citations d'accomplissement et architecture de l'evangile selon S Matthieu," *EB* 48 (1990): 47-79.

synoptic problem

2683 Henry L. Jackson, "The Present State of the Synoptic Problem," in Henry B. Sweet, ed., *Essays on Some Biblical Questions of the Day.* London: Macmillan, 1909. Pp. 421-60.

2684 W. E. Addis, "The Criticism of the Hexateuch Compared with that of the Synoptic Gospels," in William Sanday, ed., *Studies in the Synoptic Problem by Members of the University of Oxford.* Oxford: Clarendon, 1911. Pp. 367-88.

2685 W. C. Allen, "The Book of Sayings Used by the Editor of the First Gospel," in William Sanday, ed., *Studies in the Synoptic Problem by Members of the University of Oxford.* Oxford: Clarendon, 1911. Pp. 235-86.

2686 John C. Hawkins, "Probabilities as to the So-Called Double Tradition of St. Matthew and St. Luke," in William Sanday, ed., *Studies in the Synoptic Problem by Members of the University of Oxford.* Oxford: Clarendon, 1911. Pp. 95-140.

2687 John C. Hawkins, "Three Limitations to St. Luke's Use of St. Mark's Gospel," in William Sanday, ed., *Studies in the Synoptic Problem by Members of the University of Oxford.* Oxford: Clarendon, 1911. Pp. 29-94.

2688 William Sanday, "The Conditions Under Which the Gospels Were Written," in William Sanday, ed., *Studies in the Synoptic Problem by Members of the University of Oxford.* Oxford: Clarendon, 1911. Pp. 3-28.

2689 B. H. Streeter, "The Literary Evolution of the Gospels," in William Sanday, ed., *Studies in the Synoptic Problem by Members of the University of Oxford.* Oxford: Clarendon, 1911. Pp. 209-28.

2690 B. H. Streeter, "St. Mark's Knowledge and Use of Q," in William Sanday, ed., *Studies in the Synoptic Problem by Members of the University of Oxford.* Oxford: Clarendon, 1911. Pp. 165-208.

2691 B. H. Streeter, "The Original Extent of Q," in William Sanday, ed., *Studies in the Synoptic Problem by Members of the University of Oxford*. Oxford: Clarendon, 1911. Pp. 185-208.

2692 B. H. Streeter, "On the Original Order of Q," in William Sanday, ed., *Studies in the Synoptic Problem by Members of the University of Oxford*. Oxford: Clarendon, 1911. Pp. 141-64.

2693 B. H. Streeter, "Synoptic Criticism and the Eschatological Problem," in William Sanday, ed., *Studies in the Synoptic Problem by Members of the University of Oxford*. Oxford: Clarendon, 1911. Pp. 425-36.

2694 N. P. Williams, "A Recent Theory of the Origin of St. Mark's Gospel," in William Sanday, ed., *Studies in the Synoptic Problem by Members of the University of Oxford*. Oxford: Clarendon, 1911. Pp. 389-424.

2695 H. G. Wood, "Some Characteristics of the Synoptic Writers," in F. J. Foakes Jackson, ed., *The Parting of the Roads: Studies in the Development of Judaism and Early Christianity*. London: Edward Arnold, 1912. Pp. 133-71.

2696 Paul Fiebig, "Die Mündliche Überlieferung als Quelle der Syoptiker," in Hans Windisch, ed., *Neutestamentliche Studien Georg Heinrici zu seinem 70. Geburtstag*. Leipzig: Hinrichs'sche, 1914. Pp. 79-91.

2697 C. J. Callan, *The Four Gospels*. New York: Wagner, 1917.

2698 Reinhold Hartstock, "Visionsberichte in den synoptischen Evangelien," in *Festgabe für D. Dr. Julius Kaftan zu seinem 70. Geburtstage*. Tübingen: Mohr, 1920. Pp. 130-45.

2699 C. A. Bernoulli, "Queleques difficultés non résolues du problème synoptique et leur interprétation psychologique," in P.-L. Counchoud, *Congrès d'historie du Christianisme: Jubilé Alfred Loisy*. Paris: Rieder, 1928. 1:178-87.

2700 P.-L. Couchoud, "Notes de Critique verbale sur St Marc et St. Matthieu," *JTS* 34 (1933): 113-38.

2701 J. Rezevskis, "Wie haben Matthäus und Lukas den Markus benutzt?" in *Voldemaro Maldonis . . . septuagenario dedicant collegae amici discipuli*. Rīgā: Studentu Padomes Grāmatrīca, 1940. Pp. 117-34.

2702 H. Grimme, "Drei Evangelienberichte in neuer Auffassung," *TGl* 34 (1942): 83-90.

2703 B. C. Butler, *The Originality of St. Matthew: A Critique of the Two-Documents Hypothesis*. Cambridge: University Press, 1951.

2704 E. D. Smith, "A Relating of Several Formulations from General Semantics to Certain Teachings and Communication Methods of Jesus as Reported in the Synoptic Gospels of Matthew, Mark and Luke," doctoral dissertation, University of Denver, Denver CO, 1952.

2705 A. W. Argyle, "Agreements Between Matthew and Luke," *ET* 73 (1961): 19-22.

2706 John Pairman Brown, "The Form of 'Q' Known to Matthew," *NTS* 8 (1961): 27-42.

2707 A. W. Argyle, "Evidence for the View that St. Luke Used St. Matthew's Gospel," *JBL* 83/4 (1964): 390-96.

2708 William R. Farmer, "The Two-Document Hypothesis as a Methodological Criterion in Synoptic Research," *ATR* 48 (1966): 380-96.

2709 D. B. J. Campbell, *The Synoptic Gospels*. New York: Seabury, 1969.

2710 E. P. Sanders, "The Argument from Order and the Relationship Between Matthew and Luke," *NTS* 15/2 (1969): 249-61.

2711 A. W. H. Moule, "The Pattern of the Synoptists," *EQ* 43/3 (1971): 162-71.

2712 M. Devisch, "Le document Q, source de Matthieu. Problématique actuelle," in *L'Évangile selon Matthieu*. Gembloux: Duculot, 1972. Pp. 71-97.

2713   Harold A. Guy, "Did Luke Use Matthew?" *ET* 83/4 (1972): 245-47.

2714   Hugo Meynell, "A Note on the Synoptic Problem," *DR* 90 (1972): 196-206.

2715   David R. Catchpole, "The Synoptic Divorce Material as a Traditio-Historical Problem," *BJRL* 57/1 (1974): 92-127.

2716   Robert Banks, *Jesus and the Law in the Synoptic Tradition.* Cambridge: University Press, 1975.

2717   Frans Neirynck, "The Sermon on the Mount in the Gospel Synopsis," *ETL* 52 (1976): 350-57.

2718   Robert L. Thomas, "An Investigation of the Agreements between Matthew and Luke against Mark," *JETS* 19/2 (1976): 103-12.

2719   M. E. Boismard, "The Two Source Theory at an Impasse," *NTS* 26/1 (1979): 1-17.

2720   F. Neirynck, "Deuteromarcus et les accords Matthieu-Luc," *ETL* 56 (1980): 397-408.

2721   James Breckenridge, "Evangelical Implications of Matthean Priority," *JETS* 26 (1983): 117-21.

2722   Malcolm Lowe and D. Flusser, "Evidence Corroborating a Modified Proto-Matthean Synoptic Theory," *NTS* 29/1 (1983): 25-47.

2723   C. M. Tuckett, "On the Relationship Between Matthew and Luke," *NTS* 30/1 (1984): 130-42.

2724   Richard B. Vinson, "The Significance of the Minor Agreements as an Argument against the Two-Document Hypothesis," doctoral dissertation, Duke University, Durham NC, 1984.

2725   Frank Wheeler, "Textual Criticism and the Synoptic Problem: A Textual Commentary on the Minor Agreements of Matthew and Luke against Mark," doctoral dissertation, Baylor University, Waco TX, 1985.

2726   Stephenson H. Brooks, "The History of the Matthean Community as Reflected in the M Sayings," doctoral dissertation, Columbia University, New York NY, 1986.

2727   S. McKnight, "Jesus and the End-Time: Matthew 10:23," *SBLSP* 25 (1986): 501-20.

2728   Victor S. Yoon, "Did the Evangelist Luke Use the Canonical Gospel of Matthew?" doctoral dissertation, Graduate Theological Union, Berkeley CA, 1986.

2729   H. B. Green, "Matthew, Clement and Luke: Their Sequence and Relationship," *JTS* 40/1 (1989): 1-25.

2730   J. J. McDonnell, *Acts to Gospels: A New Testament Path.* Lanham, MD: University Press of America, 1989.

2731   E. P. Sanders and M. Davies, *Studying the Synoptic Gospels.* London: SCM, 1989.

2732   É. Massaux, *The Influence of the Gospel of Saint Matthew on Christian Literature before Saint Irenaeus.* Vol. 1. *The First Ecclesiastical Writers.* N. J. Belval and S. Hecht, trans. Macon, GA: Mercer University Press, 1990.

2733   Gerald F. Downing, "A Paradigm Perplex: Luke, Matthew and Mark," *NTS* 38/1 (1992): 15-36.

2734   Ronald V. Huggins, "Matthean Posteriority: A Preliminary Proposal," *Int* 34/1 (1992): 1-22.

2735   J. W. Wenham, *Redating Matthew, Mark and Luke: A Fresh Assault on the Synoptic Problem.* Downers Grove: InterVarsity, 1992.

temptations
2736   G. H. P. Thompson, "Called-Proved-Obedient: A Study in the Baptism and Temptation Narratives of Matthew and Luke," *JTS* 10 (1960): 1-12.

2737   C. U. Wolf, "The Continuing Temptation of Christ in the Church: Searching and Preaching on Matthew 4:1-11," *Int* 20 (1966): 288-301.

2738   Dieter Zeller, "Die Versuchungen Jesu in der Logienquelle," *TTZ* 89 (1980): 61-73.

2739   William R. Stegner, "Early Jewish Christianity—A Lost Chapter?" *ATJ* 44/2 (1989): 17-29.

textual criticism
2740   G. Erdmann, *Die Vorgeschichten des Lukas- und Matthäus-Evangeliums und Vergils vierte Ekloge.* Göttingen: Vandenhoeck & Ruprecht, 1932.

2741   A. Souter, "Portions of an Old-Latin Text of Saint Matthew's Gospel," in R. P. Casey, et al., eds. *Quantulacumque* (festschrift for Kirsopp Lake). London: Christophers, 1937. Pp. 349-54.

2742   K. W. Kim, "The Matthean Text of Origen in his Commentary on the Gospel of Matthew," doctoral dissertation, University of Chicago, Chicago IL, 1947.

2743   C. D. Dicks, "The Matthean Text of Chrysostom in his Homilies on Matthew," *JBL* 67 (1948): 365-76.

2744   K. W. Kim, "The Matthean Text of Origen in his Commentary on Matthew," *JBL* 68 (1949): 125-39.

2745   K. W. Kim, "Codices 1582, 1739, and Origen," *JBL* 69 (1950): 167-75.

2746   D. S. Wallace-Hadrill, "Analysis of Some Quotations from the First Gospel in Eusebius' Demonstratio Evangelica," *JTS* 1 (1950): 168-75.

2747   K. W. Kim, "Origen's Text of Matthew in his Against Celsus," *JTS* 4 (1953): 42-49.

2748   C. Roberts, "An Early Papyrus of the First Gospel," *HTR* 46 (1953): 233-37.

2749   J. Neville Birdsall, "Text of the Gospels in Photius, Pt. 1," *JTS* 7 (1956): 42-55, 190-98.

2750   Julius Gross, "Die Schluesselgewalt nach Haimo von Auxerre," *ZRGG* 9 (1957): 30-41.

2751   B. Lindars, "Matthew, Levi, Lebbaeus and the Value of the Western Text," *NTS* 4 (1957-1958): 220-22.

2752   Sebastian Bartina, "Another New Testament Papyrus," *CBQ* 20 (1958): 280-81.

2753   Marvin J. Hilton, "A Textual Evaluation of the Gospel According to Matthew (chapters 1-7)," master's thesis, Midwestern Baptist Theological Seminary, Kansas City KS, 1958.

2754   Robert P. Markham, et al., eds., "A Symposium on the Bible Societies' Greek New Testament," *BT* 18/1 (1961): 3-19.

2755   B. Schwank, " Die Matthäustexte des Lektionars 1837 im Palimpsestkodex Paris. B.N. Suppl. Grec 1232," *ZNW* 53 (1962): 194-205.

2756   R. J. Kürzinger, "Irenäus und sein Zeugnis zur Sprache des Matthäusevangeliums," *NTS* 10 (1963-1964): 108-15.

2757   F. Gryglewicz, "The St. Adalbert Codex of the Gospels," *NTS* 11 (1964-1965): 259-69.

2758   R. Merkelbach and D. Hagedorn, "Ein Neues Fragment aus Porphyrios 'Gegen die Christen'," *VC* 20/2 (1966): 86-90.

2759   I. A. Sparks, "A New Uncial Fragment of St. Matthew," *JBL* 88 (1969): 201-202.

2760   K. Junack, "Zu einem neuentdeckten Unzialfragment des Mathäus-Evangeliums," *NTS* 16 (1969-1970): 284-88.

2761   C. M. Martini, "La problématique générale du texte de Matthieu," in *L'Évangile selon Matthieu.* Gembloux: Duculot, 1972. Pp. 21-36.

2762   E. Bammel, "P[64] (67) and the Last Supper," *JTS* 24/1 (1973): 189.

2763   C. P. Hammond, "Some Textual Points in Origen's Commentary on Matthew" *JTS* 24/2 (1973): 380-404.

2764   Alfred Stuiber, "Ein Griechischer Textzeuge für das Opus
          Imperfectum in Matthäum," *VC* 27/2 (1973): 146-47.

2765   Jean Doignon, "Citations singulières et leçons rares du
          texte latin de l'Évangile de Matthieu dans l' In Matthaeum
          d'Hilaire de Poitiers," *BLE* 76 (1975): 187-96.

2766   B. M. Metzger, "An Early Coptic Manuscript of the Gospel
          According to Matthew," in J. K. Elliott, ed., *Studies in New
          Testament Language and Text* (festschrift for George
          Kilpatrick). Leiden: Brill, 1976. Pp. 301-12.

2767   Samuel Tobias Lachs, "Some Textual Observations on the
          Sermon on the Mount," *JQR* 69/2 (1978): 98-111.

2768   D. J. Fox, ed., *The Matthew-Luke Commentary of
          Philoxenus*. SBLDS 43. Atlanta: Scholars Press, 1979.

2769   G. D. Kilpatrick, "Three Problems of New Testament
          Text," *NovT* 21 (1979): 289-92.

2770   José O'Callaghan, "La Variante eis/Elthon en Mt. 9,18,"
          Bib 62/1 (1981): 104-106.

2771   James A. Borland, "Re-Examining New Testament
          Textual-Critical Principles and Practices Used to Negate
          Inerrancy," *JETS* 25 (1982): 499-506.

2772   Jacob van Bruggen, "The Lord's Prayer and Textual
          Criticism," *CalJT* 17/1 (1982): 78-87.

2773   George Howard, "Revision Toward the Hebrew in the
          Septuagint Text of Amos," *E-I* 16 (1982): 125-33.

2774   J. W. Wenham, "Why Do You Ask Me About the Good?
          A Study of the Relation between Text and Source
          Criticism," *NTS* 28/1 (1982): 116-25.

2775   Michael W. Holmes, "Early Editorial Activity and the Text
          of Codex Bezae in Matthew," doctoral dissertation,
          Princeton Theological Seminary, Princeton NJ, 1984.

2776   Frank Wheeler, "Textual Criticism and the Synoptic
          Problem: A Textual Commentary on the Minor Agreements

of Matthew and Luke against Mark,'' doctoral dissertation, Baylor University, Waco TX, 1985.

2777   Leslie A. Jackson, ''The Textual Character of the Gospels of Luke and John in Codex Psi,'' doctoral dissertation, Southwestern Baptist Theological Seminary, Fort Worth TX, 1987.

2778   George Howard, ''A Note on the Shorter Ending of Matthew,'' *HTR* 81/1 (1988): 117-20.

2779   George Howard, ''A Primitive Hebrew Gospel of Matthew and the Tol'doth Yeshu,'' *NTS* 34/1 (1988): 60-70.

2780   G. Aranda Pérez, ''La versiónn sahídica de San Mateo en Bodmer XIX y Morgan 569,'' *EB* 46 (1988): 217-30.

2781   David A. Black, ''Conjectural Emendations in the Gospel of Matthew,'' *NovT* 31/1 (1989): 1-15.

2782   Matthew Black, ''The Use of Rhetorical Terminology in Papias on Mark and Matthew,'' *JSNT* 37 (1989): 31-41.

2783   George Howard, ''The Textual Nature of Shem-Tob's Hebrew Matthew,'' *JBL* 108/2 (1989): 239-57.

2784   P. M. Head, ''Observations on Early Papyri of the Synoptic Gospels, especially on the 'Scribal Habits','' *Bib* 71/2 (1990): 240-47.

2785   J. E. Powell, ''The Genesis of the Gospel,'' *JSNT* 42 (1991): 5-16.

2786   Andreas Schmidt, ''Der mögliche Text von P. Oxy. III 405, Z 39-45,'' *NTS* 37 (1991): 160.

textual studies
2787   James Lee Flanagan, ''An Investigation of Twentieth-Century Reactions to the Greek Text and Textual Theories of Westcott and Hort,'' doctoral dissertation, Southwestern Baptist Theological Seminary, Fort Worth TX, 1982.

2788   Gerald L. Corley, "The Textual Relationships of the Gospel Manuscript Gregory 1010," doctoral dissertation, Southwestern Baptist Theological Seminary, Fort Worth TX, 1983.

theology
2789   Heinrich Graffmann, "Das Gericht nach den Werken im Matthäus-evangelium," in *Theologische Aufsätze: Karl Barth zum 50. Geburtstag.* München: Kaiser, 1936. Pp. 124-35.

2790   Walter R. Edwards, "The Doctrine of Stewardship in the Synoptic Gospels," doctoral dissertation, Midwestern Baptist Theological Seminary, Kansas City KS, 1945.

2791   R. Walker, *Die Heilsgeschichte im ersten Evangelium.* Göttingen: Vandenhoeck & Ruprecht, 1967.

2792   B. Rigaux, " 'Lier et délier': Les ministères de réconciliation dans l'Église des Temps apostoliques," *MD* 117 (1974): 86-135.

2793   A. Sand, *Das Gesetz und die Propheten: Untersuchungen zur Theologie des Evangeliums nach Matthäus.* Regensburg: Pustet, 1974.

2794   Daniel C. Arichea, " 'Faith' in the Gospels of Matthew, Mark and Luke," *BT* 29/4 (1978): 420-24.

2795   Hans Huebner, "Biblische Theologie und Theologie des Neuen Testaments: Eine programmatische Skizze," *KD* 27 (1981): 2-19.

2796   Amy-Jill Levine, "The Matthean Program of Salvation History: A Contextual Analysis of the Exclusivity Logia," doctoral dissertation, Duke University, Durham NC, 1984.

2797   Willem A. Visser't Hooft, "Triumphalism in the Gospels," *SJT* 38/4 (1985): 491-504.

2798   Robert N. Wilkin, "Repentance as a Condition for Salvation in the New Testament," doctoral dissertation, Dallas Theological Seminary, Dallas TX, 1985.

2799	Robert L. Mowery, "God, Lord, and Father: The Theology of the Gospel of Matthew," *BR* 33 (1988): 24-36.
2800	K. F. Plum, "The Female Metaphor: The Definition of Male and Female—An Unsolved Problem?" *ScanJT* 43/1 (1989): 81-89.

transfiguration
2801	C. E. Carlston, "Transfiguration and Resurrection," *JBL* 80 (1961): 233-40.
2802	Ronald Lynn Farmer, "The Significance of the Transfiguration for the Synoptic Accounts of the Ministry of Jesus," doctoral dissertation, Southwestern Baptist Theological Seminary, Fort Worth TX, 1982.

translation
2803	F. V. Filson, "Capitalization in English Translations of the Gospel of Matthew," in D. E. Aune, ed., *Studies in New Testament and Early Christian Literature* (festschrift Allen Wikgren). Leiden: Brill, 1972. Pp. 25-30.
2804	Stephen Prickett, "What Do the Translators Think They Are Up To?" *Theology* 80 (1977): 403-10.
2805	J. M. Ross, "Problems of Translation in Matthew," *BT* 29/3 (1978): 336-37.

violence/nonviolence
2806	Jan Lambrecht, "The Sayings of Jesus on Nonviolence," *LouvS* 12/4 (1987): 291-305.
2807	Walter Wink, "Beyond Just War and Pacifism: Jesus' Nonviolent Way," *RevExp* 89 (1992): 197-214.

virgin birth
2808	William H. Cook, "A Comparative Evaluation of the Place of the Virgin Birth in Twentieth-Century Literature," doctoral dissertation, Southwestern Baptist Theological Seminary, Fort Worth TX, 1960.
2809	J. Wilkinson, "Apologetic Aspects of the Virgin Birth of Jesus Christ," *SouJT* 17/2 (1964): 159-81.

2810   C. E. B. Cranfield, "Some Reflections on the Subject of the Virgin Birth," *SJT* 41 (1988): 177-89.

wisdom
2811   M. J. Suggs, *Wisdom, Christology, and Law in Matthew's Gospel*. Cambridge: Harvard University Press, 1970.

2812   Richard Jeske, "Wisdom and the Future in the Teaching of Jesus," *Dia* 11/2 (1972): 108-17.

2813   C. Deutsch, "Wisdom in Matthew: Transformation of a Symbol," *NovT* 32 (1990): 13-47.

women
2814   C. M. Martini, *Women in the Gospels*. New York: Crossroad, 1990.

2815   J. P. Heil, "The Narrative Roles of the Women in Matthew's Genealogy," *Bib* 72 (1991): 538-45.

word studies
2816   A. H. McNeile, "*Tote* in St. Matthew," *JTS* 12 (1911): 127-28.

2817   Clifton J. Allen, "A Study of ΔΙΚΑΙΟΣ and ΔΙΚΑΙΟΣΥΝΗ in the Synoptic Gospels," doctoral dissertation, Southern Baptist Theological Seminary, Louisville KY, 1932.

2818   G. G. Fox, "The Matthean Misrepresentation of *tephillîn*," *JNES* 1 (1942): 373-77.

2819   J. Blinzler, "*Eisin eunoukhoi*," *ZNW* (1957): 254-70.

2820   Donald S. Deer, "The Implied Agent in Greek Passive Verb Forms in the Gospel of Matthew," *BT* 18/4 (1967): 167.

2821   Manfred Ossege, "Einige Aspekte zur Gliederund des neutestamentlichen Wortschatzes (am Beispiel von δικαιοσύνη bei Matthäus)," *LB* 34 (1975): 37-101.

2822   Joseph A. Comber, "The Verb θεραπεύω in Matthew's Gospel," *JBL* 97 (1978): 431-34.

2823   Jack Dean Kingsbury, "The Verb *Akolouthein* as an Index of Matthew's View of His Community," *JBL* 97 (1978): 56-73.

2824   Michael W. Baird, "Jesus' Use of the Decalogue in the Synoptics: An Exegetical Study," doctoral dissertation, Southwestern Baptist Theological Seminary, Fort Worth TX, 1982.

2825   G. Schwarz, "ἀπὸ μακρόθεν/ἐπὶ τῆς ὁδοῦ," *BibN* 20 (1983): 56-57.

2826   Michael J. Wilkins, "The Concept of Disciple in Matthew's Gospel as Reflected in the Use of the Term *Mathētēs*," doctoral dissertation, Fuller Theological Seminary, Pasadena CA, 1986.

2827   James R. Edwards, "The Use of *Proserchesthai* in the Gospel of Matthew," *JBL* 106/1 (1987): 65-74.

2828   S. E. Porter, "Vague Verbs, Periphrastics, and Matt. 16:19," *FilN* 1/2 (1988): 155-73.

2829   Deirdre Good, "The Verb *Anachoreo* in Matthew's Gospel," *NovT* 32 (1990): 1-12.

2830   R. A. Edwards, "Narrative Implications of *Gar* in Matthew," *CBQ* 52 (1990): 636-55.

2831   Bruce W. Winter, "The Messiah as the Tutor: The Meaning of *Kathegetes* in Matthew 23:10," *TynB* 42 (1991): 152-57.

PART THREE

Commentaries

2832   J. Wellhausen, *Das Evangelium Matthaei*. Berlin: Reimer, 1904.

2833   H. Cooke, "The Gospel according to Saint Matthew," *The Self-Interpreting Bible*. 4 vols. St Louis: Thompson, 1905. 4:47-110.

2834   W. C. Allen, *A Critical and Exegetical Commentary on the Gospel According to St. Matthew*. ICC 22. New York: Scribner, 1907.

2835   R. F. A. Horton, *A Devotional Commentary on the Gospel of St. Matthew*. New York: Revell, 1907.

2836   A. Plummer, *Commentary on the Gospel according to St. Matthew*. London: Stock, 1910.

2837   E. Dimmler, *Das Evangelium nach Matthäus*. Munich: Volksvereins, 1911.

2838   J. Hastings, *Saint Matthew*. Great Texts of the Bible #8. Edinburgh: T. & T. Clark, 1914.

2839   J. Knabenbauer, *Commentarius in Evangelium secundum Mattheum*. Paris: Lethielleeux, 1922.

2840   G. H. Box and W. F. Slater, *Saint Matthew*. NCB 22. New York: Frowde, 1922.

2841   M. J. Lagrange, *Évangile selon Saint Matthieu*. EBib. Paris: Gabala, 1923.

2842   F. C. Ceulemans, *Commentarius in Evangelium secundum Matthaeum*. 3rd ed. Mechelen-lez-Deinze: Dessain, 1926.

2843   E. Klostermann, *Das Matthäusevangelium*. HNT 4. Tübingen: Mohr, 1909; 2d ed., 1927.

2844   T. H. Robinson, *The Gospel of Matthew*. MNTC 1. Garden City, N.Y.: Doubleday, 1928.

2845   J. N. Davies, "Matthew," *The Abingdon Bible Commentary*. New York: Abingdon Press, 1929. Pp. 953-95.

2846   A. Schlatter, *Der Evangelist Matthäus*. 2d ed. Stuttgart:
            Calwer, 1933.

2847   E. S. English, *Studies in the Gospel according to Matthew*.
            New York: Revell, 1935.

2848   H. L. Boles, *A Commentary on the Gospel according to
            Matthew*. Nashville: Gospel Advocate, 1936.

2849   F. W. Green, *The Gospel according to Matthew*. The
            Clarendon Bible #7. Oxford: Clarendon Press, 1936.

2850   R. S. Clymer, *The Interpretation of St. Matthew*. 2 vols.
            Quakertown, PA: Philosophical Publishing, 1945.

2851   A. Durand, *Évangile selon saint Matthieu*. Paris:
            Beauchesne, 1948.

2852   W. Michaelis, *Das Evangelium nach Matthäus*. 2 volumes.
            Zurich: Zwingli, 1948-1949.

2853   J. Dillersberger, *Matthäus*. 6 vols. Salzburg: Müller,
            1952-1954.

2854   A. Jones, "The Gospel of Jesus Christ according to Saint
            Matthew," in *A Catholic Commentary on Holy Scripture*.
            New York: Nelson, 1953. Pp. 851-904.

2855   F. W. Grosheide, *Het heilig Evangelie volgens Matthaus*.
            Commentaar op het Nieuwe Testament. Kampen: Kok,
            1954.

2856   F. C. Grant, *The Gospel of Matthew*. Harper's Annotated
            Bible Series 10-11. New York: Harper, 1955.

2857   J. Schniewind, *Das Evangelium nach Matthäus*. 8th ed.
            NTD 2. Göttingen: Vandehoeck & Ruprecht, 1956.

2858   G. E. P. Cox, *The Gospel according to St. Matthew*. 2d ed.
            Torch Bible Commentaries. London: SCM, 1958.

2859   E. Lohmeyer, *Das Evangelium des Matthäus*. W.
            Schmauch, ed. 2d ed. Kritischexegetischer Kommentar über

das Neue Testament (Sonderband). Göttingen: Vandenhoeck & Ruprecht, 1958.

2860   F. V. Filson, *A Commentary on the Gospel according to St. Matthew*. Black's New Testament Commentaries 1. London: Black, 1960.

2861   S. de Dietrich, *The Gospel according to Matthew*. Layman's Bible Commentary 16. Richmond: Knox, 1961.

2862   K. Stendahl, "Matthew," in *PCB*, pp. 769-798. M. Black and H. Rowley, eds. New York: Nelson, 1962.

2863   A. W. Argyle, *The Gospel according to Matthew*. Cambridge Bible Commentary. Cambridge: Cambridge University Press, 1963.

2864   J. C. Fenton, *The Gospel of Saint Matthew*. The Pelican Gospel Commentaries. Baltimore: Penguin, 1963.

2865   P. Gaechter, *Das Matthäus-Evangelium*. Innsbruck: Tyrolia, 1963.

2866   F. Earle, *Matthew, Mark, Luke*. Beacon Bible Commentary 6. Kansas City, MO: Beacon Hill, 1964.

2867   R. Earle, "The Gospel according to St. Matthew,' *Matthew-Acts* The Wesleyan Bible Commentary 4. Grand Rapids: Eerdmans, 1964. Pp. 5-125.

2868   F. W. Dillemore, "The Gospel according to Matthew," *Westminster Study Bible*. New York: Collins, 1965. Pp. 23-65.

2869   Hershel H. Hobbs, *An Exposition of the Gospel of Matthew*. Grand Rapids: Baker, 1965.

2870   A. H. McNeile, *The Gospel according to St. Matthew*. London: Macmillan, (1915) 1965.

2871   J. Schmid, *Das Evangelium nach Matthäus*. Regensburger NT 1. Regensburg: Putset, 1965.

2872   C. R. Erdman, *The Gospel of Matthew*. Philadelphia: Westminster, 1966.

2873   G. Gander, *L'Évangile de l'église: Commentaire de l'évangile selon Matthieu*. Geneva: Labor et Fides, 1967.

2874   Ulrich Luz, *Matthew 1-7: A Commentary*. Minneapolis: Augsburg, 1967.

2875   W. Grundmann, *Das Evangelium nach Matthäus*. THKNT #1. Berlin: Evangelische Verlagsanstalt, 1968.

2876   H. L. Ellison, "The Gospel according to Matthew," *A New Testament Commentary*. Grand Rapids: Zondervan, 1969. Pp. 141-76.

2877   W. Trilling, *The Gospel according to St. Matthew*. New York: Herder & Herder, 1969.

2878   P. Bonnard, *L'Évangile selon saint Matthieu*. CNT. Neuchâtel: Delachaux & Niestlé, 1963; 2d edition, 1970.

2879   W. F. Albright and C. S. Mann, *Matthew*. AB 26. Garden City: Doubleday, 1971.

2880   C. J. Ellicott, "Matthew," *Ellicott's Bible Commentary in One Volume*. Grand Rapids: Zondervan, 1971. Pp. 681-757.

2881   S. Freyne and H. Wansbrough, *Mark and Matthew*. Scripture Discussion Commentary 7. Chicago: Acts Foundation, 1971.

2882   Ortensio Da Spinetoli, *Matteo. Commento al "Vangelo della Chiesa."* Assisi: Cittadella editrice, 1971.

2883   David Hill, *The Gospel of Matthew*. NCB #1. London: Oliphants, 1972.

2884   J. Radermakers, *Au fil de l'Évangile selon saint Matthieu*. 2 volumes. Heverlee-Louvain: Institur d'études théologiques, 1972.

2885   W. Hendriksen, *The Gospel of Matthew*. Edinburgh: Banner of Truth Trust, 1974.

2886 H. B. Green, *The Gospel according to Matthew*. The New Clarendon Bible, NT #1. Oxford: University Press, 1975.

2887 E. Schweizer, *The Good News according to Matthew*. Atlanta: John Knox, 1975.

2888 F. F. Bruce, "Saint Matthew," *Daily Bible Commentary*. 4 vols. Philadelphia: Holman, 1977. 3:10-103.

2889 B. C. Johnson, *Matthew and Mark*. Waco, TX: Word Books, 1978.

2890 L. Sabourin, *L'Évangile selon saint Matthieu et ses principaux parallèles*. Rome: Biblical Institute Press, 1978.

2891 G. Maier, *Matthäus-Evangelium*. Bibel-Kommentar, volumes 1 & 2. Neuhausen-Stuttgart: Hanssler, 1979.

2892 F. W. Beare, *The Gospel accord to Matthew: A Commentary*. Oxford: Blackwell, 1981.

2893 J. P. Meier, *Matthew*. New Testament Message 3. Wilmington: Glazier, 1981.

2894 R. H. Gundry, *Matthew: A Commentary on His Literary and Theological Art*. Grand Rapids: Eerdmans, 1982.

2895 P. S. Minear, *Matthew: The Teacher's Gospel*. New York: Pilgrim, 1982.

2896 D. J. Harrington, *The Gospel according to Matthew*. Collegeville Bible Commentary #1. Collegeville, MN: Liturgical Press, 1983.

2897 D. A. Carson, "Matthew," *The Expositor's Bible Commentary*. 12 vols. Reprint. Grand Rapids: Zondervan, 1984. 8:3-599.

2898 R. Earle, "Matthew," *The New International Version Study Bible*. Grand Rapids: Zondervan, 1985. Pp. 1439-89.

2899 Daniel Patte, *The Gospel According to Matthew: A Structural Commentary on Matthew's Faith*. Philadelphia: Fortress, 1987.

2900   W. D. Davies and Dale C. Allison, *A Critical and Exegetical Commentary on the Gospel According to Saint Matthew*. ICC. #1. Edinburgh: T. & T. Clark, 1988.

2901   T. Fornberg, *Matteusevangeliet 1:1-13:52*. Uppsala: EFS-Förlaget, 1989.

2902   G. T. Montague, *Companion God: A Cross-Cultural Commentary on the Gospel of Matthew*. New York: Paulist, 1989.

2903   Ulrich Luz, *Das Evangelium nach Matthäus*. 2, Teilband - *Mt. 8-17*. EKKNT. Zürich: Benziger, 1990.

2904   W. D. Davies and Dale C. Allison, *A Critical and Exegetical Commentary on the Gospel According to Saint Matthew*. ICC. #2. Edinburgh: T. & T. Clark, 1991.

2905   R. B. Gardner, *Matthew*. Believers Church Bible Commentary. Scottdale MN: Herald, 1991.

2906   D. J. Harrington, *The Gospel of Matthew*. Collegeville: Liturgical Press, 1991.

2907   R. H. Mounce, *Matthew*. New International Biblical Commentary. Peabody: Hendrickson, 1991.

2908   M. Quesnel, *Jesus-Christ selon saint Matthieu: Synthèse théologique, Jésus et Jésus-Christ*. Paris: Desclée, 1991.

Author Index

Bulman, J. M., 2387

Bultmann, R., 0404, 0695, 0915, 0979, 1419

Bundy, W. E., 2232

Bunn, J. C., 2456, 2457

Burch, V., 1207

Burchard, C., 0350, 2581, 2617

Burger, C., 0759, 1432

Burggraff, D. L., 1299, 1300, 1301

Burke, C. B., 2049

Burkitt, F. C., 0658

Burks, R. E., 2140, 2240

Burnett, F. W., 1400, 2096, 2270

Burney, C. F., 1645

Burtness, J. H., 0474

Buse, I., 2409, 2410

Bussby, F., 0510, 0603

Buth, R., 1889

Butler, B. C., 2037, 2703

Buzzetti, C., 1226

Cóbreces, I. R., 1417

Caba, J., 1318

Cadbury, H. J., 1234, 1307

Cadoux, A. T., 1646, 2386

Cahill, S. L., 2618

Caird, G. B., 0515

Callan, C. J., 2697

Calloud, J., 2438

Cameron, P. S., 0935

Campbell, C. M., 1848

Campbell, D. B. J., 2709

Campbell, K. M., 0450

Cangh, J.-M. van, 1371

Cantwell, L., 0114

Caragounis, C. C., 1006, 1011, 1020, 1995

Cargal, T. B., 1763

Cargill, R. L., 2392

Carlisle, C. R., 1103

Carlston, C. E., 0352, 0689, 1057, 2187, 2625, 2801

Carmichael, D. B., 1713

Carmignac, J., 0623, 0670, 1174

Carmody, T. R., 2097

Carrière, J.-M., 2593

Carroll, K. L., 1209

Carson, D. A., 2274, 2582, 2583, 2897

Carton, G., 0238, 1891

Casalini, N., 0004, 0038, 0218, 0292

Casalis, G., 0613

Casciaro Ramirez, J. M., 1277, 1988, 2005

Casey, M., 0787

Casey, P. M., 0786, 0946, 1019

Caspari, W., 0208, 2482

Cassidy, R. J., 1270

Catchpole, D. R., 1060, 1337, 1670, 1734, 1738, 2715

Catherinet, F.-M., 2134

Cave, C. H., 0012, 1918

Cawley, M., 0918, 2463

Cerfaux, L., 1051

Cernuda, A. V., 0030

Ceulemans, F. C., 2842

Chapman, J., 2131

Charbel, A., 0164, 0169, 0170, 1931, 1932, 1949

Charette, B., 0846, 0985

Charles, J. D., 0230

Charpentier, É., 0779

Chavel, C. B., 2403

Chevallier, M. A., 1659, 2035

Chouraqui, A., 2526

Chow, D. T. W., 0348, 0496, 2607

Christ, F., 0941, 0966, 1556, 1561

Christiaens, M., 2076, 2348

Clark, C. A., 1514

Clark, D. J., 0638, 2317, 2673

Clark, K. W., 2136

Clark, R., 0875, 0876, 2087, 2090

Clark, S., 2158

Clavier, H., 0521, 1218, 1251

Cleary, M., 2281

Clymer, B. S., 2850

Coakley, J. F., 1708

Coggan, F. D., 0245

Cohen, M., 0995, 2045, 2272

Cohn-Sherbok, D. M., 1511

Coiner, H. G., 0536, 1353, 2064, 2336

Cole, C. E., 2099

Colella, P., 1712

Collin, M., 0735, 0970

Collins, A. Y., 2239

Collins, L. L., 2501

Collins, O., 1350, 2061, 2333

Collins, R. F., 0835, 0919, 1003, 1139

Collison, J. G. F., 2026

Colwell, E. C., 0508

Comber, J. A., 0948, 2822

Combrink, H. J. B., 2377

Combs, W. W., 2126

Conrad, A., 1750

Conte, N., 1610

Conti, M., 0739, 0858, 0859, 0863, 1628

Cook, M. J., 2508

Cook, W. H., 1914, 2808

Cooke, H., 2833

Cooper, R. M., 2454

Cope, L., 1094, 1652, 2277, 2361

Copeland, E. L., 1869

Coppens, J., 03, 2571

Corbin, M., 0434

Cordero, M. G., 1196

Corley, G. L., 2788

Correns, D., 1540

Cote, P.-R., 1384

Couchoud, P.-L., 2700

Couffignal, R., 0148

Court, J. M., 1676, 2384

Cowling, D., 1867

Cox, G. E. P., 2858

Cox, J. J. C., 0987

Craddock, F. B., 1467, 1484, 1506, 1544

Crampton, L. J., 1407

Cranfield, C. E. B., 2810

Cranford, L. L., 2641

Crawford, B. S., 2290

Cripps, K. R., 1501, 2560

Crossan, D., 0086, 0727, 1459, 2249, 2395

Crouch, W. H., 2382

Crouzel, H., 0541, 1360

Crowder, W. J., 1881

Culbertson, P., 1416, 1454

Cullmann, O., 0447, 1179

Culver, R. D., 1827, 1870

Cunningham, S., 2368

Curnock, G. N., 0986

Currie, S. D., 0522

Curtis, K. P. G., 2424

Curtis, W. A., 1403, 2256

Czerski, J., 1862

D'Urso, G., 0036

Dahl, N. A., 1700

Dahlberg, B. T., 1158

Dambricourt, G., 2193

Daniel, C., 0719, 0928, 1370, 2565

Danieli, G., 0002, 0015, 2177, 2646

Darby, J. N., 2132

Darby, R. R., 2405

Daube, D., 0188, 0564, 2665

Daumoser, I., 2486

Dautzenberg, G., 0552

David, D. H., 1164

Davies, J. N., 2845

Davies, M., 2731

France, R. T., 0197, 0198, 0247, 1907, 1946, 2219

Frankemölle, H., 0346, 0370, 1905, 2019, 2178, 2182, 2183, 2184, 2363, 2602

Fransen, I., 0756

Franzmann, M. H., 0285, 0945, 2056

Frein, B. C., 2306

Frenz, A., 1438

Fresenius, W., 0608

Freyne, S., 2050, 2519, 2881

Fridrichsen, A., 0244

Friedrich, G., 1866

Friedrich, J., 1668

Frizzi, G., 2462

Frost, M., 0772

Frutiger, S., 1173, 1695

Fuchs, A., 0832, 2173

Fuchs, E., 0581, 0697, 1329, 1405

Fuchs, W., 1679

Fueter, P. D., 2212

Fuillet, J., 0327

Fuller, G. C., 1603

Fuller, R. C., 0831

Fuller, R. H., 0091, 1394, 1961

Fullkrug-Weitzel, C., 1133

Funk, R. W., 1068, 1900

Gaechter, P., 0155, 2160, 2161, 2865

Gaide, G., 1168

Galbiati, E., 0010, 0029, 0150, 0824

Galizzi, M., 1724

Gallman, R. L., 2141

Galot, J., 1159

Gamba, G. G., 0020, 0281, 1374

Gander, G., 2873

Gangel, K. O., 0961

Ganne, P., 1177

García Martínez, F., 1302

Gardner, R. B., 2905

Gardner-Smith, P., 2479

Garland, D. E., 1271, 2327

Garritt, C. E., 1121

Gartner, B., 2470

Gaston, L., 1978

Gatzweiler, K., 1127

Geldard, M., 0543, 1358, 2071, 2343

Gench, F. T., 1993

Genuyt, F., 0277, 0811, 0847

Géoltrain, P., 1568

George, A., 0588, 0923, 0925, 1007

Gerhardsson, B., 0253, 0589, 0679, 1733, 1969, 1974

Germano, J. M., 0090, 0126, 0134, 0143, 0144

Gese, H., 1772

Gewalt, D., 1655, 1742

Giavini, G., 0538

Gibbs, J. A., 1077

Gibbs, J. M., 0005, 2266, 2497

Giblin, C. H., 0882, 1507, 1792, 1835

Giesen, H., 2214

Gil, L., 0625

Gill, D., 0560

Gilmann, F. M., 1761

Gingrich, R. E., 1073, 1583, 1588, 1590

Giordani, I., 1968

Gispen, W. H., 1472

Glasson, T. F., 0721, 1605

Glasswell, M. E., 2202

Glazener, C. G., 1976

Glombitza, O., 1022, 1477

Glorieux, P., 1222

Glover, F. C., 1424

Gnilka, J., 0426, 1202, 2474

Gnuse, R. K., 1947

Goldingay, J., 0003, 2509

Gonzalez Ruiz, J. M., 0530, 1348, 2060, 2332

Good, D., 2829

Matera, F. J., 1703, 1744, 1762, 1779, 2115, 2679

Matthews, V. H., 0431

Matthey, J., 1840

Matthias, E., 0165

Mattill, A. J., 0744, 1661

Mattison, R. D., 1994

Matura, T., 1373, 1509, 2069, 2341

May, E., 0883, 2375

Meadors, G. T., 2611

Mee, A. J., 0444

Meier, J. P., 0912, 1093, 1134, 1261, 1838, 1874, 1986, 2028, 2036, 2108, 2116, 2189, 2278, 2299, 2893

Menahem, R., 0226

Menestrina, G., 0332, 2578

Menken, M. J. J., 0200, 1175, 1753, 2512

Menninger, R. E., 2516

Mercurio, R., 1032

Merino, L. D., 1888

Merkel, H., 1452

Merkelbach, R., 1264, 2758

Metzger, B. M., 0079, 0081, 1219, 2004, 2766

Meurer, S., 1411

Meyer, B. F., 1504

Meyer, L. H., 1673

Meyer, P. W., 1079, 1441, 2110

Meynell, H., 2714

Meynet, R., 1001

Michael, K. A., 0996

Michaelis, C., 0407

Michaelis, W., 2852

Michaels, J. R., 1449, 1648

Michel, O., 2663

Miguens, M., 1565

Milikowsky, C., 0888, 2101

Miller, G. L., 1016, 2098

Miller, R. J., 0354, 0627, 1545, 2466, 2629

Milton, H., 0047

Milward, P., 1194, 2448

Minear, P. S., 0551, 0556, 0592, 1538, 1804, 1964, 2053, 2895

Mitton, C. L., 0926, 1406, 2084

Mizell, E. S., 2372

Moiser, J., 0761

Molin, G., 0577

Molldrem, M. J., 1343, 2082, 2354

Moloney, F. J., 1338

Moltmann, J., 0342, 2596

Montagnini, F., 0347, 2604

Montague, G. T., 2902

Montefiore, H., 1267

Montgomery, J. A., 0864

Moo, D. J., 2367

Moore, E., 0676

Moore, S. D., 2304

Moore, W. E., 0932, 0936

Mora, V., 2528

Moraldi, L., 0239

Moreton, M., 1895

Moreton, M. J., 0050

Morgan-Wayne, J. E., 2362

Mork, C., 1957

Morosco, R. E., 0838, 2054

Morrice, W. G., 1085

Morrison, J. H., 0445

Moule, A. W. H., 2711

Moule, C. F. D., 0471, 0500, 0502, 0507, 2316, 2447, 2498, 2564

Mounce, R. H., 2907

Mowery, R. L., 0269, 0273, 0805, 1736, 2799

Muñoz Iglesias, S., 0007, 0025

Muñoz León, D., 1720

Muddiman, J., 2481

Mulholland, M. R., 1948

Mulholland, M. R. Jr., 0032
Muller, M., 1431
Munck, J., 2154
Murphy-O'Connor, J., 1099
Murray, G., 1111, 1393
Mussner, F., 0939
Mutch, J., 1642

Nacpil, E. P., 0738
Nagano, P. M., 1664
Nagórny, J., 0349, 2612
Neirynck, F., 0125, 0280, 0333, 0807, 1097, 1256, 1740, 1819, 2213, 2302, 2417, 2717, 2720
Nellesen, E., 0364
Nelson, D. A., 1413
Nerbum, K. M., 2279
Nestle, E., 1908
Nettelhorst, R. P., 0061
Neugebauer, F., 0559
Neuhäusler, E., 0369, 0683
New, D. S., 1054
Newell, J. E., 1468
Newell, R. R., 1468
Newman, B. M., 0044, 0379, 1042, 2287, 2575
Newman, R. C., 1510
Newport, K. G. C., 1525
Nickelsburg, G. W., 1984
Niedner, F. A., 2523
Nielsen, H. K., 1643
Nineham, D. E., 0055, 1939
Nolland, J., 1539
Norton, A., 0309
Nötscher, F., 0706
Nyberg, H. S., 1030

Oaks, J. P., 1015
Oberweis, M., 1958
O'Brien, P. T., 1864

Obrist, F., 1208
O'Callaghan, J., 0817, 0828, 0830, 0861, 0906, 0944, 1046, 1047, 1049, 1095, 1098, 1101, 1116, 1143, 1252, 1259, 1260, 1273, 1399, 1402, 1427, 1428, 1429, 1524, 2770
Oepke, A., 1188, 1759
Ogawa, A., 1448
Oglesby W. B., 1061
Oglesby, W. B., 1043
O'Grady, J. F., 2244
Okeke, G. E., 2102
Olivera, F., 0110
Omanson, R., 0827
O'Neill, J. C., 0822, 1458, 1735
Onwu, N., 2103, 2113
Oporto, S. G., 1028
Orbe, A., 1410
Orchard, B., 0649
Ordon, H., 0518
Ornella, A., 0747
O'Rourke, J. J., 0532, 1351
Osborn, E. F., 1397
Osborn, H., 1457
Osborne, G. R., 1836
Osborne, R. E., 2179
Osburn, C. D., 1361
Ossege, M., 2537, 2821
Oudersluys, R. C., 1658, 2093
Oulton, J. E. L., 1217
Overman, J. A., 2651

Padilla, C. R., 0842, 1756
Pamment, M., 2289
Panosian, E. M., 2166
Pantelis, J., 0401
Pantle-Schieber, K., 2033
Papone, P., 0937
Paramo, S. del, 1072

Rausch, J., 0558

Ray, W. A., 2011, 2091

Read, D. H. C., 0184, 0476, 1775

Reese, J. M., 2247

Refoulé, F., 0612, 1184

Rehkopf, F., 1727

Reicke, B., 0898, 1496, 1580

Reid, B. E., 1254

Reiner, E., 1711

Rembry, J. G., 0211

Renard, J. P., 0485

Rengstorf, K. H., 1495, 2492

Resenhofft, R. W., 1494

Rezevskis, J., 2701

Rice, F. A., 1162

Richards, C., 2222

Richards, H., 0149

Richards, H. J., 1910

Richards, M. H., 2254

Richards, W. L., 1453

Richardson, P., 2534

Riches, J. K., 2650

Ricoeur, P., 0736

Rieckert, S. J., 1697

Riesenfeld, H., 0682

Riew, Y. K., 2374

Rigaux, B., 1594, 2792

Rigaux, R., 1810

Ringe, S. H., 2261

Roark, D. M., 2089

Robbins, V. K., 1284

Roberts, B. J., 2472

Roberts, C., 2748

Roberts, J. W., 1223, 2016

Roberts, T. A., 0894

Robinson, B. P., 1201

Robinson, J. A. T., 0927, 1647

Robinson, T. H., 2844

Robinson, W. C., 1533, 1922

Rodd, C. S., 1008

Rodhe, J., 2180

Rodzianko, V., 0412

Rolland, P., 0820, 1092, 2669

Romaniuk, K., 0284

Rosenbaum, S. M., 2364

Rosenberg, R. A., 0172

Ross, J. M., 0246, 1547, 2805

Rothfuchs, W., 2499

Roulin, P., 0238, 1891

Rüger, H. P., 0215, 0690, 0716

Runzo, J., 1297

Rusche, H., 0439

Ryan, T. J., 1138

Ryckmans, G., 0181, 1909

Ryrie, C. C., 0526, 1339, 2074, 2346

Sabourin, L., 0462, 0584, 2504, 2890

Sahlin, H., 0561, 0566, 0943

Saldarini, G., 0045, 0239

Salguero, J., 0365

Salvoni, F., 0162

Samuel, S. J., 0242

Sand, A., 2105, 2793

Sanday, W., 2688

Sanders, E. P., 2710, 2731

Sanders, H. A., 1716

Sanders, J. A., 0212

Sandt, H. W. M. van de, 0475

Saunders, E. W., 0360, 2638

Sawicki, M., 0913

Saydon, P. P., 0699, 1627

Sayer, J., 1686

Scaer, D. P., 1847

Schäfer, O., 0617

Schöllig, H., 0052, 1928

Schürmann, H., 0484, 0607, 0854, 0877

Schaberg, J., 0043

Scheffer, H., 1880

Schelkle, K. H., 0017, 0048

Schempp, P., 0418